# America at the Polls
## 1994

# America at the Polls
## 1994

*Everett Carll Ladd, editor*
*and Staff and Associates of the Roper Center*
*for Public Opinion Research*

*Roper Center • University of Connecticut*

**Occasional Papers and Monographs Series #2**

To the Memory of

*George Gallup and Elmo Roper*

*Pro debitis plurimis seras gratias*

# Contents

Preface      ix

**Chapter 1**
**1994 Vote: The Story in the Numbers**      1

**Chapter 2**
**1994 Vote: Against the Backdrop of Continuing Realignment**   19
*Commentary by Everett Carll Ladd*

**Chapter 3**
**1994 Vote: Where Was Public Thinking at Vote Time?**

     31

**Chapter 4**
**1994 Vote: How Social Groups Voted**      47
The Gender Factor
    *Commentary by Karlyn H. Bowman*
The Education Factor
    *Commentary by Jim Norman*
The Age Factor
The Race Factor
    *Commentary by Daryl Harris*
The Region Factor
    *A conversation on the vote in the South with Claibourne Darden*
The Religious Factor
As Independents Go...

**Chapter 5**
**1994 Vote: Key Races**      77
Four Pollsters' Perspectives
    *A conversation with: Micheline Blum, Texas*
                        *John Brennan, California*
                        *Scott Keeter, Virginia*
                        *Lee M. Miringoff, New York*

New York Votes: *Analysis by Jennifer M. Necci*
Texas Votes: *Analysis by John M. Barry*
Virginia Votes: *Analysis by Rob Persons*
Washington's 5th District Votes: *Analysis by G. Donald Ferree, Jr.*
Maryland Votes: *Analysis by Catherine P. Flavin*
Pennsylvania Votes: *Analysis by Regina M. Dougherty*

**Chapter 6**
**1994 Vote:  Direct Democracy Ballot Issues**                    111
*Commentary by Thomas E. Cronin*

**Chapter 7**
**1994 Vote:  The Money Story**                                   127
*Commentary by Michael J. Malbin*

**Chapter 8**
**1994 Vote:  "How I Won"**                                       141
*Conversations with Congressman John Hostettler (R-IN) and*
*Congressman Tim Holden (D-PA)*

**Contributors**                                                  149

**Appendix—The 1994 Exit Polls**                                  155

# **P**reface

It's with great pleasure that my colleagues and I at the Roper Center present this volume on the 1994 US elections to our friends and colleagues in political science (and their students), in the press, survey research, and elsewhere in the public affairs and politics communities. We hope you will find this a useful resource book, one that brings together the information you need—survey and aggregate vote data alike—in one place. The Center plans to publish comparable volumes on each succeeding national election.

*America at the Polls 1994* also provides analysis of the election results. I'm especially appreciative of the efforts of those colleagues outside the Center who took time from very busy schedules to provide expert commentary. Their names are shown, of course, on the Contents page and by their respective contributions. It took a major effort by these friends and associates, and as well by many Center staff members, to produce a volume of this scope in so short a span.

We've tried not to editorialize. It's not possible, or desirable, to eschew judgment in analyzing an election's results. It is possible, and desirable, in a "databook" of this kind to keep commentary tightly focused on what is known—as opposed to matters of speculation—most of the time. We've tried to do this. It's also possible to avoid commentary which is mere preference-stating, and we've tried hard to do this.

A number of people who did not contribute directly to the writing and production of *America at the Polls 1994* made contributions of an indirect sort that are no less essential. I want to thank first Murray Edelman and Lee C. Shapiro at Voter News Surveys, who provided access to the VNS exit poll data. This publication owes much to their generosity. My colleagues and I also acknowledge the kindness of Warren Mitofsky and Rob Farbman, of Mitofsky International, who on the morning of November 9 made getting Roper Center staff exit poll material a higher priority than getting sleep. Barbara Carvalho of the Marist Institute for Public Opinion, Sean Herbert of CBS News, Bob Balkin and James Kaleigh of the Political Campaign Hotline, Del Ali of Mason-Dixon Political/Media Research, G. Terry Madonna at Millersville University and Patrick Stroh at Carnegie Mellon University provided valuable data on the key races highlighted in Chapter 5, as did Brant Fitzgerald and Charlotte Ottavelli of the Elections Division of the Secretary of State's Office, Washington State. Elizabeth Bender of Americans for Tax Reform, Tommy Neal of the National Conference of State Legislatures, and Joan Ponessa from the Public Affairs Research Institute of New Jersey, helped us tell the referenda story. Robert Biersack of the Federal Election Commission provided campaign finance data. Trish Reilly, Press Secretary for Congressman Tim Holden and David Dougherty, Campaign Manager, "Holden for Congress" were instrumental in helping schedule our interview with Congressman Holden while John Forester at the *Reading Eagle Times* provided valuable background information on the district. Jeff Knight, Campaign Chairman, "Hostettler for Congress" facilitated our interview with Congressman John Hostettler.

Closer to home, Christy R. Sacks took time out from her Center duties in the field of data management and analysis to focus trained eyes on the final manuscript. She helped enormously with the error-catching. So, too, did Nikki A. LeSage and Renee M. Ladouceur.

Lastly but not leastly, I want to express my deep appreciation for the efforts of Frank Williams and his staff at the Hall and Bill Printing Company—especially for doing so much to keep us on a very tight schedule.

As editor of *America at the Polls 1994* , I have, then, a great many debts to acknowledge. At the same time, as I seem to remember some politician saying, "The buck stops here." For any errors of fact or interpretation which may have survived, I am responsible.

**ECL**
Storrs, Connecticut
January 3, 1995

# C hapter 1
## 1994 Vote: The Story in the Numbers
### Nationally, A Rising Republican Tide Lifted Many Party Boats

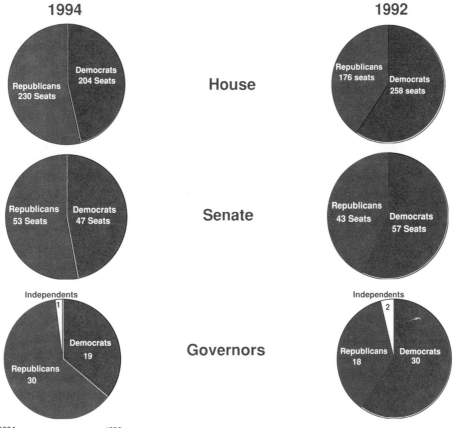

| 1994 | | 1992 | |
|---|---|---|---|
| | House | | |
| Republicans 230 Seats / Democrats 204 Seats | | Republicans 176 seats / Democrats 258 seats | |
| | Senate | | |
| Republicans 53 Seats / Democrats 47 Seats | | Republicans 43 Seats / Democrats 57 Seats | |
| | Governors | | |
| Independents 1 / Democrats 19 / Republicans 30 | | Independents 2 / Republicans 18 / Democrats 30 | |

| 1994 | | 1992 | |
|---|---|---|---|
| Republicans | Democrats | Republicans | Democrats |
| | | | |
| Members of State Legislatures | | | |
| 3491 | 3846 | 3005 | 4342 |
| | | | |
| Control of State Legislative Chambers by Party | | | |
| 47 | 48 | 29 | 66 |
| | | | |
| States with both Legislative House and Governor of Same Party | | | |
| 15 | 7 | 3 | 16 |

### Number of Incumbents Losing, 1994

| | Republicans | Democrats |
|---|---|---|
| Senators | 0 | 2 |
| House Members | 0 | 35 |
| Governors | 0 | 5 |

# Popular Vote for U.S. Representatives 1932-1994

**The 1994 vote was only the third since 1930, and the first since 1946, in which Republicans won a majority of the vote for Congress.**

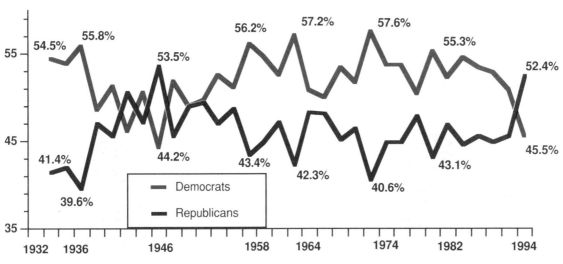

| | Democrats | Republicans |
|------|-----------|-------------|
| 1932 | 54.5% | 41.4% |
| 1934 | 53.9 | 42.0 |
| 1936 | 55.8 | 39.6 |
| 1938 | 48.6 | 47.0 |
| 1940 | 51.3 | 45.6 |
| 1942 | 46.1 | 50.6 |
| 1944 | 50.6 | 47.2 |
| 1946 | 44.2 | 53.5 |
| 1948 | 51.9 | 45.5 |
| 1950 | 49.0 | 49.0 |
| 1952 | 49.7 | 49.4 |
| 1954 | 52.5 | 47.0 |
| 1956 | 51.1 | 48.7 |
| 1958 | 56.2 | 43.4 |
| 1960 | 54.7 | 44.8 |
| 1962 | 52.5 | 47.2 |
| 1964 | 57.2 | 42.3 |
| 1966 | 50.9 | 48.3 |
| 1968 | 50.0 | 48.2 |
| 1970 | 53.4 | 45.1 |
| 1972 | 51.7 | 46.4 |
| 1974 | 57.6 | 40.6 |
| 1976 | 53.7 | 44.9 |
| 1978 | 53.7 | 44.9 |
| 1980 | 50.4 | 47.9 |
| 1982 | 55.3 | 43.1 |
| 1984 | 52.3 | 46.8 |
| 1986 | 54.6 | 44.5 |
| 1988 | 53.4 | 45.5 |
| 1990 | 52.9 | 44.9 |
| 1992 | 50.9 | 45.5 |
| 1994 | 45.5 | 52.4 |

**Editor's Note:** It's a quite extraordinary string, isn't it? It was an unprecedentedly long span (for a competitive democracy) that one party, the Democrats, dominated US House of Representatives voting—both the popular vote as shown above, and the House seats side shown on the next page.

# Party Shares of Seats in the U.S. House of Representatives, 1932-1994

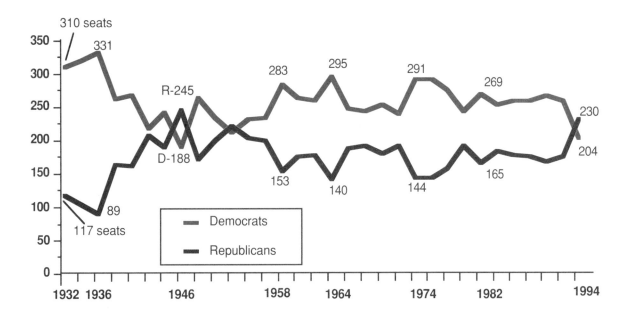

**Editor's Note**: In fact, the Democratic margin in the popular vote for the House is greater than the data suggest. The vote in uncontested seats is not included for any of the years prior to 1994, because no official tally is made in such races. Since the Democrats had many more uncontested seats than did the Republicans for most of the period, many more of their popular votes were in fact excluded from the official counts.

The popular vote figure for 1994 is one which Center staff have made using the best available estimates. First, we tallied the latest National Elections Service figures for all of the contested races. To this we added an estimate of the uncounted absentee ballots, following the estimate made by Curtis Gans and his colleagues at the Center for the Study of the American Electorate in their 1994 election report. The estimated 1.7 million uncounted ballots (uncounted as of the time the NES tally was completed) were distributed between the parties in the same proportion as that of the tallied vote. Lastly, the vote for candidates in uncontested races was estimated as the average vote cast for candidates of the same party in contested House races in the state in question. In 1994 this added a bit to the Republican proportion, since many more of the uncontested seats were in the Republican column—in marked contrast to historical experience when they were disproportionately Democratic. As the chart on pp. 8-11 shows, the 1994 uncontested races were still disproportionately in the South, with Florida easily surpassing all other states in this measure.

# Seats in the House:
# The Parties Swap Regions
## In 1994, For the First Time, Republicans Won A Majority of House Seats from the South

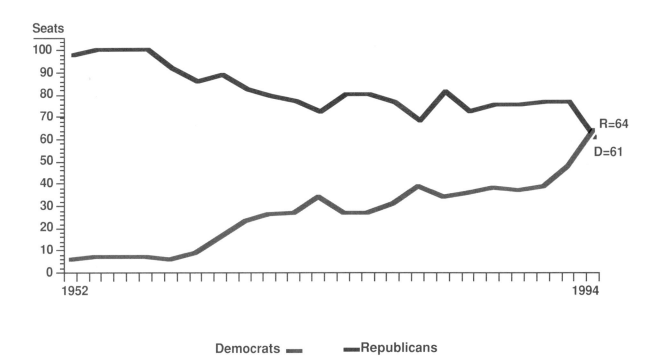

Democrats ▬     ▬Republicans

## The Northeast Has Long Since Swung Democratic
## —And Remained Democratic in House Seats in 1994

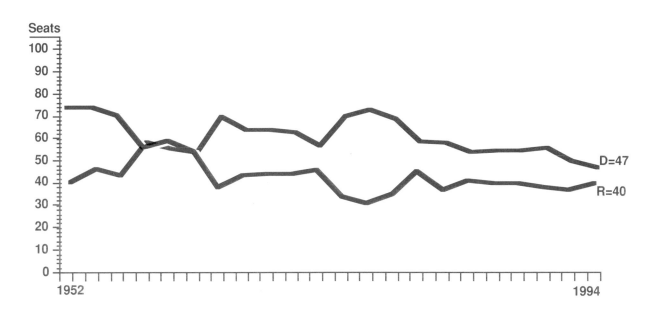

# Changing Regional Make-Up of the Congressional Parties

### Percentage of All House Republicans from Each Region

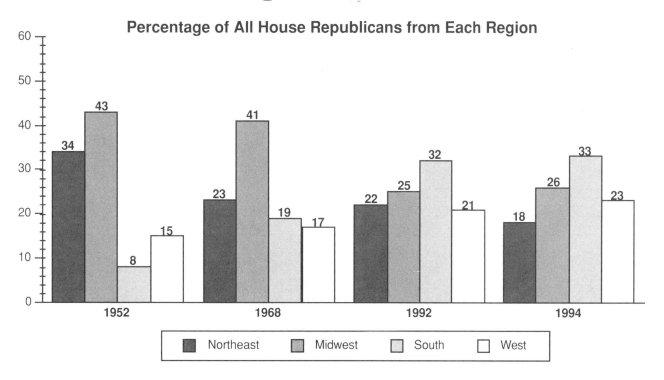

### Percentage of All House Democrats from Each Region

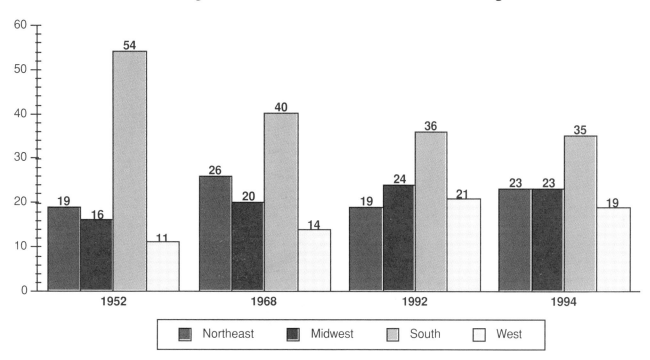

# The 1994 House Results in Historical Perspective

## Seat Change, 1882-1994

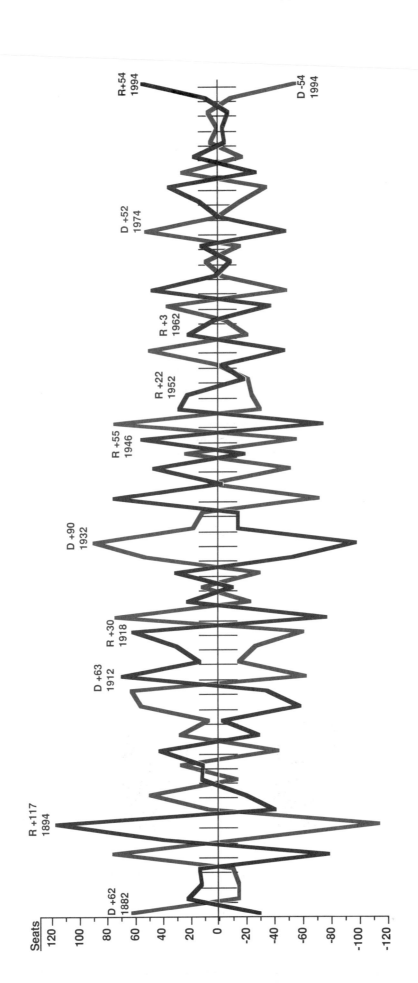

# Party Control of the Governorships, 1952-1994

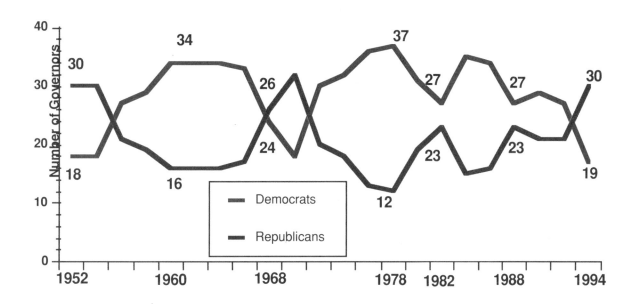

## Party Control of the Governorships of the Ten Largest States, selected years, 1952-1994

|      | Democrats | Republicans |
|------|-----------|-------------|
| 1994 | 2 | 8 |
| 1992 | 5 | 5 |
| 1980 | 6 | 4 |
| 1972 | 5 | 5 |
| 1970 | 2 | 8 |
| 1960 | 8 | 2 |
| 1952 | 6 | 4 |

# House **Republican** Winners, by region

| Region/State | District | Winner | Total % of Vote | Margin |
|---|---|---|---|---|
| *NEW ENGLAND* | | | | |
| *(Republicans hold 8 of 23 Seats)* | | | | |
| Maine | 1st | Longley | 52% | 4% |
| New Hampshire | 1st* | Zeliff | 66% | 37% |
| | 2nd* | Bass | 51 | 5 |
| Vermont | (0 Seats)* | | | |
| Massachusetts | 3rd | Blute | 55% | 11% |
| | 6th | Torkildsen | 51 | 4 |
| Rhode Island | (0 Seats) | | | |
| Connecticut | 4th | Shays | 74% | 50% |
| | 5th | Franks | 52 | 7 |
| | 6th* | Johnson | 64 | 32 |
| | | | | |
| *MIDDLE ATLANTIC* | | | | |
| *(Republicans hold 32 of 65 Seats)* | | | | |
| New York | 1st | Forbes | 53% | 7% |
| | 2nd* | Lazio | 68 | 40 |
| | 3rd | King | 59 | 19 |
| | 4th* | Frisa | 50 | 13 |
| | 13th* | Molinari | 71 | 46 |
| | 19th* | Kelly | 52 | 16 |
| | 20th* | Gilman | 68 | 39 |
| | 22nd | Solomon | 73 | 46 |
| | 23rd* | Boehlert | 70 | 47 |
| | 24th | McHugh | 78 | 56 |
| | 25th | Walsh | 57 | 14 |
| | 27th | Paxton | 76 | 52 |
| | 30th | Quinn | 67 | 34 |
| | 31st | Houghton | 84 | n/a |
| New Jersey | 2nd | LoBiondo | 65% | 30% |
| | 3rd* | Saxton | 66 | 35 |
| | 4th | Smith | 68 | 37 |
| | 5th* | Roukema | 74 | 52 |
| | 7th | Franks | 59 | 20 |
| | 8th | Martini | 50 | 2 |
| | 11th | Frelinghuysen | 71 | 43 |
| | 12th | Zimmer | 68 | 37 |
| Pennsylvania | 5th | Clinger | Uncontested | --- |
| | 7th | Weldon | 70% | 40% |
| | 8th* | Greenwood | 66 | 39 |
| | 9th | Shuster | Uncontested | --- |
| | 10th* | McDade | 66 | 35 |
| | 13th* | Fox | 49 | 4 |
| | 16th | Walker | 70 | 40 |
| | 17th | Gekas | Uncontested | --- |
| | 19th | Goodling | Uncontested | --- |
| | 21st* | English | 49 | 2 |
| | | | | |
| *EAST NORTH CENTRAL* | | | | |
| *(Republicans hold 42 of 74 Seats)* | | | | |
| Ohio | 1st | Chabot | 56% | 12% |
| | 2nd | Portman | 77 | 54 |
| | 4th | Oxley | Uncontested | --- |
| | 5th | Gillmor | 73 | 46 |
| | 6th | Cremeans | 51 | 2 |
| | 7th | Hobson | Uncontested | --- |
| | 8th | Boehner | Uncontested | --- |
| | 10th* | Hoke | 52 | 13 |
| | 12th | Kasich | 62 | 24 |
| | 15th | Pryce | 68 | 36 |
| | 16th | Regula | 75 | 50 |
| | 18th | Ney | 53 | 6 |
| | 19th* | LaTourette | 48 | 5 |
| Indiana | 2nd | McIntosh | 54% | 8% |
| | 4th | Souder | 55 | 10 |
| | 5th | Buyer | 70 | 42 |
| | 6th | Burton | 77 | 54 |
| | 7th | Myers | 65 | 30 |
| | 8th | Hostettler | 52 | 4 |
| Illinois | 5th | Flanagan | 55% | 10% |
| | 6th* | Hyde | 74 | 50 |
| | 8th | Crane | 65 | 30 |
| | 10th | Porter | 75 | 50 |
| | 11th | Weller | 61 | 22 |
| | 13th | Fawell | 73 | 46 |
| | 14th | Hastert | 76 | 52 |
| | 15th | Ewing | 68 | 36 |
| | 16th | Manzullo | 71 | 42 |
| | 18th | LaHood | 60 | 20 |

| Region/State | District | Winner | Total % of Vote | Margin |
|---|---|---|---|---|
| Michigan | 2nd | Hoekstra | 75% | 51% |
| | 3rd* | Ehlers | 74 | 50 |
| | 4th | Camp | 73 | 48 |
| | 6th | Upton | 73 | 47 |
| | 7th* | Smith | 65 | 32 |
| | 8th* | Chrysler | 52 | 7 |
| | 11th | Knollenberg | 68 | 38 |
| Wisconsin | 1st | Neumann | 50% | 1% |
| | 2nd | Klug | 69 | 40 |
| | 3rd* | Gunderson | 56 | 15 |
| | 6th | Petri | Uncontested | --- |
| | 8th | Roth | 64 | 28 |
| | 9th | Sensenbrenner | Uncontested | --- |
| | | | | |
| *WEST NORTH CENTRAL* | | | | |
| *(Republicans hold 17 of 31 Seats)* | | | | |
| Minnesota | 1st | Gutknecht | 55% | 10% |
| | 3rd | Ramstad | 74 | 48 |
| Iowa | 1st | Leach | 60% | 22% |
| | 2nd | Nussle | 56 | 12 |
| | 3rd | Lightfoot | 58 | 17 |
| | 4th | Ganske | 53 | 7 |
| | 5th | Latham | 61 | 22 |
| Missouri | 2nd | Talent | 67% | 36% |
| | 7th* | Hancock | 57 | 17 |
| | 8th | Emerson | 70 | 43 |
| North Dakota | (0 Seats) | | | |
| South Dakota | (0 Seats) | | | |
| Nebraska | 1st | Bereuter | 63% | 26% |
| | 2nd | Christensen | 51 | 2 |
| | 3rd | Barrett | 79 | 58 |
| Kansas | 1st | Roberts | 77% | 54% |
| | 2nd | Brownback | 66 | 32 |
| | 3rd | Meyers | 57 | 14 |
| | 4th | Tiahrt | 53 | 6 |
| | | | | |
| *SOUTH ATLANTIC* | | | | |
| *(Republicans hold 44 of 75 Seats)* | | | | |
| Maryland | 1st | Gilchrest | 68% | 36% |
| | 2nd | Ehrlich | 63 | 26 |
| | 6th | Bartlett | 66 | 32 |
| | 8th | Morella | 70 | 40 |
| Delaware | At large* | Castle | 71% | 44% |
| Virginia | 1st | Bateman | 74% | 51% |
| | 6th | Goodlatte | Uncontested | --- |
| | 7th | Bliley | 84 | 68 |
| | 10th* | Wolf | 88 | --- |
| | 11th* | Davis | 52 | 6 |
| West Virginia | (0 Seats) | | | |
| North Carolina | 2nd | Funderburk | 56% | 12% |
| | 3rd | Jones | 53 | 6 |
| | 4th | Heineman | 50 | 0 |
| | 5th | Burr | 57 | 14 |
| | 6th | Coble | Uncontested | --- |
| | 9th | Myrick | 65 | 30 |
| | 10th | Ballenger | 72 | 44 |
| | 11th | Taylor | 60 | 20 |
| South Carolina | 1st | Sanford | 66% | 34% |
| | 2nd | Spence | Uncontested | --- |
| | 3rd | Graham | 60 | 20 |
| | 4th | Inglis | 74 | 48 |
| Georgia | 1st | Kingston | 76% | 52% |
| | 3rd | Collins | 66 | 32 |
| | 4th | Linder | 58 | 16 |
| | 6th | Gingrich | 64 | 28 |
| | 7th | Barr | 52 | 4 |
| | 8th | Chambliss | 63 | 26 |
| | 10th | Norwood | 66 | 32 |
| Florida | 1st | Scarborough | 61% | 22% |
| | 4th | Fowler | Uncontested | --- |
| | 6th | Stearns | Uncontested | --- |
| | 7th | Mica | 73 | 46 |
| | 8th | McCollum | Uncontested | --- |
| | 9th | Bilirakis | Uncontested | --- |
| | 10th | Young | Uncontested | --- |
| | 12th | Canady | 65 | 30 |
| | 13th | Miller | Uncontested | --- |
| | 14th | Goss | Uncontested | --- |
| | 15th | Weldon | 54 | 8 |
| | 16th | Foley | 58 | 16 |
| | 18th | Ros-Lehtinen | Uncontested | --- |
| | 21st | Diaz-Balart | Uncontested | --- |
| | 22nd | Shaw | 63 | 26 |

# House Democratic Winners, by region

| Region/State | District | Winner | Total % of Vote | Margin |
|---|---|---|---|---|
| **NEW ENGLAND** | | | | |
| *(Democrats hold 14 of 23 Seats)* | | | | |
| Maine | 2nd* | Baldacci | 46% | 5% |
| New Hampshire | (0 Seats) | | | |
| Vermont* | (0 Seats) | | | |
| Massachusetts | 1st | Olver | Uncontested | --- |
| | 2nd* | Neal | 59% | 23% |
| | 4th | Frank | Uncontested | --- |
| | 5th | Meehan | 70 | 40 |
| | 7th | Markey | 64 | 28 |
| | 8th | Kennedy | Uncontested | --- |
| | 9th | Moakley | 70 | 40 |
| | 10th | Studds | 69 | 38 |
| Rhode Island | 1st | Kennedy | 54% | 8% |
| | 2nd | Reed | 68 | 36 |
| Connecticut | 1st | Kennelly | 73% | 48% |
| | 2nd* | Gejdenson | 43 | 1 |
| | 3rd | DeLauro | 63 | 26 |
| **MIDDLE ATLANTIC** | | | | |
| *(Democrats hold 33 of 65 Seats)* | | | | |
| New York | 5th | Ackerman | 55% | 11% |
| | 6th | Flake | 80 | 60 |
| | 7th* | Manton | 87 | --- |
| | 8th | Nadler | 81 | 65 |
| | 9th | Schumer | 71 | 42 |
| | 10th | Towns | 89 | 80 |
| | 11th | Owens | 89 | 79 |
| | 12th | Velázquez | 92 | 86 |
| | 14th | Maloney | 63 | 27 |
| | 15th* | Rangel | 96 | --- |
| | 16th | Serrano | 98 | --- |
| | 17th* | Engel | 74 | 56 |
| | 18th | Lowey | 57 | 16 |
| | 21st | McNulty | 71 | 44 |
| | 26th | Hinchey | 49 | 1 |
| | 28th* | Slaughter | 57 | 17 |
| | 29th | LaFalce | 55 | 12 |
| New Jersey | 1st | Andrews | 72% | 44% |
| | 6th | Pallone | 60 | 23 |
| | 9th | Torricelli | 62 | 26 |
| | 10th* | Payne | 76 | 54 |
| | 13th* | Menendez | 71 | 46 |
| Pennsylvania | 1st | Foglietta | 81% | 62% |
| | 2nd | Fattah | 86 | 72 |
| | 3rd | Borski | 63 | 26 |
| | 4th | Klink | 64 | 28 |
| | 6th | Holden | 57 | 14 |
| | 11th | Kanjorski | 67 | 34 |
| | 12th | Murtha | 69 | 38 |
| | 14th* | Coyne | 64 | 31 |
| | 15th | McHale | 48 | 0 |
| | 18th | Doyle | 55 | 10 |
| | 20th | Mascara | 53 | 6 |
| **EAST NORTH CENTRAL** | | | | |
| *(Democrats hold 32 of 74 Seats)* | | | | |
| Ohio | 3rd | Hall | 59% | 18% |
| | 9th | Kaptur | 75 | 50 |
| | 11th | Stokes | 77 | 54 |
| | 13th* | Brown | 49 | 3 |
| | 14th | Sawyer | 52 | 4 |
| | 17th | Traficant | 77 | 54 |
| Indiana | 1st | Visclosky | 56% | 12% |
| | 3rd | Roemer | 55 | 10 |
| | 9th | Hamilton | 52 | 4 |
| | 10th | Jacobs | 53 | 6 |
| Illinois | 1st | Rush | 75% | 50% |
| | 2nd | Reynolds | Uncontested | --- |
| | 3rd | Lipinski | 54 | 8 |
| | 4th | Gutierrez | 75 | 50 |
| | 7th | Collins | 79 | 58 |
| | 9th | Yates | 66 | 32 |
| | 12th | Costello | 66 | 32 |
| | 17th | Evans | 55 | 10 |
| | 19th | Poshard | 58 | 16 |
| | 20th | Durbin | 55 | 10 |
| Michigan | 1st | Stupak | 57% | 15% |
| | 5th* | Barcia | 65 | 33 |
| | 9th | Kildee | 51 | 4 |
| | 10th | Bonior | 62 | 14 |
| | 12th | Levin | 52 | 5 |
| | 13th* | Rivers | 52 | 7 |
| | 14th | Conyers | 82 | 65 |
| | 15th | Collins | 84 | 70 |
| | 16th | Dingell | 59 | 19 |
| Wisconsin | 4th | Kleczka | 54% | 9% |
| | 5th | Barrett | 62 | 26 |
| | 7th | Obey | 54 | 8 |
| **WEST NORTH CENTRAL** | | | | |
| *(Democrats hold 14 of 31 Seats)* | | | | |
| Minnesota | 2nd* | Minge | 52% | 7% |
| | 4th* | Vento | 55 | 13 |
| | 5th | Sabo | 62 | 24 |
| | 6th | Luther | 50 | 0(>1%) |
| | 7th | Peterson | 51 | 2 |
| | 8th | Oberstar | 66 | 32 |
| Iowa | (0 Seats) | | | |
| Missouri | 1st* | Clay | 63% | 30% |
| | 3rd* | Gephardt | 58 | 18 |
| | 4th | Skelton | 68 | 36 |
| | 5th | McCarthy | 57 | 14 |
| | 6th | Danner | 66 | 32 |
| | 9th* | Volkmer | 51 | 6 |
| North Dakota | At large* | Pomeroy | 52% | 7% |
| South Dakota | At large * | Johnson | 60% | 23% |
| Nebraska | (0 Seats) | | | |
| Kansas | (0 Seats) | | | |
| **SOUTH ATLANTIC** | | | | |
| *(Democrats hold 31 of 75 Seats)* | | | | |
| Maryland | 3rd | Cardin | 71% | 42% |
| | 4th | Wynn | 75 | 50 |
| | 5th | Hoyer | 59 | 18 |
| | 7th | Mfume | 81 | 62 |
| Delaware | (0 Seats) | | | |
| Virginia | 2nd | Pickett | 59% | 18% |
| | 3rd | Scott | 79 | 58 |
| | 4th | Sisisky | 62 | 24 |
| | 5th | Payne | 53 | 6 |
| | 8th | Moran | 59 | 20 |
| | 9th | Boucher | 59 | 18 |
| West Virginia | 1st | Mollohan | 70% | 40% |
| | 2nd | Wise | 64 | 28 |
| | 3rd | Rahall | 64 | 28 |
| North Carolina | 1st | Clayton | 61% | 22% |
| | 7th | Rose | 52 | 4 |
| | 8th | Hefner | 52 | 4 |
| | 12th | Watt | 66 | 32 |
| South Carolina | 5th | Spratt | 52% | 4% |
| | 6th | Clyburn | 64 | 28 |
| Georgia | 2nd | Bishop | 66% | 32% |
| | 5th | Lewis | 69 | 38 |
| | 9th | Deal | 58 | 16 |
| | 11th | McKinney | 66 | 32 |
| Florida | 2nd | Peterson | 62% | 24% |
| | 3rd | Brown | 58 | 16 |
| | 5th | Thurman | 57 | 14 |
| | 11th | Gibbons | 52 | 4 |
| | 17th | Meek | Uncontested | --- |
| | 19th | Johnston | 66 | 32 |
| | 20th | Deutsch | 61 | 22 |
| | 23rd | Hastings | Uncontested | --- |

*An **independent** candidate received at least 2% of the vote.

# House Republican Winners, by region/cont.

| Region/State | District | Winner | Total % of Vote | Margin |
|---|---|---|---|---|
| *EAST SOUTH CENTRAL* | | | | |
| *(Republicans hold 13 of 27 Seats)* | | | | |
| Kentucky | 1st | Whitfield | 51% | 2% |
| | 2nd | Lewis | 60 | 20 |
| | 4th | Bunning | 74 | 48 |
| | 5th | Rogers | 79 | 58 |
| Tennessee | 1st* | Quillen | 73% | 48% |
| | 2nd* | Duncan | 91 | No Dem |
| | 3rd | Wamp | 52 | 6 |
| | 4th | Hilleary | 56 | 14 |
| | 7th | Bryant | 60 | 21 |
| Alabama | 1st | Callahan | 67% | 34% |
| | 2nd | Everett | 74 | 48 |
| | 6th | Bachus | 79 | 58 |
| Mississippi | 1st | Wicker | 63% | 26% |
| *WEST SOUTH CENTRAL* | | | | |
| *(Republicans hold 21 of 47 Seats)* | | | | |
| Arkansas | 3rd | Hutchinson | 68% | 36% |
| | 4th | Dickey | 52 | 4 |
| Louisiana | 1st | Liingston | Uncontested | --- |
| | 5th | McCrery | Uncontested | --- |
| | 6th | Baker | Uncontested | --- |
| Oklahoma | 1st | Largent | 63% | 26% |
| | 2nd | Coburn | 52 | 4 |
| | 4th* | Watts | 52 | 9 |
| | 5th* | Istook | 78 | No Dem |
| | 6th | Lucas | 70 | 40 |
| Texas | 3rd* | Johnson | 91% | No Dem |
| | 6th | Barton | 76 | 54% |
| | 7th | Archer | Uncontested | --- |
| | 8th* | Fields | 92 | No Dem |
| | 9th | Stockman | 52 | 6 |
| | 13th | Thornberry | 56 | 12 |
| | 19th | Combest | Uncontested | --- |
| | 21st* | Smith | 90 | No Dem |
| | 22nd | DeLay | 74 | 50 |
| | 23rd | Bonilla | 62 | 24 |
| | 26th | Armey | 76 | 54 |
| *MOUNTAIN* | | | | |
| *(Republicans hold 18 of 24 Seats)* | | | | |
| Montana | (0 Seats) | | | |
| Idaho | 1st | Chenoweth | 56% | 12% |
| | 2nd | Crapo | 75 | 50 |
| Wyoming | At large* | Cubin | 53% | 12% |
| Colorado | 3rd | McInnis | 70% | 40% |
| | 4th | Allard | 72 | 44 |
| | 5th | Hefley | Uncontested | -- |
| | 6th | Schaefer | 70 | 42 |
| New Mexico | 1st | Schiff | 73% | 46% |
| | 2nd* | Skeen | 63 | 31 |
| Arizona | 1st* | Salmon | 56% | 17% |
| | 3rd | Stump | 70 | 40 |
| | 4th* | Shadegg | 60 | 24 |
| | 5th* | Kolbe | 68 | 39 |
| | 6th* | Hayworth | 54 | 12 |
| Utah | 1st | Hansen | 65% | 30% |
| | 2nd* | Waldholtz | 46 | 10 |
| Nevada | 1st* | Ensign | 48% | 0 |
| | 2nd* | Vucanovich | 63 | 34 |

| Region/State | District | Winner | Total % of Vote | Margin |
|---|---|---|---|---|
| *PACIFIC* | | | | |
| *(Republicans hold 35 of 69 Seats)* | | | | |
| Oregon | 2nd* | Cooley | 56% | 16% |
| | 5th | Bunn | 50 | 3 |
| Alaska | At large* | Young | 57% | 24% |
| California | 1st | Riggs | 53% | 6% |
| | 2nd* | Herger | 64 | 38 |
| | 4th* | Doolittle | 61 | 26 |
| | 10th | Baker | 59 | 20 |
| | 11th* | Pombo | 62 | 27 |
| | 19th* | Radanovich | 57 | 18 |
| | 21st* | Thomas | 69 | 42 |
| | 22nd | Seastrand | 49 | 0 |
| | 23rd* | Gallegly | 66 | 38 |
| | 25th* | McKeon | 65 | 33 |
| | 27th* | Moorehead | 52 | 9 |
| | 28th* | Dreier | 67 | 36 |
| | 36th* | Brooks | 48 | 0 |
| | 38th* | Horn | 59 | 22 |
| | 39th | Royce | 66 | 37 |
| | 40th | Lewis | 71 | 42 |
| | 41st | Kim | 62 | 24 |
| | 43rd* | Calvert | 55 | 16 |
| | 44th* | Bono | 56 | 18 |
| | 45th | Rohrabacher | 69 | 38 |
| | 46th* | Dornan | 57 | 20 |
| | 47th* | Cox | 72 | 47 |
| | 48th* | Packard | 73 | 51 |
| | 49th* | Bilbray | 49 | 3 |
| | 51st* | Cunningham | 67 | 39 |
| | 52nd* | Hunter | 64 | 33 |
| Washington | 1st | White | 51% | 2% |
| | 2nd | Metcalf | 54 | 8 |
| | 3rd* | Smith | 52 | 7 |
| | 4th | Hastings | 52 | 4 |
| | 5th | Nethercutt | 51 | 2 |
| | 8th | Dunn | 67 | 34 |
| | 9th | Tate | 51 | 2 |
| Hawaii | (0 Seats) | | | |

# House Democratic Winners, by region/cont.

| Region/State | District | Winner | Total % of Vote | Margin |
|---|---|---|---|---|
| *EAST SOUTH CENTRAL* | | | | |
| *(Democrats hold 14 of 27 Seats)* | | | | |
| Kentucky | 3rd* | Ward | 44% | 0% |
| | 6th | Baesler | 59 | 18 |
| Tennessee | 5th | Clement | 60% | 21% |
| | 6th | Gordon | 51 | 2 |
| | 8th | Tanner | 64 | 28 |
| | 9th | Ford | 58 | 16 |
| Alabama | 3rd | Browder | 64% | 28% |
| | 4th | Bevill | Uncontested | --- |
| | 5th | Cramer | 51 | 2 |
| | 7th | Hilliard | 77 | 54 |
| Mississippi | 2nd* | Thompson | 53% | 14% |
| | 3rd | Montgomery | 68 | 36 |
| | 4th | Parker | 68 | 36 |
| | 5th | Taylor | 60 | 20 |
| *WEST SOUTH CENTRAL* | | | | |
| *(Democrats hold 26 of 47 Seats)* | | | | |
| Arkansas | 1st | Lambert | 54% | 8% |
| | 2nd | Thornton | 57 | 14 |
| Louisiana | 2nd | Jefferson | Uncontested | --- |
| | 3rd | Tauzin | Uncontested | --- |
| | 4th | Fields | Uncontested | --- |
| | 7th | Hayes | Uncontested | --- |
| Oklahoma | 3rd | Brewster | 74% | 48% |
| Texas | 1st* | Chapman | 55% | 14% |
| | 2nd | Wilson | 57 | 14 |
| | 4th | Hall | 59 | 19 |
| | 5th | Bryant | 50 | 2 |
| | 10th* | Doggett | 56 | 16 |
| | 11th | Edwards | 59 | 18 |
| | 12th | Geren | 69 | 38 |
| | 14th | Laughlin | 56 | 12 |
| | 15th | de la Garza | 59 | 20 |
| | 16th | Coleman | 57 | 14 |
| | 17th | Stenholm | 54 | 8 |
| | 18th | Lee | 72 | 48 |
| | 20th | Gonzalez | 62 | 24 |
| | 24th | Frost | 53 | 6 |
| | 25th* | Bentsen | 52 | 7 |
| | 27th | Ortiz | 59 | 18 |
| | 28th | Tejeda | 71 | 43 |
| | 29th | Green | 73 | 46 |
| | 30th | Johnson | 73 | 47 |
| *MOUNTAIN* | | | | |
| *(Democrats hold 6 of 24 Seats)* | | | | |
| Montana | At large* | Williams | 49% | 7% |
| Idaho | (0 Seats) | | | |
| Wyoming | (0 Seats) | | | |
| Colorado | 1st | Schroeder | 60% | 20% |
| | 2nd | Skaggs | 57 | 14 |
| New Mexico | 3rd | Richardson | 64% | 30% |
| Arizona | 2nd* | Pastor | 62% | 29% |
| Utah | 3rd | Orton | 59% | 19% |
| Nevada | (0 Seats) | | | |

| Region/State | District | Winner | Total % of Vote | Margin |
|---|---|---|---|---|
| *PACIFIC* | | | | |
| *(Democrats hold 34 of 69 Seats)* | | | | |
| Oregon | 1st* | Furse | 50% | 5% |
| | 3rd* | Wyden | 74 | 56 |
| | 4th | DeFazio | 68 | 36 |
| Alaska | (0 Seats) | | | |
| California | 3rd* | Fazio | 49% | 2% |
| | 5th* | Matsui | 68 | 39 |
| | 6th* | Woolsey | 58 | 20 |
| | 7th* | Miller | 70 | 43 |
| | 8th | Pelosi | 82 | 64 |
| | 9th* | Dellums | 72 | 49 |
| | 12th | Lantos | 67 | 34 |
| | 13th | Stark | 64 | 34 |
| | 14th | Eshoo | 61 | 22 |
| | 15th | Mineta | 60 | 20 |
| | 16th | Lofgren | 65 | 30 |
| | 17th* | Farr | 52 | 7 |
| | 18th* | Condit | 65 | 33 |
| | 20th | Dooley | 56 | 12 |
| | 24th* | Beilenson | 49 | 2 |
| | 26th* | Berman | 63 | 31 |
| | 29th* | Waxman | 68 | 40 |
| | 30th* | Becerra | 66 | 38 |
| | 31st | Martinez | 59 | 18 |
| | 32nd | Dixon | 78 | 61 |
| | 33rd | Roybal-Allard | 81 | 62 |
| | 34th* | Torres | 62 | 28 |
| | 35th | Waters | 78 | 56 |
| | 36th | Harman | 49 | 1 |
| | 37th | Tucker | 78 | 56 |
| | 42nd | Brown | 51 | 2 |
| | 50th* | Filner | 57 | 22 |
| Washington | 6th | Dicks | 58% | 16% |
| | 7th | McDermott | 76 | 52 |
| Hawaii | 1st* | Abercrombie | 54% | 11% |
| | 2nd* | Mink | 70 | 46 |

\* An **independent** candidate received at least 2% of the vote.

# The Winners: 1994 Senate Races, by region

| Region | State | Winner | Party | Total Vote | Percent |
|---|---|---|---|---|---|
| NEW ENGLAND | | | | | |
| | Maine | Snowe | R | 304,516 | 60* |
| | Vermont | Jeffords | R | 102,978 | 50* |
| | Massachusetts | Kennedy | D | 1,257,945 | 58 |
| | Rhode Island | Chaffee | R | 213,896 | 64 |
| | Connecticut | Lieberman | D | 685,460 | 67* |
| MIDDLE ATLANTIC | | | | | |
| | New York | Moynihan | D | 2,548,697 | 55* |
| | New Jersey | Lautenberg | D | 1,017,751 | 50 |
| | Pennsylvania | Santorum | R | 1,732,526 | 49* |
| EAST NORTH CENTRAL | | | | | |
| | Ohio | DeWine | R | 1,816,722 | 53* |
| | Indiana | Lugar | R | 1,029,421 | 67 |
| | Michigan | Abraham | R | 1,577,865 | 52 |
| | Wisconsin | Kohl | D | 912,826 | 58 |
| WEST NORTH CENTRAL | | | | | |
| | Minnesota | Grams | R | 873,849 | 49* |
| | Missouri | Ashcroft | R | 1,058,320 | 60* |
| | North Dakota | Conrad | D | 135,668 | 58 |
| | Nebraska | Kerrey | D | 314,442 | 55 |
| SOUTH ATLANTIC | | | | | |
| | Maryland | Sarbanes | D | 788,052 | 59 |
| | Delaware | Roth | R | 110,886 | 56 |
| | Virginia | Robb | D | 925,500 | 46* |
| | West Virginia | Byrd | D | 288,353 | 69 |
| | Florida | Mack | R | 2,874,424 | 71 |
| EAST SOUTH CENTRAL | | | | | |
| | Tennessee (A) | Frist | R | 828,975 | 57 |
| | Tennessee (B) | Thompson | R | 878,443 | 61 |
| | Mississippi | Lott | R | 411,733 | 69 |
| WEST SOUTH CENTRAL | | | | | |
| | Oklahoma | Inhofe | R | 542,390 | 55* |
| | Texas | Hutchison | R | 2,596,379 | 61 |
| MOUNTAIN | | | | | |
| | Montana | Burns | R | 212,618 | 62 |
| | Wyoming | Thomas | R | 118,061 | 59 |
| | Utah | Hatch | R | 356,345 | 69 |
| | New Mexico | Bingaman | D | 243,759 | 54 |
| | Arizona | Kyl | R | 577,934 | 52* |
| | Nevada | Bryan | D | 193,444 | 53 |
| PACIFIC | | | | | |
| | California | Feinstein | D | 3,608,497 | 47* |
| | Washington | Gorton | R | 796,233 | 55 |
| | Hawaii | Akaka | D | 256,189 | 72* |

* An **independent** candidate received at least 2% of the vote.

# The Winners:  1994 Gubernatorial Races, by region

| Region | State | Winner | Party | Total Vote | Percent |
|--------|-------|--------|-------|-----------|---------|
| *NEW ENGLAND* | | | | | |
| | Maine | King | I | 178,606 | 36* |
| | New Hampshire | Merrill | R | 216,755 | 70* |
| | Vermont | Dean | D | 142,998 | 70* |
| | Massachusetts | Weld | R | 1,521,561 | 71 |
| | Rhode Island | Almond | R | 164,130 | 47* |
| | Connecticut | Rowland | R | 411,887 | 36* |
| *MIDDLE ATLANTIC* | | | | | |
| | New York | Pataki | R | 2,477,986 | 49* |
| | Pennsylvania | Ridge | R | 1,622,885 | 45 |
| *EAST NORTH CENTRAL* | | | | | |
| | Ohio | Voinovich | R | 2,392,319 | 72* |
| | Illinois | Edgar | R | 1,973,239 | 64 |
| | Michigan | Engler | R | 1,839,520 | 62 |
| | Wisconsin | Thompson | R | 1,052,776 | 67 |
| *WEST NORTH CENTRAL* | | | | | |
| | Minnesota | Carlson | R | 1,100,289 | 64 |
| | Iowa | Branstad | R | 562,918 | 57 |
| | South Dakota | Janklow | R | 172,500 | 55 |
| | Nebraska | Nelson | D | 420,048 | 74 |
| | Kansas | Graves | R | 524,502 | 64 |
| *SOUTH ATLANTIC* | | | | | |
| | Maryland | Glendening | D | 638,995 | 50 |
| | South Carolina | Beasley | R | 469,595 | 51 |
| | Georgia | Miller | D | 787,835 | 51 |
| | Florida | Chiles | D | 2,125,984 | 51 |
| *EAST SOUTH CENTRAL* | | | | | |
| | Tennessee | Sundquist | R | 801,664 | 54 |
| | Alabama | James | R | 601,882 | 51 |
| *WEST SOUTH CENTRAL* | | | | | |
| | Arkansas | Tucker | D | 427,970 | 60 |
| | Oklahoma | Keating | R | 486,740 | 47 |
| | Texas | Bush | R | 2,350,389 | 54 |
| *MOUNTAIN* | | | | | |
| | Idaho | Batt | R | 214,506 | 52* |
| | Wyoming | Geringer | R | 117,491 | 59 |
| | Colorado | Romer | D | 617,581 | 55 |
| | New Mexico | Johnson | R | 224,411 | 50 |
| | Arizona | Symington | R | 570,501 | 52* |
| | Nevada | Miller | D | 199,891 | 54* |
| *PACIFIC* | | | | | |
| | Oregon | Kitzhaber | D | 501,539 | 53* |
| | California | Wilson | R | 4,351,584 | 55 |
| | Alaska | Knowles | D | 54,936 | 41 |
| | Hawaii | Cayetano | D | 134,978 | 37* |

\* An **independent** candidate received at least 2% of the vote

# Voter Turnout, in 1994
## compared to 1990, by state
# Up Modestly Overall

| | 1994 | 1990 | 1994 compared to 1990 |
|---|---|---|---|
| **National** | **38%** | **37%** | **+1** |
| Alabama | 38% | 41% | -3% |
| Alaska | 43 | 51 | -8 |
| Arizona | 37 | 39 | -2 |
| Arkansas | 39 | 40 | -1 |
| California | 34 | 35 | -1 |
| Colorado | 41 | 42 | -1 |
| Connecticut | 46 | 45 | +1 |
| Delaware | 37 | 36 | +2 |
| District of Columbia | 40 | 36 | +4 |
| Florida | 38 | 35 | +4 |
| Georgia | 30 | 30 | -* |
| Hawaii | 41 | 42 | -1 |
| Idaho | 51 | 45 | +6 |
| Illinois | 35 | 38 | -3 |
| Indiana | 36 | 37 | -1 |
| Iowa | 47 | 48 | -1 |
| Kansas | 43 | 43 | +* |
| Kentucky | 27 | 33 | -6 |
| Louisiana | 27 | 47 | -20 |
| Maine | 54 | 57 | -2 |
| Maryland | 36 | 31 | +6 |
| Massachusetts | 47 | 50 | -3 |
| Michigan | 44 | 37 | +7 |
| Minnesota | 53 | 56 | -3 |
| Mississippi | 32 | 20 | +12 |
| Missouri | 45 | 35 | +10 |
| Montana | 56 | 55 | +1 |
| Nebraska | 48 | 52 | -3 |
| Nevada | 35 | 35 | +* |
| New Hampshire | 37 | 35 | +1 |
| New Jersey | 34 | 33 | +1 |
| New Mexico | 39 | 38 | +1 |
| New York | 37 | 30 | +7 |
| North Carolina | 28 | 41 | -13 |
| North Dakota | 50 | 51 | -1 |
| Ohio | 41 | 43 | -2 |
| Oklahoma | 42 | 39 | +2 |
| Oregon | 41 | 52 | -11 |
| Pennsylvania | 39 | 34 | +5 |
| Rhode Island | 46 | 47 | -1 |
| South Carolina | 34 | 29 | +5 |
| South Dakota | 60 | 52 | +8 |
| Tennessee | 38 | 21 | +16 |
| Texas | 33 | 32 | +2 |
| Utah | 42 | 40 | +2 |
| Vermont | 48 | 50 | -2 |
| Virginia | 41 | 24 | +16 |
| Washington | 37 | 36 | +1 |
| West Virginia | 30 | 30 | +* |
| Wisconsin | 41 | 38 | +3 |
| Wyoming | 59 | 50 | +8 |

**Source**: The estimates in this table were made by Curtis Gans and his colleagues, in their *1994 Report* of the Committee for the Study of the American Electorate.

# Turnout in 1994,
## Compared to Past Off-Year Elections
(in percent)

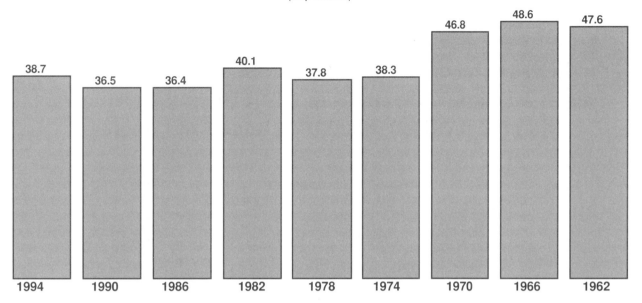

| 1994 | 1990 | 1986 | 1982 | 1978 | 1974 | 1970 | 1966 | 1962 |
| --- | --- | --- | --- | --- | --- | --- | --- | --- |
| 38.7 | 36.5 | 36.4 | 40.1 | 37.8 | 38.3 | 46.8 | 48.6 | 47.6 |

## The Turnout Muddle

For a nation which has been holding free elections for more than two centuries, we Americans have a terrible time getting the voter turnout story straight. Everyone recognizes, to be sure, that voter turnout—whether in presidential years, or in off-year elections—reached its 20th-century high in the early 1960s, and stands at a significantly lower level today.

This said, our basic turnout data are seriously flawed. I believe that the estimates developed by Curtis Gans and his colleagues at the Center for the Study of the American Electorate are the best available—better than those developed by the U.S. Bureau of the Census and published in the *Statistical Abstract*—but Gans himself notes problems with the percentages which his organization releases, shown in the table on the left and in the above figure. Gans notes in his *1994 Report*, for example, that the base for determining turnout which he uses, following the Census lead, is voting-age population. The problem here is that many resident adults by law cannot vote—and these people should not be considered "non-voters." Gans writes: "They are, however, flawed figures, insofar as they include approximately 11 million documented aliens, 2 million undocumented aliens, convicted felons and people in mental institutions who cannot vote...." I would add that the figure on "undocumented aliens" in the resident population is almost certainly far too low. Overall, as many as 18 or 19 million people who by law cannot vote are categorized as "non-voters" in the most widely used turnout statistics.

Each year analysts are presented with this same puzzle: Should they use a more accurate turnout measure for the current year, but then present a number which is not comparable to the previous year's estimates, or should they continue calculating turnout as usual, maintaining the time-line but again yielding estimates known to be flawed? In my judgment, there is no excuse for the Census to continue to base its turnout statistics on a substantially erroneous base. The base has to be: American ctitizens of voting age who are not otherwise deprived, by law, of the franchise.

—ECL—

# The Partisan Composition
## of the Electorate, 1994 compared to 1992

**Around the country, the percentage of the electorate calling themselves Republican in 1994—a big GOP year—was little different from 1992, when the Democrats won the presidency and both houses of Congress.**

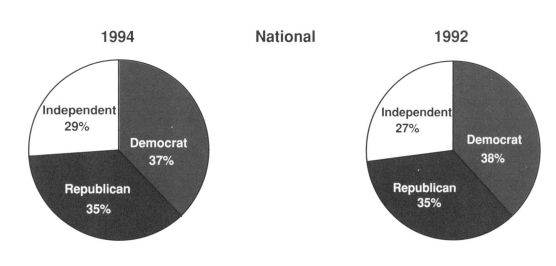

| 1994 | National | 1992 |

*(Pie charts)*

**1994 National:** Democrat 37%, Republican 35%, Independent 29%

**1992 National:** Democrat 38%, Republican 35%, Independent 27%

### New York

|      | Republican | Democrat | Independent |
|------|-----------|----------|-------------|
| **1994** | 32% | 39% | 29% |
| **1992** | 32 | 42 | 26 |

|      | Conservative | Liberal | Moderate |
|------|-------------|---------|----------|
| **1994** | 33% | 23% | 43% |
| **1992** | 25 | 23 | 52 |

### Ohio

|      | Republican | Democrat | Independent |
|------|-----------|----------|-------------|
| **1994** | 39% | 35% | 26% |
| **1992** | 36 | 38 | 27 |

|      | Conservative | Liberal | Moderate |
|------|-------------|---------|----------|
| **1994** | 37% | 18% | 45% |
| **1992** | 33 | 18 | 49 |

### New Jersey

|      | Republican | Democrat | Independent |
|------|-----------|----------|-------------|
| **1994** | 35% | 31% | 34% |
| **1992** | 38 | 35 | 27 |

|      | Conservative | Liberal | Moderate |
|------|-------------|---------|----------|
| **1994** | 38% | 16% | 46% |
| **1992** | 26 | 20 | 54 |

### Michigan

|      | Republican | Democrat | Independent |
|------|-----------|----------|-------------|
| **1994** | 34% | 34% | 32% |
| **1992** | 34 | 36 | 30 |

|      | Conservative | Liberal | Moderate |
|------|-------------|---------|----------|
| **1994** | 40% | 16% | 44% |
| **1992** | 33 | 21 | 46 |

# The "Philosophic" Composition of the Electorate, 1994 compared to 1992

**At the same time, the proportion of the electorate calling themselves *conservative* increased substantially this year—7 points in the national exit poll sample, and by proportions ranging from 3 points (Texas) to 14 points (Illinois) in the "Big Eight" states.**

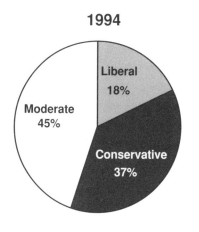

## National

### 1994

Liberal 18%
Moderate 45%
Conservative 37%

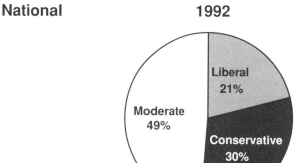

### 1992

Liberal 21%
Moderate 49%
Conservative 30%

### Illinois

|  | Republican | Democrat | Independent |
|---|---|---|---|
| **1994** | 35% | 37% | 28% |
| **1992** | 35 | 38 | 27 |

|  | Conservative | Liberal | Moderate |
|---|---|---|---|
| **1994** | 40% | 17% | 43% |
| **1992** | 26 | 22 | 52 |

### Florida

|  | Republican | Democrat | Independent |
|---|---|---|---|
| **1994** | 40% | 39% | 20% |
| **1992** | 37 | 41 | 23 |

|  | Conservative | Liberal | Moderate |
|---|---|---|---|
| **1994** | 39% | 17% | 44% |
| **1992** | 33 | 20 | 47 |

### California

|  | Republican | Democrat | Independent |
|---|---|---|---|
| **1994** | 39% | 40% | 20% |
| **1992** | 36 | 41 | 23 |

|  | Conservative | Liberal | Moderate |
|---|---|---|---|
| **1994** | 36% | 20% | 44% |
| **1992** | 26 | 23 | 50 |

### Texas

|  | Republican | Democrat | Independent |
|---|---|---|---|
| **1994** | 39% | 35% | 27% |
| **1992** | 36 | 37 | 27 |

|  | Conservative | Liberal | Moderate |
|---|---|---|---|
| **1994** | 43% | 16% | 42% |
| **1992** | 40 | 17 | 43 |

# Chapter 2
# 1994 Vote: Against the Backdrop of Continuing Realignment

### By Everett Carll Ladd

"This book is an attempt to take the mystery out of present-day American politics," Samuel Lubell wrote in *The Future of American Politics*." Our political life, he argued, had been reshaped by a "new, baffling set of political forces"; the "'traditional' pattern of American politics" had disappeared. "There are two basic reasons, I believe, why the American voter has become such an enigma to even the experts and the professional politicians," Lubell went on. "First, we have moved into a new political era in which the old rules and axioms no longer apply. Second, we are in a period of party realignment, with millions of voters being tugged in conflicting directions at the same time."[1]

Later in the book, Lubell introduced his famous—if astronomically confused—"Sun" and "Moon" analogy. The Democratic Party was, of course, the "Sun" in this New Deal cosmology, the Republicans a mere satellite in orbit. The key feature of Democratic dominance, Lubell thought, was not so much its winning most of the elections of the era, but its dictating the substance of political debate.

"If this theory is valid, it follows that the *key to the political warfare of any particular period will be found in the conflict among the clashing elements in the majority party*. This conflict controls the movements of the minority party as well as of the third parties which may appear. The Moon and the lesser planets revolve around the majority Sun."[2]

Sam Lubell caught the "New Deal era" in mid-passage. The party system, which at once reflected and defined the era, indeed differed from those of the past. If dominance by Republican-led coalitions had been "traditional," then political tradition had been busted. More precisely, by the time Lubell wrote in 1951, a new tradition had long-since been forming. Nonetheless, he was right in arguing that many analysts had not accepted the completeness of the New Deal transformation. Franklin Roosevelt had played the key leadership role in shaping it, but its reach and durability far transcended this great architect. There would be no going back. The Democrats were as much the "Sun" in New Deal politics as the Republicans had been in the decades preceding the Depression.

Our own time in at least one sense resembles that which shaped Lubell's book: We, too, haven't gotten entirely accustomed to the fact that politics has been transformed. Lubell's readers had been startled by Harry Truman's 1948 victory—which provided the immediate backdrop. How could it have happened? Very easily, Lubell argued. One had only to understand the magnitude of the partisan changes of the preceding 15 years. A coalition with the reach of the Democrats' could win even in an "off" year. By 1948, its form should have been familiar to all. Similarly, we have often been "startled" by our era's electoral outcomes—but we shouldn't be.

In getting used to our still relatively new parties and election system, it helps to scrap the idea that it must include a new Sun. For two decades now it has been correct to say that the Democrats have lost their majority party status—yet incorrect to describe the Republicans as the majority. We've experienced political change as sweeping as that of the New Deal years. Thus far, though, it has not resulted in either party's unambiguous ascendancy.

### The Immediate Past of American Politics

Lubell's book is a valuable one, but not because it saw the future of American politics. Instead, it shed light on the past. It's true that careful description of what has been happening politically provides background essential in efforts to grasp and respond to present circumstances. It also provides a variety of hints about the political future, since many trends evident in the recent past are likely to continue. At the same time, since the political future is always to be shaped by future actions and events, it remains beyond our grasp. We should be content to describe what has occurred. My colleagues and I hope this volume on the 1994 elections will help researchers and students better understand the political period through which we have been passing.

For a quarter-century we've been seeing a new political era emerge. Writing in 1969, a young Kevin Phillips saw elements of this partisan transformation.[3] In 1975, I began an account of the changes by observing that in rapid fashion "the New Deal has become 'history'."[4] I then described various shifts involving the party system—among them, that "the Democrats have lost the presidential majority status which they enjoyed during the New Deal era," and that "the electorate is far more weakly tied to political parties...than at any time in the past century."[5] These observations still seem to me an accurate account of changes which had already occurred by the mid-1970s—and which remain part of our political present. The political era in which we are living has introduced itself slowly.

In many ways the 1994 vote was a "political earthquake." Just two years after a Democratic president won election, with substantial majorities in both houses of Congress and in the state houses, the GOP has gained its most complete victory since the Great Depression. The "unthinkable" has happened: The Republicans have won the House of Representatives—and, what's more, as this is written they are proclaiming loudly their intention to make something of their newly acquired political strength. My friend James Barnes of the *National Journal* is fortunately positioned to describe this development—being able to say that "on November 8 something happened that I had never seen in my lifetime." Barnes is 38 years old. He was -2 years when the Republicans last saw House majority status.

Nonetheless, I argue that we learned in the 1994 balloting relatively little which is new about our era. It was a striking shift in political power, which will have all manner of consequences, that we will observe in the months and (at least two) years ahead. But the GOP's victory last November 8 only added emphatic punctuation to a political story which has long been unfolding.

## On *Realignment* and Realignment

I have been a bit frustrated with "realignment" as the concept has been applied by my discipline. The word itself is an entirely serviceable one in discussions of partisan change. The *Random House Dictionary of the English Language* (second edition, unabridged) defines "alignment" as "a state of agreement or cooperation among persons, groups...with a common cause or viewpoint." "Realignment" occurs, then, when such an alliance is signficantly changed or, inferentially, when conflict among compet-

---

*Nonetheless, I argue that we learned in the 1994 balloting relatively little which is new about our era. It was a striking shift in political power, which will have all manner of consequences, that we will observe in the months and (at least two) years ahead. But the GOP's victory last November 8 only added emphatic punctuation to a political story which has long been unfolding.*

---

ing alliances is transformed. This simple construction provides, I think, an entirely satisfactory beginning point for political research on changes which may have occurred in the party system.

Have we experienced partisan realignment? Certainly. In one sense, of course, realignment is continuously occurring: Various groups in the population are never completely static in their partisan preferences, and political conflict constantly evinces new dimensions. A straightforward application of the standard dictionary meaning of realignment would insist, though, that for the development to occur there must be *substantial change* from the preceding alignment of social groups and in the shape of political argument. In this sense the US began experienc-

ing political realignment in the late 1960s.

I titled my 1975 book on the subject "tranformations" of the American party system, rather than "realignment," because the latter term had assumed other properties which I did not think were part of the partisan shifts I was describing. It was not, in important regards, like the transformation which we associate with the New Deal. Most notably, it lacked an event of comparably unambiguous impact as the Great Depression. The depth of the Depression crisis broke "politics as usual" loose from its moorings more rapidly and completely than has any event in our own time.

Even so, the New Deal realignment was less compact than often depicted. It had roots reaching much deeper than the New Deal itself. Developments in the Progressive era were precursors. The presidency of Theodore Roosevelt has no real precedents in 19th century America; but, while the course followed by his cousin Franklin differed from TR's, the two reflect important commonalities of response to industrialization. At the other end temporally, as James Sundquist has shown, the New Deal shifts were not neatly consummated in the 1930s. Many occurred well after, as Sundquist says through his metaphor on "aftershocks" of the New Deal.[6]

Still, the New Deal realignment *was* far more compact than the one we have been experiencing, because the Depression really was a huge political event—as well as a massive social and economic one. Its magnitude understandably fueled political science's occupation with the idea of "critical elections." I won't review the labyrinthian developments whereby a narrow model of partisan change, based on an historically unique circumstance—the enormity and sweep of the Depression—shaped the discipline's focus. That has already been attended to elsewhere.[7] Three elements are central to the political science construction of the realignment model:

### Figure 1
### The Republicans Enjoyed a Sharp Spike in Party Identification
### following the 1994 Vote

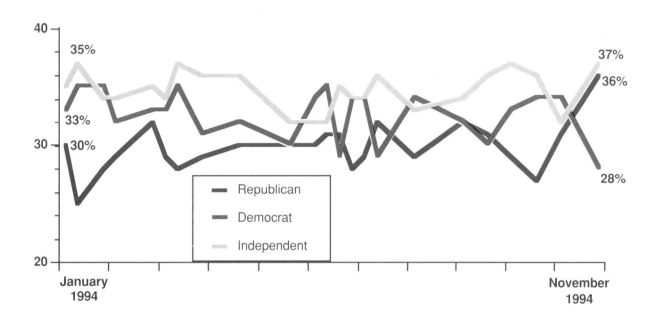

### Figure 2
### President Clinton's Approval Scores Languished Throughout
### the Second Half of 1994

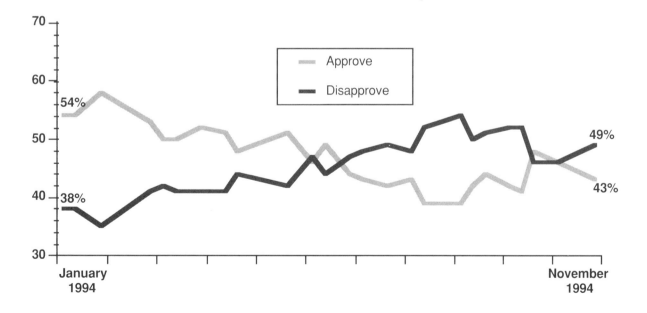

**Source**: [Both Figures] Surveys by the Gallup Organization for CNN and *USA Today*.

(1)That certain elections are of special importance to partisan change; (2) that these critical elections occur in a rather precise frequency or periodicity—usual every 32 to 36 years; and (3) that with realignment a decisive, unidirectional shift occurs in partisan control over the agencies of government, as a new majority party appears at all levels and relegates its predecessor to the dustbin of history.[8]

Criticizing this approach to partisan change, I wrote in 1989 that "the realignment perspective requires us to ask why the partisan 'Big Change' hasn't occurred (and when will it?)... [I]t continues to tease us with the promise that an enormously complex reality will submit to a very simple and highly parsimonious theoretic organization. But the political world stubbornly refuses to comply. [That world] requires of us the task—laborious and prosaic—of charting the many shifts that have occurred in the party system, and seeking *their diverse sources and implications*."[9]

The 1994 election was a "big election" and its results will surely ripple across American politics. It was not a "critical" election, and it showed us relatively little which is new about the vast partisan realignment which has been occurring. Its results followed naturally from important features of that realignment, although they could not have been precisely predicted from it.

In partisan terms, the Republicans have obviously been advantaged by this transformation. They were, decisively, the minority party in the New Deal era. Their position is far stronger today, as many different types of data attest. Gallup found, for example, in its last pre-election poll of 1994 that registered voters were evenly divided in partisan identification—46% Democratic, 46% Republican. By way of contrast, Gallup had found huge Democratic leads in its final pre-election polls most of the time during the New Deal era. In 1962, for example, Democrats outnumbered Republicans by 56% to 38% among registered voters. The

fact that the GOP has achieved essentially parity status in our own time means that the party now competes on an even playing field.

Whether the Republicans will become the majority party as the Democrats were in the New Deal years remains to be seen. What we need to understand, I believe, is that realignment involves a shift in the substance of politics, following upon a shift in socioeconomic structure. In that sense, American politics has been realigned in our time. The precise nature of partisan gains and losses is not specified by the claim that a major realignment has occurred. Some shifts in the partisan balance are evident already; more may be expected. In fundamental regards, the realignment itself is a *fait accompli*.

---

*The "New Deal party system" was a creature of the industrial era. In such an environment, enlargement of the authority and reach of the national government was widely thought—not just by New Deal Democrats—to be appropriately "countervailing."*

---

**From the Industrial to the Post-Industrial Era**

Since I began work on *American Political Parties* in the late 1960s, I've believed that the concept of *postindustrialism* is essential for understanding our era, and in particular for charting developments in the party system.[10] My best effort at a name for the new setting in that volume was "the technological society." Actually, Daniel Bell, the social theorist who has given the term currency, had used *postindustrialism* somewhat earlier. (Bell has noted that the term was first used by sociologist David Riesman in a 1958 essay, though with a somewhat

different meaning.)[11] In any case, Bell developed the concept of postindustrial society in a brilliant 1973 volume.[12] He contrasted the postindustrial period with its predecessor, writing that whereas "industrial society is the coordination of machines and men for the production of goods," postindustrial society is "organized around knowledge."[13] The key developments, Bell argued, defining postindustrialism are "the exponential growth and branching of science, the rise of a new intellectual technology, the creation of systematic research through R & D budgets, and...the codification of theoretical knowledge."[14] I have found Bell's analysis very useful, as I have said, and I've applied elements of it in my assessments of the American political system, notably the party system, in a number of works over the years.[15]

The "New Deal party system" was a creature of the industrial era. Saying this isn't to claim that all of its features grew inevitably from industrial-era social structure. In the first place, of course, industrialism developed in the context of American history, institutions, ideology, and the like. It wasn't a denatured social setting, but rather one that expressed itself in the concrete life of the country. Similarly, noting the importance of industrialism for political change in the US doesn't deny the influence of other factors—including the role of political leadership. Franklin Roosevelt really was president from March 1933 to April 1945, and he and his administration did many things that were in no sense determined by the social structural setting.

Nonetheless, the New Deal was designed to confront problems which were distinctly part of the industrial era, and it chose approaches that struck responsive cords in the population of that day. The interest groups that came together included some whose entry into the Democratic fold long pre-dated the Depression—for example, the South, which was a key part of the New Deal majority, became solidly Democratic as a result of the Civil War. But the majority assembled under FDR's leadership was in many ways a distinctively industrial-era majority—marked by the prominent place accorded big-city interests and party organizations and by the cementing of the allegiance to the Democratic party of a growing labor movement.

What's even more important, the industrial era shaped the substance of the policy debate. Central among those influences on public policy was the fact that industrialization brought with it vast concentrations of power and activity in large enterprises. This was dramatically evident in the business sphere, where the factory system had transformed work life and, in turn, generated demand for a like development in labor unions. The field of communications evinced clear parallels, including in the American experience a single dominant telephone company and, later, the "Big Three" networks' ascendancy in broadcasting.

In such an environment, enlargement of the authority and reach of the national government was widely thought—not just by New Deal Democrats—to be appropriately "countervailing." There was argument, to be sure, between the major parties over how much government there should be, doing which things. Throughout the long New Deal era the Democrats were the more committed of the two major parties to new national government programs. Still, Republicans were often a "me too" party as governmental expansion took place, something nowhere more fully seen than in "Great Society" programs. The Great Society originated in Lyndon Johnson's administration, but Richard Nixon's first term saw many extensions of this approach. The Environmental Protection Agency had its birth during Nixon's presidency, for example, with Nixon's strong support; and a major increase in federal environmental regulation ensued. It was Nixon who remarked early in 1971 that "Now I am Keynesian"—referring to the great British economist's thinking about government's role in

macro-economic management, and endorsing far more activist government than any Republican president had contemplated previously.

In an age of centralization and concentration brought on by the mature industrial order, then, the idea of expanded government had broad appeal and legitimacy. In 1909, Herbert Croly had written *The Promise of Amerian Life*, a brilliant and far-reaching essay on the American political system.[16] Croly argued that at different stages in its history, the US confronted different sorts of challenges, requiring differing responses. Though a leading Progressive—a movement

---

*If the dominant impulses of industrialization were centralizing and government-enhancing, those of the postindustrial years are polar opposites. In the economic and technological spheres, dispersion and decentralization have proceeded apace. In this new setting, centering political power in national government bureaucracies has become increasingly anomalous.*

---

not particularly friendly to the record of the Federalist party—Croly believed that great credit accrued to the Federalists in America's first epoch. They foresaw, he argued, that the promise of American life required a vigorous national government—and took the lead in divising and seeing through the new Constitution. Then, in the years leading up to the Civil War, Croly saw the nation beset by tragic drift. He celebrated Abraham Lincoln's resolute leadership in finally resolving one large part (though by no means all) of the immense crisis. Slavery was not only a great wrong; it was, in Croly's view, a challenge to American nationality itself. America could not realize the promise stated in the Declaration of

Independence, so long as it countenanced an institution which mocked those constitutive claims. Lincoln's "nationalizing" of slavery—rather than leaving it to state's rights ("popular sovereignty" in the language of Stephen Douglas and other politicians who defended it)—rescued American nationality.

The industrial era, Croly observed from his perch in 1909, required new nationalizing impulses—a bold governmental nationalism. To "make the nation more a nation" in the face of challenges stemming from industrialism, major federal intervention was needed in economic management, regulation, and social welfare. Croly saw leaders in both parties failing to chart the new course. He credited one political figure, Theodore Roosevelt, however, with seeing the necessary future of national government responsibility. TR was not the perfect politician in this regard, Croly reasoned, and the Republican party left much to be desired, but thanks to Roosevelt, the Republicans had become the best hope for reform. It was, of course, another Roosevelt and another party which achieved Croly's vision in the 1930s.

I'm not arguing that the New Deal was a carbon copy of Progressivism—because it wasn't. Whether Croly, had he seen the New Deal come to fruition, would have been among its supporters can't be known. Many of his fellow Progressives objected to elements of the New Deal. Walter Lippmann, an early collaborator of Croly's in founding *The New Republic*, became a strong critic of FDR's approach. This having been acknowledged, I will argue that the New Deal's fundamental spirit reflected the spirit of Herbert Croly's call in *The Promise of American Life*.

This doesn't mean that Croly would have seen the fundaments of the New Deal as determinative for all time. New eras breed new requirements. Croly of all people was sensitive to this, having chronicled the implications of era-change for American political development. The industrial era—the setting for Croly's book, and for Franklin Roosevelt's administration—has by now long-since passed. The postindustrial America of 1994 is as decisively different in social structural regards from industrial America of 1937, as the latter was from the predominantly agricultural America of 1867.

## Dispersion and Decentralization

If the dominant impulses of industrialization were centralizing and government-enhancing, those of the postindustrial years are polar opposites. In the economic and technological spheres, dispersion and decentralization have proceeded apace. In this new setting, centering political power in national government bureaucracies has become increasingly anomalous.

The late twentieth century is seeing a quite extraordinary movement against monopolies (and their sisters, oligopolies). A recent issue of the *New York Times* chronicled yet another event in this progression, in a story under the headline, "Electric Utilities Brace for an End to Monopolies."[17] Soon, the account informed readers, consumers will be able to choose which electric utility they buy their power from—will be able in short to "shop" for electrical power. Who would have imagined it just a few years ago?

But of course all sorts of monopolies and oligopolies are coming under successful assault. Telephones are an obvious case. Until a few years ago, experts assumed that one monopoly would survive in the telephone

buiness, even as AT&T's historic monopoly passed—namely that held by the local phone system which brings the wires into your house. However much competition there might be in other sectors of the phone business, you would have to have your home and office wired, wouldn't you, and it wouldn't make sense to have two companies wiring one town. Now, we know that developments in cellular technology have brought competition to the level of local service.

Looking to business corporations today, we read much about "corporate downsizing" and the strains it entails for many employees. We read less of the fact that downsizing reflects not merely a global marketplace and its greater competitive pressures, but as

### Table 1
### A Big Decrease in "Spending Enthusiasm"

|  | Increase | Keep Same | Decrease |
|---|---|---|---|
| **Environmental Protection** |  |  |  |
| December, 1994 | 40% | 40% | 17% |
| May, 1990 | 71 | 24 | 3 |
| **Social Security** |  |  |  |
| December, 1994 | 46 | 45 | 7 |
| May, 1990 | 63 | 32 | 3 |
| **Health Care** |  |  |  |
| December, 1994 | 52 | 33 | 11 |
| August, 1990 | 74 | 6 | 18 |
| **Farm Subsidies*** |  |  |  |
| December, 1994 | 27 | 36 | 29 |
| May, 1990 | 50 | 34 | 13 |
| **Military Defense** |  |  |  |
| December, 1994 | 31 | 44 | 23 |
| August, 1990 | 23 | 31 | 43 |

*Stated as "Aid to farmers" in trends.

**Question:** If you were making up the federal budget this year, would you increase spending for...decrease spending for...or keep spending the same for this?

**Source:** Surveys by the Times Mirror Center for The People and The Press.

### Table 2
### Conservatism Was "In" in 1994:
### Assessing the Republicans' Conservatism and the Democrats' Liberalism

|  | Too Conservative | Too Liberal | About Right |
|---|---|---|---|
| **The Republican Party** |  |  |  |
| November 28-29, 1994 | 31% | 11% | **54%** |
| August 19-20, 1992 | 39 | 12 | **38** |
| **The Democratic Party** |  |  |  |
| November 28-29, 1994 | 13 | 50 | **32** |
| August 19-20, 1992 | 8 | 37 | **46** |

**Question:** In general, do you think the political views of [the party] are too conservative, too liberal, or about right?

**Source:** Survey by the Gallup Organization for CNN and *USA Today*.

well the end of the kind of exclusivity and dominance which certain big corporations had experienced. International Business Machines is a prime case here. IBM was never a monopoly, but for a time it so dominated the computer market as to give it extraordinary resources—which among other things sustained a management and employee structure that could not possibly be maintained in a truly competitive marketplace. When the continued unfolding of computer technology eroded IBM's mainframe dominance, this quasi-monopoly, and its employment practices, had to end.

In general, "Fortune 500" firms have for many years now been losing ground in their share of US employment. Job growth, which has been impressive overall in the past 15 years, continuing now into the Clinton Administration, has occurred primarily through a vast expansion of small enterprises. Individual entrepreneurial activity has been flourishing—in part because many features of the postindustrial socioeconomic structure, including many manifestations of computer technology, have encouraged it.

In the face of these changes across the social and economic system, major political shifts were inevitable. Elements have proceeded in stages—centering in a vast transformation of public thinking on the role and place of government. Caught up as we are in this debate, and inevitably choosing sides in ongoing partisan arguments, we easily lose sight of the fact that pressures for decentralization and dispersion are occurring across the society and are in no sense limited to the governmental sphere. There's a proper partisan argument over just what government should be doing. Nonetheless, thinking about government was bound to be substantially impacted.

## The Debate Transformed

The transformation in thinking about government, which I see as social-structurally related to the move into postindustrialism, doesn't posit a certain partisan winner— though in the short-term it has evidently weakened the Democrats' position. Consider US experience during rapid industrialization. For much of the era Republicans gave disproportionate leadership to industrial development—to the extent, that is, that government was engaged. As noted, writing in 1909 Herbert Croly believed that the Republicans were more likely than the Democrats to lead in the second stage of industrial-era policy reform. An astute observer of American politics, Samuel Beer, has posed a big"what if " question. Beer asked, what if Alfred E. Smith had won the election of 1928 and Herbert Hoover had been able to assume office in 1933 without being seen, then, as the architect of the Great Depression?[18] One need not accept all of Joan Hoff Wilson's argument in her study, *Herbert Hoover: Forgotten Progressive*, to accept, as I do, her portrayal of the 31st president in terms starkly different from the imagery of "Hoovervilles."[19]

In short, there was nothing inevitable in the social-structural realities of the industrial era requiring a Democratic majority—although centralizing, nationalizing, and government-enhancing tendencies were inevitable in this setting. The latter had manifested themselves in Republican thinking. Now, the question of the partisan custody of the next 25 years of American experi-

### Table 3
### "Liberalism" was Notably out of Favor at Election Time 1994

|  | Average Thermometer Score | % "Warm" | % "Cool" |
|---|---|---|---|
| **Conservatives (overall rating)** | **57** | **47** | **25** |
| Rated by: |  |  |  |
| Independents | 55 | 43 | 25 |
| Democrats | 48 | 30 | 35 |
| Republicans | 68 | 68 | 15 |
| **Liberals (overall rating)** | **41** | **23** | **47** |
| Rated by: |  |  |  |
| Independents | 44 | 25 | 44 |
| Democrats | 49 | 32 | 30 |
| Republicans | 30 | 11 | 67 |

**Question**: ...I'd like to rate your feelings toward some people and organziations, with one hundred meaning a "very warm, favorable" feeling; zero meaning a "very cold, unfavorable" feeling; and fifty meaning not particularly warm or cold. You can use any number from zero to one hundred, the higher the number the more favorable your feelings are toward that person or organization.

**Source**: Survey by Greenberg Research for the Democratic Leadership Council, November 8-9, 1994.

ence as a postindustrial society hasn't been fixed. Much of the playing field on which that competition will be fought is, however, well laid out. Both political parties will have to compete on this terrain.

Thus far, the role-of-government argument has played itself out in certain stages—Proposition 13 and the early "taxpayers' revolts," then the

### Table 4
### A Big Comparative Gain (at least temporarily) in GOP Favorability

|  | Favorable | Unfavorable |
|---|---|---|
| **July, 1994** |  |  |
| Republican Party | 63% | 33% |
| Democratic Party | 62 | 34 |
| **December, 1994** |  |  |
| Republican Party | 67 | 27 |
| Democratic Party | 50 | 44 |

**Source**: Surveys by the Times Mirror Center for The People and the Press.

"Reagan Revolution," on to the "anti-government mood" of the 1990s and, last month, the GOP's big victories in congressional balloting and in state house contests. The magnitude of this change is at once exaggerated and trivialized by calling present thinking "anti-government." Americans evidently do not want to dismantle the modern state. It's nonsensical to claim that we are "against government." It's equally silly, though, to say that our thinking about government has not changed substantially over the last 20 years. Americans continue to want a lot of government. We will continue to want a lot. But we have shifted our views. I have tried to chronicle this evolution in a number of publications.[20]

While not turning against government, Americans have become more skeptical about its efficacy, less inclined to agree when a politician approaches them saying, in effect, "We have a terrible problem, and this new government program is what's needed." The new mood of doubt or skepticism about extending the modern state is vastly different from what "anti-government" connotes . It's also certainly the case that among the many things which people want government to continue to do are those which benefit them directly. In an interview published later in this volume, John Brennan of the *Los Angeles Times* points out, for example, that large segments of the middle class are in no sense eager to see their "middle-class entitlements" gutted.

This acknowledged,"more government" is a vastly harder sell now than it was from the Depression on through the Great Society. The healthcare debate evinced important elements of the shift. It began centering on one question: Do we have major problems, especially involving escalating costs and how to pay for them? The public's emphatic answer was, and is, yes. In the latter stages, though, the debate focused on a very different question: Do you favor extended governmental management of the healthcare system? Here, the answer was an emphatic no. The Democrats won the debate when it focused on the first question, and lost it when it shifted to the second.[21]

## The "Contract With America"

A related topic involves the impact of the House Republicans' "Contract with America." Surveys have shown that most voters had little if any specific knowledge about the proposals. This does not mean, however, that they did not see the Republicans as more inclined than the Democrats to challenge the efficacy of governmental action. Seven of the ten "planks" in the contract deal directly with the role of government and call for reductions in national government activity. Did the idea of the Contract strengthen public sentiment that the GOP was "serious" about doing something in this area—even though specific knowledge of the proposals was absent? I know of no survey data which are conclusive here, but that hardly disposes of the question.

What we do know is that public sentiment during the 1994 campaign was strongly negative on government's current performance and skeptical about the longer-term utility of more government. Various data presented in Chapter 3 of this volume attest to this. A few additional tables presented in this chapter help round out the picture. When Americans are asked whether they want more, less, or about the existing amount of public spending for things they strongly favor—such as education and Social Security—they typically have said "spend more." It's against this backdrop that the answers to a December 1994 Times Mirror survey are so striking. Asked whether or not "if you were making up the federal budget this year," you would "increase or decrease spending on various programs and activities," respondents were vastly less inclined to say "spend more" than respondents had been in previous surveys (Table 1). Relatedly, I think,

the public at election time was more inclined to call the Republican party's conservatism "about right" than previously and, in the same vein, less inclined to endorse the Democrats' liberalism (Table 2). In a survey done by Greenberg Research for the Democratic Leadership Council (DLC) on election day and the day following, respondents gave conservatives a far higher "feeling thermometer" endorsement than they did liberals (Table 3). Almost certainly related to and following from this, the GOP's favorability ratings vis-a-vis the Democrats were much improved around election time and immediately following than they had been most of the time in the past

---

*Thus far, the role-of-government argument has played itself out in certain stages—Proposition 13 and the early "taxpayers' revolts," then the "Reagan Revolution," on to the "anti-government mood" of the 1990s and, last month, the GOP's big victories in congressional balloting and in state house contests. The magnitude of this change is at once exaggerated and trivialized by calling present thinking "anti-government."*

---

(Table 4; Figure 1). This is in part the "rosy glow" that accompanies winning—and certainly it's no guarantee that the favorable response which the Republican effort got at the ballot box on November 8, will be sustained. It does seem, as I've said, that a large shift in public thinking about government has taken place, that it provided an essential part of the backdrop for the 1994 balloting, and that voters were as a result more inclined to "take a chance" on the GOP than they otherwise would have been.

## Short-Term Factors

An American election is not, of course, simply the playing out of broad social-structure-related changes. Bill Clinton has had a rocky presidency. His approval ratings for the first two years of his administration are the lowest for any president over the same span since such polling data became available. The Gallup data on Clinton's approval during 1994 (Figure 2) show that he never got out of the "high doldrums." His average approval—for 1994 alone, or for his entire presidency—is firmly ensconced in the 40s. Clinton's marks immediately before and after the 1994 vote were notably low—as these CBS News/ *New York Times* data in Table 5 attest.

The President's relative unpopularity was evidently a factor in 1994. The Democrats' electoral fate would almost certainly have been more fortunate had their president been getting better marks. In part, to be sure, Clinton's low ratings were not for "Clinton" himself but involved his administration's approach to public policy—i.e., Democratic policy. Nonetheless, other contributing elements to Clinton's low standing derive from things entirely apart from program substance—the so-called "character dimension," and the sense that he is indecisive and vacilating. The former factor hasn't been measured with precision, but my reading of poll data from the time Clinton became a major national candidate through to the present suggests that John Brennan's estimate (Chapter 5) of a ten-percentage-point "character drag" in Clinton's standing is close to the mark.

So, yes, definitely, "things could have been different in 1994" even given the basic unfolding of thinking on government. But short-term factors always shape elections. This doesn't stop us from seeing larger and longer term elements at play. We know that partisan developments of the New Deal era were not just products of Franklin Roosevelt's personal charm and skillful leadership. Public thinking about government and what it should do, which had been shifting over several decades, moved sharply following the Depression—toward support for a broader federal role. Similarly, I believe, it has been shifting in our own time, though in a different direction. This underlies many of the electoral problems that the Democrats have been having—problems which came into focus first in presidential voting.

## The Established View of Congressional Elections Wasn't Wrong

Political scientists and other analysts have explored why the Democratic party had such dominance in congressional balloting for so long. It's been noted, for example, that incumbents—of whom the Democrats have had more, thanks in part to such Republican calamities as Watergate—have enjoyed disproportionate advantages over their challengers in campaign resources. Nothing about the 1994 experience challenges this assessment. In Chapter 7, Michael Malbin, a leading expert on these matters, examines 1994 campaign finance data and shows that more challengers in 1994 had "sufficiency" in resources, although most were still outspent by incumbents. Malbin has long argued that the goal in campaign finance should be *sufficiency* for credible challengers, not *parity*. But the fact that there was more "sufficiency" in 1994 hardly challenges the interpretation that a campaign finance structure favoring incumbents—which has dominated modern congressional electioneering—has contributed to modern results.

Similarly, I have argued elsewhere that Americans are highly ambivalent about modern government. They are strongly critical of its performance, far

more so than they used to be. At the same time, they want a lot of services and see no alternatives to a large governmental role. This ambivalence is clearly demonstrated in survey findings.[21] I have speculated that it has provided one important underlay of our long experience with divided government—the presidency of one party, Congress of the other. This division has manifested itself most of the time in a Republican presidency and a Democratic Congress, but surely the "cognitive Madisonian" assessment, if valid, need not work out that way. A

**Table 5**
**The President's Standing Was Especially Low at Election Time**

| | | 12/94 | 11/94 | 10/94 |
|---|---|---|---|---|
| Overall Clinton Approval: | Approve | 38% | 40% | 43% |
| | Disapprove | 49 | 50 | 48 |
| Handling Foreign Policy: | Approve | 36 | 42 | 49 |
| | Disapprove | 50 | 44 | 40 |
| Handling Economy: | Approve | 41 | 39 | 37 |
| | Disapprove | 49 | 52 | 56 |

**Source**: Surveys by CBS News and the *New York Times.*

Democratic presidency and a Republican Congress will do just fine, thank you. Analyst William Schneider quipped some years ago that the Republicans would not win control of Congress until they lost the presidency. It's a clever remark—and also one with real substance behind it.[22]

Americans have not resolved their ambivalence about the modern state. Data show that skepticism about governmental answers is greater now than at any point since the onset of the New Deal. This hardly means, though, that the tensions in sentiment about the state have been removed. Doubts on government's role and record co-exist with high public expectations that large national problems be vigorously addressed. Americans will not be satisfied with the overall record as they see

it in health care. They believe that much more needs to be done to curb crime. They continue to favor a strong national defense. They endorse free public education, and they want more done to improve its quality. In these and many other areas, we see large governmental responsibility. We are receptive to more *nongovernmental* answers, but we remain insistent that *there be answers*. The public will continue to be cross-pulled, even while the underlying balance of sentiment has shifted in the postindustrial era.

## Continuity More Than Change

The Republicans' gaining control of the national legislature for the first time since 1954 is a big change. The aggressive efforts of House Republicans to reframe the national debate and transform their institution deserves the attention it's getting as I write. Nonetheless, the election results of 1994 display important continuities with the past—in many ways far more impressive than the differences.

Writing just after the 1992 elections, I observed that the key features of social group voting that had become common features of the political scene since the late 1960s continued in evidence in 1992, even though Bill Clinton regained the presidency for the Democrats. The South continued its long-term move from the Democratic camp, even though African Americans, South as well as North, were overwhelmingly Democratic. Catholics, along with southern white Protestants, a mainstay of earlier Democratic coalitions, continued in 1992 their long drift from decisive Democratic loyalties. The gender gap was a prominent part of the 1992 balloting. Among white Americans, Republicans did far better among the "churched" part of the electorate than among the "unchurched."[23] These and many other patterns carried over in 1992 from the 1980s continued in 1994.

We show this in Chapter 4, where patterns of social group voting are examined. Again, there was a large gender gap, with women more Democratic, men more Republican. Again, the relationship of education in the vote forms a U-curve—with the Democrats doing best among those with little formal education, and then among those with the most years of school. The South continued its long odyssey toward the GOP. In 1994, for the first time ever, a majority of House members from the South are Republicans. But the basic dynamic of the southern realignment is our longest-running realignment story. (The South still has a way to go. Democrats still hold more than 1100 of the region's 1800 state legislative seats—about 63%. This is almost certainly an unsustainable margin, given current partisan preferences of southerners.)

The United States is somewhere in the middle stages of a major political realignment, one precipitated in large part by the shift from an industrial to a postindustrial setting. Important features of the new party system are clearly defined. Party coalitions are drastically different from those of the New Deal years. Party organization plays a far lesser role in the current system than in any of its predecessors, and the electronic media are a central instrumentality of the new politics. The Democratic party lost its once-clear majority status in the realignment's early stages. Whether any party will be able to claim firm majority status remains to be seen—though we do know that voter ties to parties are weaker than in times past, and almost certainly, permanently so.

After every national election a partisan battle for the future begins. It is one of the glories of our democracy. *America at the Polls 1994* is a description of the past—which we hope will assist those who will observe and participate in the shaping of the future.

## Endnotes

[1] Samuel Lubell, *The Future of American Politics* (Garden City, NY: Doubleday,

2nd edition revised 1956; first published 1951), p. 1.

[2] *The Future of American Politics*, p. 217.

[3] Kevin Phillips, *The Emerging Republican Majority* (New Rochelle, NY: Arlington House, 1969).

[4] Ladd, with Charles D. Hadley, *Transformations of the American Party System: Political Coalitions from the New Deal to the 1970s* (New York: W. W. Norton, 1975, second edition, 1978), p. xxi.

[5] *Transformations of the American Party System*, pp. 26-27.

[6] James L. Sundquist, *Dynamics of the Party System* revised ed. (Washington, DC: Brookings, 1983).

[7] See, for example, David G. Lawrence and Richard Fleisher, "Puzzles and Confusions: Political Realignment in the 1980s" *Political Science Quarterly*, Spring 1987, pp. 79-92; Jerome M. Clubb, William H. Flanagan, and Nancy H. Zingale, *Partisan Realignment: Voters, Party and Government in American History* (Beverly Hills, CA: Sage Publications, 1980), especially pp. 19-45; and Edward G. Carmines and James A. Stimson, "The Dynamics of Issue Evolution: the United States," in *Electoral Change in Advanced Industrial Democracies*, ed. Russell J. Dalton, (Princeton, NJ: Princeton University Press, 1984), pp. 134-158.

[8] See my essay, "Like Waiting for Godot: The Uselessness of *Realignment* for Understanding Change in Contemporary American Politics." This was first prepared as a paper presented at the 1989 meeting of the American Political Science Association in Atlanta. It was subsequently published in two different forums: *Polity*, Volume XXII, No. 3, Spring, 1990, pp. 511-25; and in Byron E. Shafer, ed., *The End of Realignment? Atrophy of a Concept and Death of a Phenomenon* (Madison: University of Wisconsin Press, 1991), Chapter 2.

[9] "Like Waiting for Godot," p. 34.

[10] Ladd, *American Political Parties: Social Change and Political Response* (New York: W. W. Norton, 1970). I was reminded of just how long I have been occupied with this question (and inclined to a particular approach) when I looked at the cover of my copy from the first printing: The price is there imprinted—$3.95.

[11] David Riesman, "Leisure and Work in Postindustrial Society," printed in the compendium of essays, *Mass Leisure* (Glencoe, IL: The Free Press, 1958).

[12] Daniel Bell, *The Coming of Postindustrial Society* (New York: Basic Books, 1973).

[13] *The Coming of Postindustrial society*, p. 20.

[14] Ibid., p. 44.

[15] *Transformations of the American Party System: Political Coalitions from the New Deal to the 1970s*, with Charles D. Hadley (New York: W. W. Norton, 1975); *Where Have All the Voters Gone?: The Fracturing of America's Political Parties* (New York: W.W. Norton, 1978, revised edition, 1982); "The Shifting Party Coalitions: 1932-1976," in S.M. Lipset, ed., *Emerging Coalitions in American Politics* (San Fransisco: Institute for Contemporary Studies, 1978), pp. 81-102; "The New Lines Drawn: Class Ideology in America," *Public Opinion* (July/August 1978), pp. 48-53; "Class Ideology, Part II," *Public Opinion* (September/October 1978), pp. 14-20; "The American Party System Today," in S.M. Lipset, ed., *The Third Century: America as a Post Industrial Society* (Stanford: Hoover Institution Press, 1979), pp. 153-182; "The Brittle Mandate: Electoral Dealignment and the 1980 Presidential Election," *Political Science Quarterly* (Spring 1981), pp. 1-25; "The Shifting Party Coalitions from the 1930s to the 1970s," in S.M. Lipset, ed., *Party Coalitions in the 1980s* (San Fransisco: Institute for Contemporary Studies, 1981); "Politics in the 1980s: an Electorate at Odds with Itself," *Public Opinion* (December/January 1983), pp. 2-6; "The Reagan Phenomenon and Public Attitudes Towards Government," in Lester M. Salamon and Michael S. Lund, eds., *The Reagan Presidency and the Governing of America* (Washington, D.C.: Urban Institute Press, 1984); "On Mandates, Realignments, and the 1984 Presidential Election," *Political Science Quarterly* (Spring 1984), pp. 1-25; "Party Reform and the Public Interest," in A. James Reichley, ed., *Elections American Style* (Washington, D.C.: The Brookings Institution, 1987); "The 1988 Election: Continuation of the Post-New Deal System," *Political Science Quarterly* (Spring 1989), pp. 1-18; "Like Waiting for Godot," *Polity*, Spring 1990, pp. 511-25; "The 1992 Vote for President Clinton: Another Brittle Mandate," *Political Science Quarterly* (Spring 1993), pp. 1-28; "Political Parties and Presidential Elections in the Postindustrial Era," in Harvey Shantz, ed., *Presidential Elections Throughout the Years* (Albany: State University of New York Press, 1995); "We'll Have More Perots and Religion-based Politics," *Cosmos Journal* (April 1994); "On the Argument for Parties Strong and 'Great': A Dissent," in John K. White and John C. Green, eds., *The Politics of Ideas* (Forthcoming, 1995).

[16] Herbert Croly, *The Promise of American Life* (Boston, MA: Northeastern University Press, 1989, first published 1909).

[17] *The New York Times*, August 8, 1994.

[18]Samuel H. Beer, "Liberalism and the National Idea," *The Public Interest*, Fall 1966, p. 75.

[19] Joan Hoff Wilson, *Herbert Hoover: Forgotten Progressive* (Boston: Little Brown, 1975).

[20] See Ladd, with S. M. Lipset, "Public Opinion and Public Policy: Trends and the Likely Climate for the 1980s," in P. Duignan and A. Abushka, eds., *The United States in the World of the 1980s* (Stanford: Hoover Institution Press, 1980). See following by Ladd: "Politics in the 1980s: An Electorate at Odds with Itself," *Public Opinion* (December/January 1983); "The Reagan Phenomenon and Public Attitudes Towards Government," in Lester M. Salamon and Michael S. Lund, eds., *The Reagan Presidency and the Governing of America* (Washington, D.C.: Urban Institute Press, 1984); "Tax Attitudes," *Public Opinion* (February/March 1985), pp. 8-10; "Attitudes Toward Government: What the Public Says," with Karlyn H. Keene, *Government Executive* (January 1988), pp. 11-16; "Public Attitudes on the U.S. Military: A Case Study in Continuity," with Karlyn H. Keene, *Government Executive* (June 1989); "Public Opinion and The 'Congress Problem'," *The Public Interest* (Summer 1990), pp. 1-11.

[21] In Chapter 3 of this volume, we have presented some summary data on the public's response throughout the healthcare debate. For fuller coverage, see the Roper Center's magazine, *The Public Perspective*, Sept./Oct., '94, pp. 23-28, 109; July/Aug., '94, pp. 94-95; May/June, '94, pp. 84-90; and March/April, '94, pp. 74-76.

[22]See Ladd, "The 1988 Elections: Continuation of the Post-New Deal System," *Political Science Quarterly*, Spring 1989, especially pp. 2-7.

[23] Ladd, "The 1992 Vote for President Clinton: Another Brittle Mandate?", *Political Science Quarterly*, Spring 1993, pp. 3-13.

# Chapter 3
## 1994 Vote: Where Was Public Thinking at Vote Time?

As the 1994 midterm elections approached, the American public was dissatisfied with the status quo. A call for "change," so familiar from the campaigning two years earlier, was again in the air. For many people, the federal government seemed to be failing in its attempt to correct various social and economic ills facing the nation. Surveys had documented before the election that the public was leaning in a conservative direction on many major issues. On items ranging from the size of government, to crime control, to job creation and welfare reform, majorities felt the GOP was best able to deal with these problems.

The underlying theme which served as the foundation for the public's dissatisfaction was a loss of confidence in government. As the data in this chapter show, trust in government reached historic lows in 1994. In the 1950s, roughly three quarters of the public said they trusted the government "to do what is right" all or most of the time. By 1994, less than one-quarter said that. The same progression holds true for Congress, which in 1994 had a lower confidence rating than just about any other public, business or media institution in the nation. Complaining is part of human nature, and Americans have been criticizing their government in some form or another since the nation's founding. However, complaining about the condition of government reached a vociferous peak in 1994.

As for specific issues, people were worried about crime, health care, government taxing and spending, declining morals, and the economy. On each of these matters, the data in this chapter show a growing acceptance among the public of conservative solutions. For example, a large majority of the public in 1994 was demanding that government take a more retributive stance toward those who commit crimes. On welfare, most wanted benefits limited and work requirements expanded. The public favored health care reform, but did not want it to result in large-scale government involvement. State exit polls on election day offered similar evidence. In state after state, respondents showed strong support for smaller government, changes in the welfare system, term limits, and a "modest" approach to health care reform. By November 1994, on just about every issue, a plurality of the public looked more favorably on the Republicans than on the Democrats or the Clinton Administration.

In 1992, the American people wanted change and turned to a self-described "moderate," "change-oriented" Democrat. By 1994, the public, shifting to the right on many issues, was still not satisfied. Voters elected an increasingly conservative Republican party to become the majority force within the Congress for the first time in four decades.

—George Pettinico

# Public Confidence in Government, Especially the Federal Government, Was Very Low in 1994...And Had Been Declining for Some Time

**Question**: Do you agree or disagree with the following statements?..."

**The government is run for benefit of the few and the special interests, not the people.**

**Government is the problem, not the solution to our problems.**

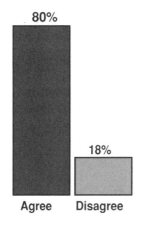

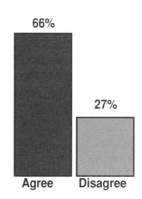

**Source**: Survey by the Tarrance Group & Mellman, Lazarus & Lake for *U.S. News and World Report*, October 21-23, 1994.

**Question**: Which comes closer to your view: Government should do more to solve national problems or **government is doing too many things** better left to businesses and individuals?"

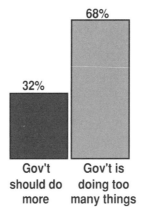

**Source**: Survey by CBS News/*New York Times*, October 29-November 1, 1994.

# No, It Wasn't Always This Way

## From the New Deal years up through the mid-1960s, Americans generally had high hopes and expectations for the federal government.

### 1941

**Question**: Do you think there is too much power in the hands of the government in Washington?

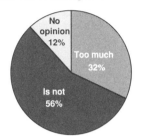

**Source**: Survey by the Gallup Organization, April 10-15.

### 1948

**Question**: Most people agree that a good many activities and responsibilities that were formerly left up to the states are now centered in the national government in Washington. Generally speaking, do you think...**the centering of more activities in Washington has been a good thing for the country?**

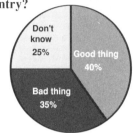

**Source**: Survey by the Roper Organization for *Fortune*, September 13-20, 1948.

### 1954

**Question**: One problem is keeping any group in the United States from getting too big and too powerful. Where do you feel this problem is greatest today...?

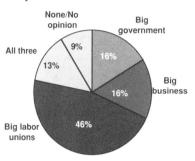

**Source**: Survey by the Opinion Research Corporation, August 23-September 3, 1954.

### 1960

**Question**: On the whole, do the activities of the national government tend to improve conditions in this country or would we be better off without them?

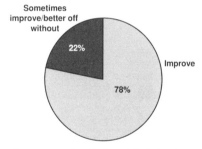

**Source**: Survey by the National Opinion Research Center of International Studies, Princeton University, March, 1960.

### 1964

**Question**: Which one of the statements listed on this card comes closest to your own views about governmental power today?

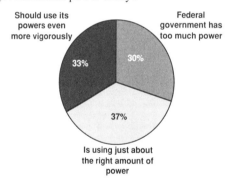

**Source**: Survey by the Gallup Organization for Potomac Associates, October 1964.

**Question**: How much of the time do you think you can trust the government to do what is right—just about always, most of the time, or only some of the time?

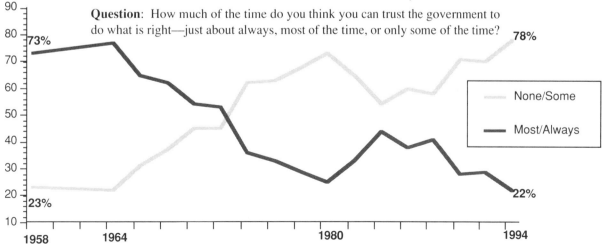

**Source**: University of Michigan National Election Study (NES) for years 1958-1992; 1994 asking from the CBS/*New York Times* Poll, October 1994.

# Federal Government, Much More Than State Government, Under Fire

**Question**:  From which level of government do you feel you get the most for your money?

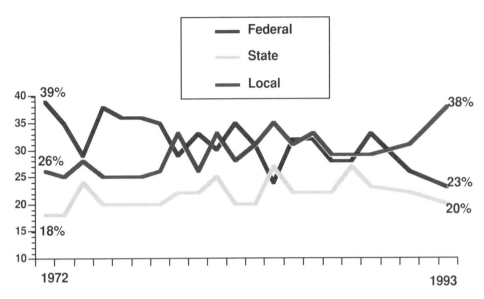

**Source**:  "Changing Public Attitudes on Governments and Taxes," by the Gallup Organization for the Advisory Commission on Intergovernmental Relations, 1993.

**Question**:  Overall, how much trust and confidence do you have in...[the federal/your state/your local government] to do a good job in carrying out its responsibilities? A great deal, a fair amount, not very much, none at all.  (Percentages shown are the combined total of "a great deal" and "a fair amount" responses.)

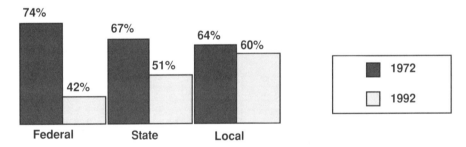

**Source**:  Surveys by the Opinion Research Corporation (1972) and the Gallup Organization (1992) for the Advisory Commission on Intergovernmental Relations.

**Question**:  Thinking of the national government of the United States, would you say you are very satisfied, somewhat satisfied, somewhat dissatisfied, or very dissatisfied with its overall performance?

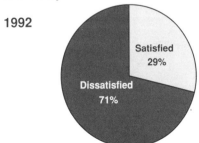

**Source**:  Survey by the Angus Reid Group for CNN, March 1992.

**Question**:  Do you think that, in general, the federal government creates more problems than it solves, or do you think it solves more problems than it creates?

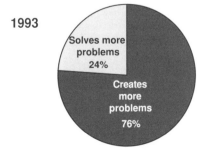

**Source**:  Survey by CBS News for the *New York Times*, January 12-14, 1993.

# In Particular, Criticism of Congress Was Very Strong, and Had Been Building

**Question**: ...[W]hich of these descriptions apply and which do not apply to the members of Congress...?

**...Care about the average American**

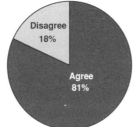

Applies 29%

Does not apply 71%

**...Can get things done**

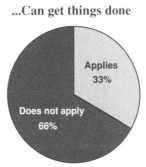

Applies 33%

Does not apply 66%

**...Are bringing needed change to government**

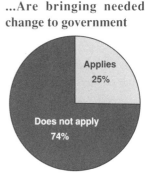

Applies 25%

Does not apply 74%

**Source**: Survey by Yankelovich Partners, Inc. for *Time*/CNN, August 17-18, 1994.

**Question**: ... [Do you agree or disagree]...those we elect to Congress in Washington lose touch with the people pretty quickly....

Disagree 18%

Agree 81%

**Source**: Survey by ABC News/*Washington Post*, June 23-26, 1994.

**Question**: Do you think that most members of Congress are more interested in serving the people they represent, or more interested in serving special interest groups?

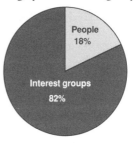

People 18%

Interest groups 82%

**Source**: Survey by CBS News/*New York Times*, October 29-November 1, 1994.

**Question**: ...Please tell me how much confidence you have in each [institution]...—a great deal, quite a lot, some, or very little? (Figures show those who answered "great deal"/"quite a lot".)

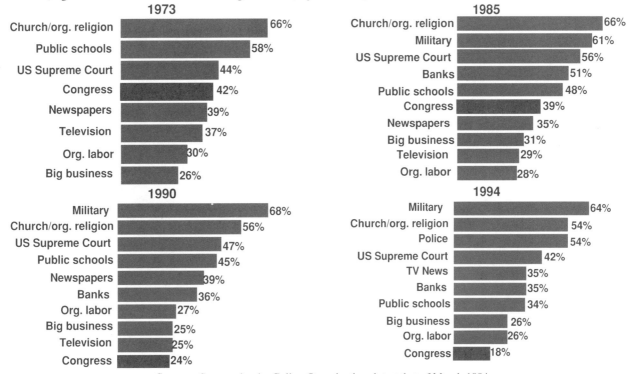

**1973**

| | |
|---|---|
| Church/org. religion | 66% |
| Public schools | 58% |
| US Supreme Court | 44% |
| Congress | 42% |
| Newspapers | 39% |
| Television | 37% |
| Org. labor | 30% |
| Big business | 26% |

**1985**

| | |
|---|---|
| Church/org. religion | 66% |
| Military | 61% |
| US Supreme Court | 56% |
| Banks | 51% |
| Public schools | 48% |
| Congress | 39% |
| Newspapers | 35% |
| Big business | 31% |
| Television | 29% |
| Org. labor | 28% |

**1990**

| | |
|---|---|
| Military | 68% |
| Church/org. religion | 56% |
| US Supreme Court | 47% |
| Public schools | 45% |
| Newspapers | 39% |
| Banks | 36% |
| Org. labor | 27% |
| Big business | 25% |
| Television | 25% |
| Congress | 24% |

**1994**

| | |
|---|---|
| Military | 64% |
| Church/org. religion | 54% |
| Police | 54% |
| US Supreme Court | 42% |
| TV News | 35% |
| Banks | 35% |
| Public schools | 34% |
| Big business | 26% |
| Org. labor | 26% |
| Congress | 18% |

**Source**: Surveys by the Gallup Organization, latest that of March 1994.

# Thinking About the Economy

## Decidedly Mixed Views on the Nation's Position

**Question**: How would you rate the condition of the national economy these days? Is it very good, fairly good, fairly bad, or very bad?

**Question**: Do you think the economy is getting better, getting worse, or staying about the same?

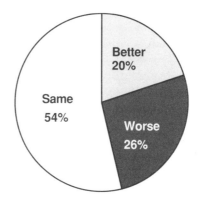

**Source**: Survey by CBS News/*New York Times*, October 29-November 1, 1994.

## Fairly Positive Views on Personal Finances

**Question**: ...In terms of your own family's finances, how do you feel you are doing today—very well, fairly well, poorly, or very poorly?

**Question**: Compared to a year ago, are you and your family better off financially, worse off financially, or about the same?

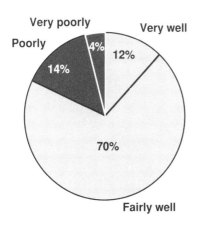

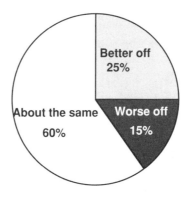

**Question**: Looking ahead two years from now (1996), do you think you and your family will be better off than now, worse off, or about the same?

**Question**: How much do you worry about losing your job—a great deal, some, only a little, or not at all?

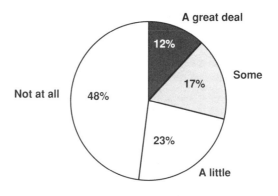

**Source**: Survey by Yankelovich Partners, Inc. for *Time*/CNN, October 11-12, 1994.

# Americans on the Issues:
# Crime:  It's *Very* Serious
## Do *Something...Tough*

**Question**:  How much of a problem is crime in the US?

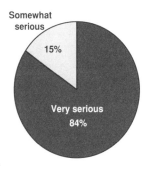

**Source**:  Survey by the Wirthlin Group, September 6-9, 1994.

**Question**:   How much of a problem is crime in your community?...an extremely serious problem, a somewhat serious problem, not very much of a problem, not at all a problem?

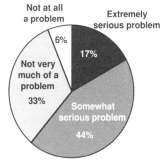

**Source**:  Survey by the Wirthlin Group, September 6-9, 1994.

**Question**:  Has the crime problem gotten better or worse in the past few years?

**Source**:  Survey by Yankelovich Partners, October 11-12, 1994.

**Question**: In general, do you think gun control laws should be made more strict, less strict, or kept as they are now?

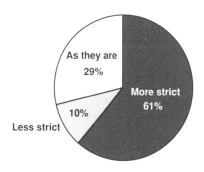

**Source**:  Survey by CBS News, November 27-28, 1994.

**Question**: Do you favor or oppose the death penalty for persons convicted of murder?

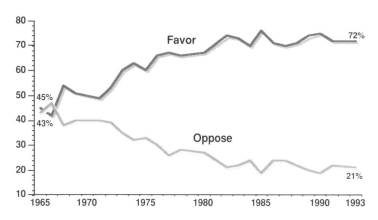

**Question**:  Which best describes how you generally feel about punishment for criminals..."An Eye for An Eye"...or "Turn the Other Cheek"?

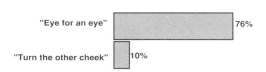

**Source**:  Survey by the Wirthlin Group, September 6-9, 1994.

**Note**:  Gallup data (1965-1971) "Are you in favor of the death penalty for persons convicted of murder?"  NORC data (1972-1993) "Do you favor or oppose the death penalty for persons convicted of murder?"

## Americans on the Issues:

# Health Care Reform: Yes to "Reform";
## No to the Clinton Plan; Concern About
## "Big Government"

**Question:** In general, do you favor or oppose **President Clinton's health care reform plan**?

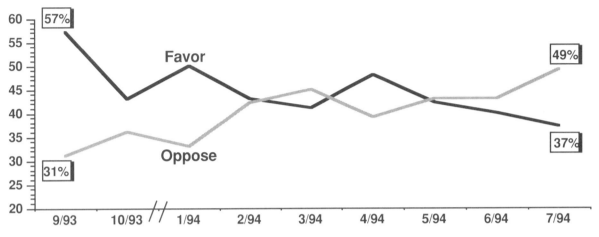

**Source:** Surveys by Yankelovich Partners for *Time*/CNN, latest that of July 13-14, 1994.

**Question:** Which of the following statements comes closest to expressing **your overall view of the health care system in this country**...There are some good things in our health care system, but fundamental changes are needed to make it better...Our health care system has so much wrong with it that we need to completely rebuild it...On the whole, the health care system works pretty well and only minor changes are necessary to make it work?

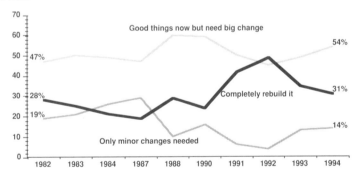

**Source:** Surveys by Louis Harris and Associates, latest that of April 4-7, 1994.

**Question:** Do you think **Clinton's [health care] plan creates too much government involvement** in the nation's health care system, not enough government involvement or about the right amount?

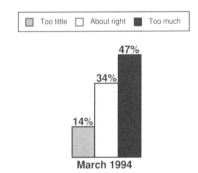

**Source:** Survey by ABC News/*Washington Post*, March 25-27, 1994.

**Question:** Has your support for reform changed in the last six months?

**Question:** Who should take the lead on reform?

**Question:** What should Congress do next on health-care reform:

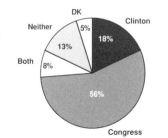

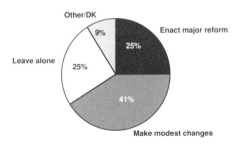

**Source:** Surveys by Kaiser/Harvard/KRC Election Night Survey, November 8, 1994.

# Americans on the Issues:
# Welfare: More Emphasis on Individual Responsibility
# Big Doubts About Existing Programs

**Question**:  Do you agree or disagree..., **"It is the responsibility of the government to take care of people who can't take care of themselves?"**

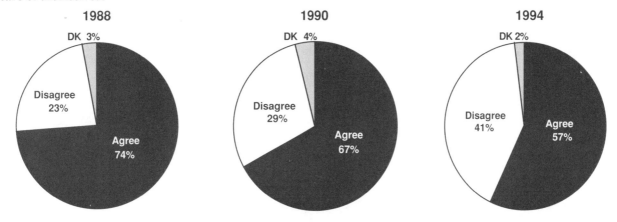

**1988**

DK 3%
Disagree 23%
Agree 74%

**1990**

DK 4%
Disagree 29%
Agree 67%

**1994**

DK 2%
Disagree 41%
Agree 57%

**Source**:  Surveys by Princeton Survey Research Associates for the Times Mirror Center, latest that of July 12-27, 1994.

**Question**: ...Do you think the actions by the federal government in the last twenty years have made this situation  (the opportunity for a poor person in this country to get ahead by working hard) better or worse?

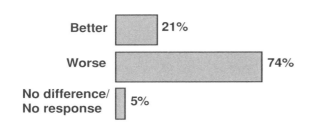

Better — 21%
Worse — 74%
No difference/ No response — 5%

**Source**:  Survey by the Gallup Organization for CNN/*USA Today*, October 22-25, 1994.

**Question**: Do you think the current welfare system encourages poor people to find work or discourages them?

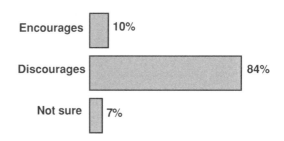

Encourages — 10%
Discourages — 84%
Not sure — 7%

**Source**:  Survey by Yankelovich Partners. for *Time*/CNN, May 18-19, 1994.

**Question**: Do you think welfare recipients should receive benefits, such as food stamps and aid to dependent children, for only two years, or do you think there should not be a two-year limit?

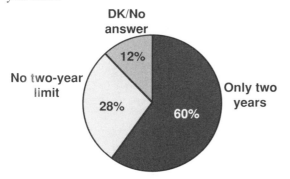

DK/No answer 12%
No two-year limit 28%
Only two years 60%

**Source**:  Survey by CBS News, November 27-28, 1994.

**Question**: (Here is a list of changes many people would like to make in the current welfare system.  For each...please tell me whether you favor or oppose that change.)...Require all able-bodied people on welfare, including women with small children, to work or learn a job skill.

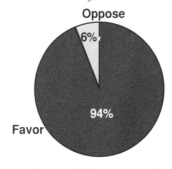

Oppose 6%
Favor 94%

**Source**: Survey by Yankelovich Partners, Inc. for *Time*/CNN, May 18-19, 1994.

# Americans on the Issues:
# The Moral Dimension:
## Concerned We're Losing Ground; Need Moral Leadership from Government; Yet, Maintain Tolerance

**Question**: How do you feel about the problem of low moral and ethical standards in this country today? Do you think this problem is about the same as it has been, that the country is making progress in this area, or that the country is losing ground in this area?

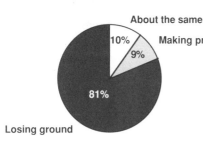

**Source**: Survey by Princeton Survey Research Associates for Times Mirror, September 9-11, 1994.

**Question**: In general, do you think the changes in values and morality which happened in the 1960s have had a positive or a negative effect on the country?

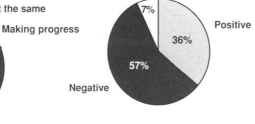

**Source**: Survey by the Gallup Organization for CNN/*USA Today*, September 6-7, 1994.

**Question**: Do you agree or disagree...Individual freedom has gotten out of hand and values are in decline?

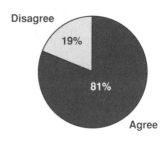

**Source**: Survey by The Tarrance Group & Mellman, Lazarus & Lake, *US News and World Report*, October 21-23, 1994.

**Question**: Some people think the government should promote traditional values in our society. Others think the government should not favor any particular set of values. Which comes closer to your view?

**Question**: Do you agree or disagree...We need more **moral** leadership in government because family values are in decline.

**Question**: Do you agree or disagree...We should be more tolerant about how people choose to live their own personal lifestyles and values?

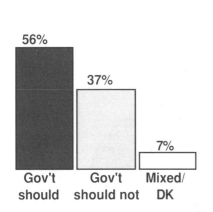

**Source**: Survey by the Gallup Organization for CNN/*USA Today*, November 2-6, 1994.

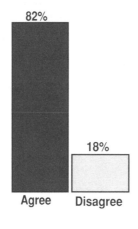

**Source**: Survey by The Tarrance Group & Mellman, Lazarus & Lake, *US News and World Report*, October 21-23, 1994.

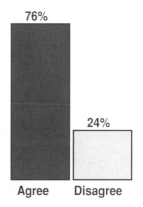

**Source**: Survey by The Tarrance Group & Mellman, Lazarus & Lake, for *US News and World Report*, October 21-23, 1994.

# Americans on the Issues:
# Florida, New Jersey, Michigan, Wisconsin:
## 1994 VNS Findings: A Yes to Less Government

**Question**: ...Would you rather have government provide more services but cost more in taxes, or government cost less in taxes but provide fewer services?

■ (a) Provide more and costs more          ☐ (b) Provide less and costs less

## All Respondents

### Florida
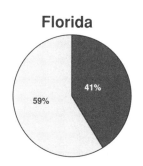

### New Jersey
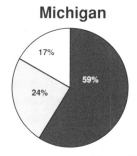

### Wisconsin
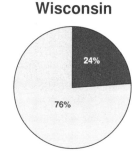

## How Respondents Voted

| Florida Governor | Chiles | Bush |
|---|---|---|
| (a) More | 68% | 32% |
| (b) Less | 42 | 58 |

| New Jersey Senate | Lautenberg | Haytaian |
|---|---|---|
| (a) More | 74% | 25% |
| (b) Less | 36 | 59 |

| Wisconsin Governor | Chvala | Thompson |
|---|---|---|
| (a) More | 51% | 47% |
| (b) Less | 24 | 72 |

**Question**: Do you think the recent changes in [Michigan's/Wisconsin's] welfare system have: been good for the state, been bad for the state, had no effect?

■ (a) Been Good          ☐ (b) Been Bad          ☐ (c) No Affect

## All Respondents

### Michigan

### Wisconsin

## How Respondents Voted

| Michigan Governor | Wolpe | Engler |
|---|---|---|
| (a) Good | 18% | 82% |
| (b) Bad | 82 | 18 |
| (c) No Aff. | 58 | 42 |

| Wisconsin Governor | Chvala | Thompson |
|---|---|---|
| (a) Good | 21% | 76% |
| (b) Bad | 51 | 46 |
| (c) No Aff. | 46 | 51 |

**Source**: For all data on pages 41-44, VNS Exit Polls, November 8, 1994.

## Americans on the Issues:

# California, Washington, Nebraska, Pennsylvania: Still a Yes to Health Care Reform; But Not "Overhaul," and Mixed Partisan Results

**Question**: How did you vote on Proposition 186, which establishes a singlepayer health care system?

### California

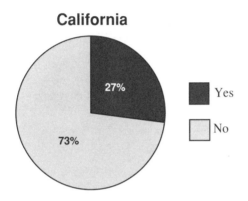

|  | How Respondents Voted | |
|---|---|---|
|  | **California Governor** | |
|  | **Brown** | **Wilson** |
| Yes | 61% | 35% |
| No | 31 | 66 |

**Question**: Do you think the health care system in the United States: Works well enough as is, Needs some changes, needs a complete overhaul?

■ No change          ▨ Some change          □ Overhaul

### Nebraska

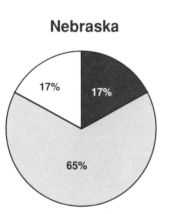

### Pennsylvania

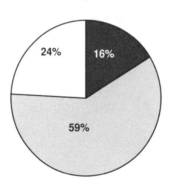

### Washington

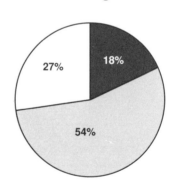

## How Respondents Voted

| Nebraska Senate | | | Pennsylvania Senate | | | Washington Senate | | |
|---|---|---|---|---|---|---|---|---|
|  | **Kerry** | **Stoney** |  | **Wofford** | **Santorum** |  | **Sims** | **Gorton** |
| No change | 29% | 71% | No change | 23% | 73% | No change | 20% | 80% |
| Some change | 55 | 45 | Some change | 45 | 50 | Some change | 41 | 59 |
| Overhaul | 76 | 24 | Overhaul | 67 | 29 | Overhaul | 64 | 36 |

# Americans on the Issues:

# The "War on The West":
## The "sagebrush rebellion," 1994 Style

**Question**: Have Clinton Administration policies on land use and natural resources helped your state, hurt your state, or not affected your state?

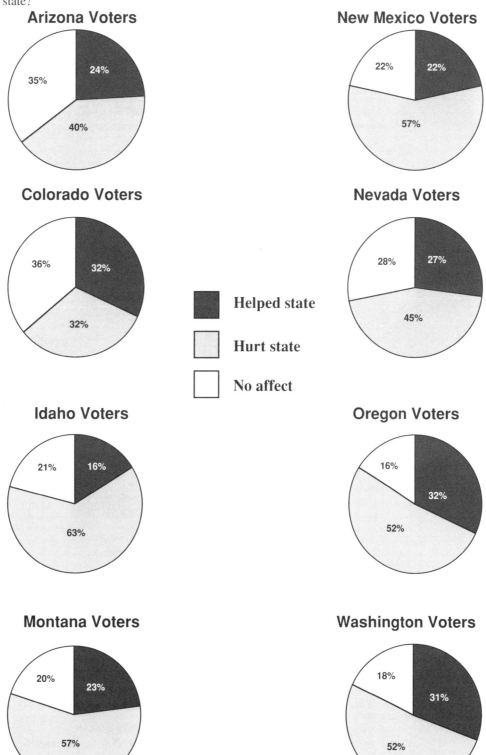

### Arizona Voters
- 24%
- 40%
- 35%

### New Mexico Voters
- 22%
- 57%
- 22%

### Colorado Voters
- 32%
- 32%
- 36%

### Nevada Voters
- 27%
- 45%
- 28%

Helped state

Hurt state

No affect

### Idaho Voters
- 16%
- 63%
- 21%

### Oregon Voters
- 32%
- 52%
- 16%

### Montana Voters
- 23%
- 57%
- 20%

### Washington Voters
- 31%
- 52%
- 18%

# Americans on the Issues:

# Abortion: A Complex, Divided Public Response

**Question**: Which comes closest to your position? Abortion should be legal in all cases, legal in most cases, illegal in most cases, illegal in all cases?

## Minnesota Respondents

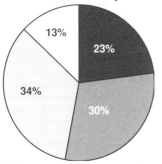

| Minnesota Governor | Marty | Carlson | | Minnesota Senate | Wynia | Grams | (I)Burke |
|---|---|---|---|---|---|---|---|
| Always legal | 47% | 52% | | Always legal | 62% | 30% | 7% |
| Mostly legal | 36 | 62 | | Mostly legal | 58 | 33 | 7% |
| Mostly illegal | 31 | 67 | | Mostly illegal | 30 | 64 | 4% |
| Always illegal | 27 | 68 | | Always illegal | 20 | 77 | 3% |

## Missouri Respondents

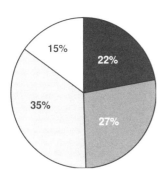

## Ohio Respondents

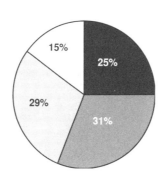

## Oregon Respondents

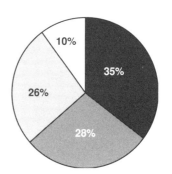

| | |
|---|---|
| ■ | Always legal |
| ▨ | Mostly legal |
| ▢ | Mostly illegal |
| □ | Always illegal |

## Oklahoma Respondents

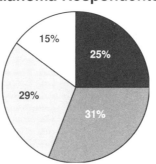

## Pennsylvania Respondents

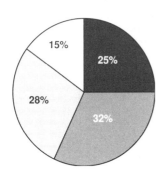

### Pennsylvania Governor

| | Singel | Ridge | (I)Luksik |
|---|---|---|---|
| Always legal | 53% | 37% | 5% |
| Mostly legal | 45 | 43 | 7% |
| Mostly illegal | 26 | 53 | 19% |
| Always illegal | 26 | 48 | 25% |

### Pennsylvania Senate

| | Wofford | Santorum |
|---|---|---|
| Always legal | 64% | 31% |
| Mostly legal | 52 | 44 |
| Mostly illegal | 33 | 63 |
| Always illegal | 30 | 67 |

# Americans on the Issues:

# Rating the Parties:A Big Swing to the GOP in 1994

**Question**: Which political party do you think can do a better job of handling the problem you have just mentioned (as the most important problem facing the country today)...the Republican party or the Democratic party?

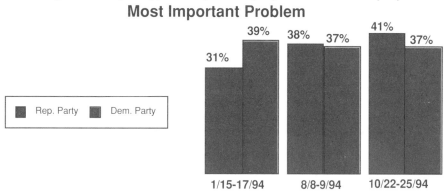

**Question**: Do you think the Republican Party or the Democratic Party would do a better job dealing with each of the following issues and problems...

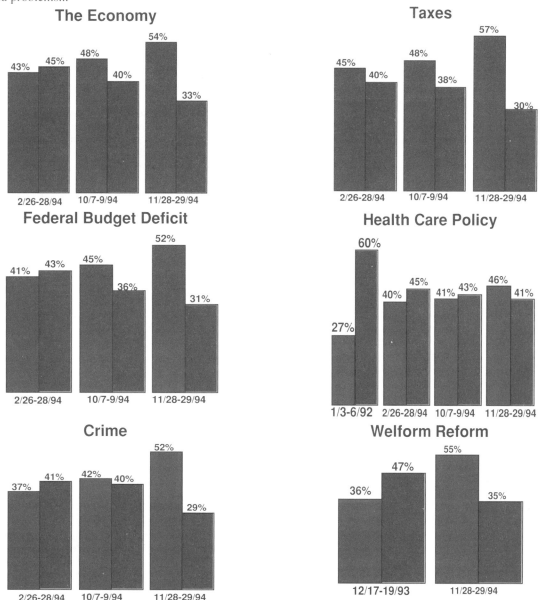

**Source**: Surveys by the Gallup Organization for CNN/*USA Today*.

# *C*hapter 4
# 1994 Vote: How Social Groups Voted

A key feature of every historic US realignment is new patterns in social group voting and partisan ties. Some patterns are always carried over from earlier periods, but each of the major realignments has involved enough new ones to give the era's politics a distinctive cast.

As time passes and a period's group alignment becomes increasingly familiar, succeeding elections seem in one basic regard replays: The absolute proportions of the vote given each party vary, of course, depending on which one is currently advantaged, but the underlying relationships in social group support remain fairly constant. They remain constant, that is, until the next big realigning cycle begins.

The 1994 balloting came fairly far into the realignment cycle which we attribute to the postindustrial setting. It's natural, then, that we saw a lot of "familiar faces" in the group patterns. In the pages that follow, Karlyn Bowman, Jim Norman, Daryl Harris, Claibourne Darden, and a number of my colleagues at the Roper Center relate in considerable detail the 1994 group story.

—ECL

# Voting for the US House of Representatives 1984-1994:
## The Group Story

|  |  | 1994 | | | 1992 | | | 1990 | |
|---|---|---|---|---|---|---|---|---|---|
|  |  | **D** | **R** | | **D** | **R** | | **D** | **R** |
| **TOTAL** | | 45.5% | 52.5% | | 50.9% | 45.5% | | 52.9% | 44.9% |
| **By Gender** | | | | | | | | | |
| Men | | 43 | 57 | | 51 | 47 | | 50 | 46 |
| Women | | 54 | 46 | | 54 | 44 | | 54 | 43 |
| **By Gender/Age** | | | | | | | | | |
| **Women** | 18-29 | 58 | 42 | | 57 | 41 | | 55 | 43 |
| | 30-44 | 52 | 48 | | 53 | 44 | | 53 | 43 |
| | 45-59 | 53 | 47 | | 53 | 45 | | 53 | 44 |
| | 60+ | 54 | 46 | | 55 | 42 | | 54 | 44 |
| **Men** | 18-29 | 43 | 57 | | 50 | 46 | | 48 | 49 |
| | 30-44 | 42 | 58 | | 50 | 47 | | 52 | 45 |
| | 45-59 | 42 | 58 | | 49 | 49 | | 48 | 49 |
| | 60+ | 45 | 55 | | 55 | 43 | | 52 | 45 |
| **By Gender/Education** | | | | | | | | | |
| **Women** | HS | 52 | 48 | | 57 | 40 | | 57 | 40 |
| | College | 58 | 42 | | 53 | 45 | | 55 | 42 |
| **Men** | HS | 49 | 51 | | 59 | 38 | | 57 | 40 |
| | College | 42 | 58 | | 45 | 53 | | 48 | 50 |
| **By Race/Ethnicity** | | | | | | | | | |
| Whites | | 42 | 58 | | 49 | 49 | | 50 | 47 |
| Blacks | | 92 | 8 | | 87 | 11 | | 78 | 20 |
| Hispanics | | 60 | 40 | | 70 | 27 | | 71 | 27 |
| Asians | | 55 | 45 | | 48 | 49 | | 62 | 36 |
| **By Race/Region** | | | | | | | | | |
| **Whites** | North | 45 | 55 | | 49 | 48 | | 50 | 46 |
| | South | 35 | 65 | | 46 | 52 | | 49 | 50 |
| **Blacks** | North | 89 | 11 | | 88 | 10 | | 77 | 21 |
| | South | 94 | 6 | | 87 | 11 | | 80 | 19 |
| **By Age** | | | | | | | | | |
| 18-29 | | 51 | 49 | | 54 | 44 | | 51 | 46 |
| 30-44 | | 47 | 53 | | 51 | 46 | | 53 | 44 |
| 45-59 | | 48 | 52 | | 51 | 47 | | 51 | 46 |
| 60+ | | 50 | 50 | | 55 | 43 | | 53 | 45 |
| **By Age/Education** | | | | | | | | | |
| 18-29 | HS | 55 | 45 | | 62 | 36 | | 60 | 37 |
| 30-44 | | 42 | 58 | | 52 | 45 | | 59 | 38 |
| 45-59 | | 51 | 49 | | 60 | 37 | | 54 | 43 |
| 60+ | | 54 | 46 | | 61 | 37 | | 56 | 41 |
| 18-29 | College | 51 | 49 | | 50 | 49 | | 52 | 45 |
| 30-44 | | 53 | 47 | | 49 | 48 | | 52 | 45 |
| 45-59 | | 51 | 49 | | 46 | 52 | | 50 | 47 |
| 60+ | | 42 | 58 | | 48 | 50 | | 48 | 50 |

| | 1988 | | | 1986 | | | 1984 | |
|---|---|---|---|---|---|---|---|---|
| | **D** | **R** | | **D** | **R** | | **D** | **R** |
| | **53.4%** | **45.5%** | | **54.6%** | **44.5%** | | **52.3%** | **46.8%** |
| | 49 | 46 | | 49 | 47 | | 46 | 53 |
| | 54 | 41 | | 52 | 44 | | 51 | 48 |
| | | | | | | | | |
| | 52 | 43 | | 51 | 43 | | 51 | 47 |
| | 54 | 41 | | 50 | 46 | | 53 | 46 |
| | 55 | 40 | | 55 | 40 | | 50 | 50 |
| | 54 | 42 | | 50 | 44 | | 48 | 52 |
| | 50 | 45 | | 46 | 49 | | 43 | 54 |
| | 48 | 47 | | 50 | 45 | | 49 | 49 |
| | 47 | 48 | | 48 | 48 | | 45 | 54 |
| | 52 | 45 | | 49 | 47 | | 44 | 55 |
| | | | | | | | | |
| | 56 | 39 | | 51 | 43 | | 51 | 48 |
| | 52 | 44 | | 55 | 42 | | 52 | 47 |
| | 54 | 40 | | 54 | 41 | | 47 | 51 |
| | 44 | 52 | | 44 | 52 | | 45 | 53 |
| | | | | | | | | |
| | 47 | 48 | | 47 | 49 | | 43 | 56 |
| | 81 | 14 | | 80 | 13 | | 91 | 8 |
| | 73 | 23 | | 70 | 23 | | 66 | 32 |
| | NA | | | NA | | | NA | |
| | | | | | | | | |
| | 46 | 49 | | 46 | 50 | | 44 | 55 |
| | 50 | 46 | | 48 | 48 | | 42 | 57 |
| | 80 | 14 | | 82 | 11 | | 90 | 9 |
| | 84 | 13 | | 77 | 15 | | 96 | 4 |
| | | | | | | | | |
| | 51 | 44 | | 48 | 46 | | 47 | 50 |
| | 51 | 44 | | 50 | 46 | | 51 | 48 |
| | 51 | 44 | | 51 | 44 | | 48 | 52 |
| | 53 | 43 | | 50 | 46 | | 46 | 54 |
| | | | | | | | | |
| | 52 | 43 | | 49 | 43 | | 43 | 54 |
| | 54 | 41 | | 50 | 44 | | 50 | 48 |
| | 56 | 39 | | 55 | 40 | | 53 | 46 |
| | 57 | 38 | | 53 | 43 | | 49 | 50 |
| | | | | | | | | |
| | 49 | 46 | | 45 | 51 | | 50 | 48 |
| | 49 | 46 | | 51 | 45 | | 52 | 46 |
| | 44 | 52 | | 50 | 46 | | 41 | 58 |
| | 48 | 48 | | 45 | 51 | | 39 | 60 |

# Voting for the US House of Representatives 1984-1994: The Group Story/continued

| | 1994 | | | 1992 | | | 1990 | |
|---|---|---|---|---|---|---|---|---|
| | **D** | **R** | | **D** | **R** | | **D** | **R** |
| **By Education** | | | | | | | | |
| Less than HS | 60 | 40 | | 65 | 32 | | 59 | 38 |
| HS Grad | 48 | 52 | | 57 | 41 | | 56 | 41 |
| Some College | 42 | 58 | | 51 | 46 | | 51 | 45 |
| College Grad | 50 | 50 | | 48 | 49 | | 51 | 46 |
| **By Income** | | | | | | | | |
| Less than $15,000 | 63 | 37 | | 67 | 30 | | 63 | 34 |
| $15,000-29,999 | 53 | 47 | | 56 | 42 | | 54 | 42 |
| $30,000-49,999 | 46 | 54 | | 51 | 47 | | 52 | 45 |
| $50,000+ | 43 | 57 | | 46 | 52 | | 49 | 48 |
| **By Denomination** | | | | | | | | |
| Protestant | 40 | 60 | | 45 | 53 | | 47 | 51 |
| Catholic | 48 | 52 | | 55 | 42 | | 55 | 41 |
| Other Christian | 50 | 50 | | 49 | 48 | | 56 | 42 |
| Jewish | 78 | 22 | | 77 | 21 | | 73 | 25 |
| None | 63 | 37 | | 66 | 29 | | 56 | 37 |
| **Union Household** | 61 | 39 | | 66 | 32 | | 63 | 34 |
| Not checked | 46 | 54 | | 49 | 48 | | 52 | 45 |
| **Married** | 43 | 57 | | 49 | 49 | | 50 | 47 |
| Not Married | 56 | 44 | | 59 | 38 | | 58 | 39 |
| **Attend Religious Services** | | | | | | | | |
| Once a week/month | Not asked | | | 46 | 52 | | 49 | 49 |
| Not checked | | | | 57 | 40 | | 57 | 40 |
| **By Party ID** | | | | | | | | |
| Democrat | 89 | 11 | | 87 | 11 | | 78 | 19 |
| Republican | 8 | 92 | | 15 | 83 | | 25 | 73 |
| Independent | 42 | 58 | | 52 | 43 | | 51 | 45 |
| **By Ideology** | | | | | | | | |
| Liberal | 82 | 18 | | 77 | 18 | | 71 | 25 |
| Moderate | 58 | 42 | | 56 | 42 | | 56 | 41 |
| Conservative | 20 | 80 | | 27 | 71 | | 38 | 59 |

| 1988 | | 1986 | | 1984 | |
|---|---|---|---|---|---|
| **D** | **R** | **D** | **R** | **D** | **R** |
| 59 | 34 | 53 | 41 | 56 | 43 |
| 54 | 41 | 52 | 43 | 48 | 51 |
| 50 | 45 | 48 | 48 | 46 | 53 |
| 48 | 48 | 49 | 48 | 48 | 51 |
| | | | | | |
| 63 | 31 | 53 | 41 | 59 | 39 |
| 53 | 43 | 50 | 45 | 49 | 50 |
| 50 | 45 | 51 | 45 | 45 | 54 |
| 43 | 52 | 45 | 51 | 37 | 61 |
| | | | | | |
| 45 | 50 | 45 | 51 | 40 | 60 |
| 53 | 43 | 52 | 43 | 55 | 43 |
| 52 | 42 | 49 | 46 | 44 | 54 |
| 66 | 31 | 67 | 29 | 70 | 28 |
| 61 | 33 | 56 | 39 | 65 | 33 |
| | | | | | |
| 60 | 35 | 60 | 36 | 61 | 38 |
| 48 | 47 | 46 | 49 | 43 | 56 |
| | | | | | |
| 49 | 46 | 49 | 47 | 46 | 53 |
| 56 | 38 | 53 | 42 | 53 | 45 |
| | | | | | |
| NA | | NA | | NA | |
| NA | | NA | | NA | |
| | | | | | |
| 80 | 16 | 77 | 19 | 83 | 16 |
| 20 | 75 | 19 | 77 | 13 | 86 |
| 51 | 43 | 49 | 45 | 45 | 52 |
| | | | | | |
| 76 | 19 | 68 | 28 | 73 | 24 |
| 55 | 41 | 55 | 40 | 54 | 45 |
| 32 | 62 | 33 | 62 | 28 | 71 |

Source: *Statistical Abstract of the United States, 1990* and *1993-1994* for final aggregate vote totals. For exit poll analysis: Voter News Service, November 8, 1994; Voter Research & Surveys, for 1990 and 1992; CBS News and *New York Times* for 1984, 1986 and 1988. Please see the appendix for further information about group sizes and comparable data from the 1994 Mitofsky International exit poll.

# The Gender Factor

## *By Karlyn H. Bowman*

The gender gap has become a permanent feature of our politics. Since 1980, men and women have voted differently in every national election. Sometimes the gap has been large as in the 1980 election. Yet, at other times, it has been modest. This election revealed the largest gender gap (22 points in House races) in any since different voting patterns appeared (see Table 2). Beyond differences in voting, men and women have responded dissimilarly to our presidents and to the Democratic and Republican parties.

The gender gap story has always had two primary components. As women have been moving in the Democratic direction, men have been looking more Republican. In the past, commentators have focused significant attention on women's voting patterns in part because their rate of voting was increasing. It equalled the men's rate for the first time in 1980. Also contributing to the publicity given to the women's side of the story was the simple demographic fact that there are more women in the population than men. Because their numbers in the voting age population are greater, a significant divergence in male and female voting could make a difference in election outcomes. In some states, women have represented a much larger share of voters than men. In Senate elections this year in Florida, 55% of all voters were women; in Virginia the number was 54%; in Pennsylvania, Oklahoma, Texas, 53%. Since the mid-1970s, significantly more women than in the past have run for office and won, and this development also focused the media spotlight on the distaff side of the equation. Table 1 and Figure 1 show how the representation of women in the House, the Senate, and state legislatures has changed over time. The Republican sweep in November turned the tables, and media commentary has zeroed in on men's affinity for the GOP.

There are many cuts in the gender gap story. The most obvious one is the national vote in House races. Men voted 57% Republican to 43% Democratic. Women were a virtual mirror image, 54% Democratic to 46% Republican. (To calculate the gender gap, subtract the percentage of men voting Republican from those voting Democratic (57-43=14) and then make the same calculation for women (46-54=-8). The gap (22 points) is the difference between 14 and -8). White women and white men cast their bal-

---

**How They Voted in House 1994 Races**

| | D | R |
|---|---|---|
| Women | 54% | 46% |
| Men | 43 | 57 |

**Gender Gap**
**22**

---

lots for Republican candidates in November, but by different margins. Women were 53% Republican to 47% Democratic, while men were 63% Republican to 37% Democratic. Furthermore, there were significant regional differences among white women. White women in the South went decisively Republican (61 to 39%). In the West and Midwest they favored the GOP by narrow margins, 52 to 48% and 51 to 49% respectively. Only in the East were they Democratic (54 to 46%).

In this election, women in every age group were at least 10 points more Democratic than men. Or, conversely, men were more Republican across the age spectrum (see Table 3). The gap was larger among younger than older voters. Eighteen-to 24-year-old women voters were 18 points more Democratic than 18-to 24-year-old male voters. In the 50- to 64-year-old group, women were 10 points more Democratic.

Women in every education group were more Democratic than men, or, expressed the other way, men in this cut were more Republican. The more education they have, the more Democratic women are. Women with a high school education or less and women with some college training split their votes in House elections in 1994. Majorities with college and post-graduate training pulled the Democratic lever. Men with some or a complete college education are the most Republican leaning (see Table 4).

Protestant and Catholic women were more Democratic than men of those faiths. Still, Protestant women and men voted for GOP candidates. Catholic women voted for Democrats in House races by a significant margin; Catholic men voted for Republicans by an overwhelming one. Jewish women were slightly less Democratic than Jewish men, but both were overwhelmingly Democratic. Voters indicating they had no religious affiliation were Democratic, but women were especially so (see Table 5).

### Senate and Gubernatorial Races

In a comprehensive study of all US Senate, House, gubernatorial contests from 1972 to 1992, and state legislative contests in 1986, 1988, 1990, and 1992, Jody Newman, executive director of the National Women's Political Caucus, concludes that when women run, they win. Her massive database found that incumbent women running for state house contests won 95% of the time compared to 94% of the time for men. In open seats in state houses, women won 52% of their elections compared to 53% for men. Female challengers won 10% of the contests for those seats compared to 9% for men. The pattern was repeated in state senate contests and in the US House. While the number of women running for the Senate and governor's offices during the period of the study was too small to make generalizations, Newman found no evidence that women were less likely to win those offices. In the much vaunted "year of the women," 1992, she says, women won no more often than men, just as they won no less often than men before that time. She concludes, the "reason there aren't more women in public office is not that women don't win, but that not enough women have been candidates in general elections."

In this election, 9 women sought Senate seats. Three were elected, bringing the number of women in the Senate to 8. The House of Representatives will have 30 Democratic and 18 Republican women in 1995, representing a slight increase in women's representation there. Only one woman, Republican Christine Todd Whitman of New Jersey, elected in 1993, is serving as a governor. More women will be serving in state legislatures than in the past. Do the gender differences that pertain in national level data extend to governor's and senate contests?

In some of the six Senate races where a woman faced a man and where exit poll data are available, no gender gap existed. Republican Kay Bailey Hutchinson of Texas won identical shares of the male and female vote (61%). Men and women voted in like numbers (60%) for Republican Olympia Snowe in Maine. In the other four Senate races where a woman faced a man, a gender gap existed. It was particularly large in the high-profile Minnesota and California senatorial contests. In both of these races, majorities of women voted for the Democrat, men for the Republican (see Table 6).

There were six governor's contests where a woman faced a man and where exit poll data are available to review. Unlike the Texas Senate contest where no gender gap existed, the gap was large (18 points) in the contest between Democrat Ann Richards and

Republican George W. Bush. In the Texas and Maryland races, majorities of women voted for the Democrat, men for the Republican (see Table 7).

Evidence from past elections indicates that women have been less likely to vote for Republican women candidates than men have. In this election women were less likely to vote for Ellen Sauerbrey in the Maryland gubernatorial race than men, but there was no difference in the male-female vote for the losing GOP gubernatorial candidate in Maine. Women were less likely than men to vote for Republican Bernardette Castro in the New York Senate contest, but they were equally likely to vote for Kay Bailey Hutchinson and Olympia Snowe in their races. Men were more disposed than women to vote for the Independent victor in the Maine gubernatorial contest than were women, just as they were more likely than women to vote for Ross Perot in 1992.

Beyond these contests, there were 21 Senate races where men faced men and for which exit poll data exist. In all but two (Delaware and Florida) the gender gap was more than 7 points. In every other race, women were more Democratic than men. White women were more Democratic than white men. Or conversely, men were more Republican everywhere. Men and women voted for winners in most of these contests. The exceptions were Michigan (men voted for the victorious Republican Abraham, women for Democrat Carr), New Jersey (a majority of women cast ballots for the Democrat winner Lautenberg, a majority of men for Haytaian), Pennsylvania (a plurality of women for Wofford in this race, a bare majority of men for the winner, Santorum), Virginia (a plurality of men voted for North in this 3-way race, a majority of women for Robb), and Washington State.

There were 23 gubernatorial races where men ran against men and data

were available. Women were more Democratic (or men more Republican) nearly everywhere. In South Carolina, a majority of men and women voted for the Republican, a candidate who had been associated with the religious right.

The VNS exit poll asked voters whether they approved or disapproved of the job Bill Clinton was doing as president. Not surprisingly, a gender gap exists here, too, as it has throughout his presidency. Women were 9 percentage points more likely to approve than men. Women in all age, education, and religious groups were more likely to approve of him than men.

**Conclusion**

Given the persistence of differences in voting, how consequential is gender for the future of both political parties? We don't know yet whether young women are going to carry their Democratic tendencies (or young men their Republican ones) with them as they age. More formal education appears to make women more Democratic. Given the fact that more men and more women (women in greater numbers in some areas) are pursuing higher education, this could suggest some peril for the GOP. Women voted for female candidates in some places, but there is no evidence that this trend is accelerating. Women are voting in greater numbers than men, and this seems especially true in races that receive significant national media attention. This year, women were more Democratic in virtually every Senate and gubernatorial contest, and men more Republican. These contrasting dispositions may be hardening. Still, in most races, both men and women voted for winners; while gender is pulling voters in different directions, many other things matter. More women are running, and they appear to be of more diverse backgrounds. Seven of the 11 women newly elected to the House of Representatives this year are Republicans.

### Table 2
### The Gender Gap in Off-Year Elections (House Races)
### 1978-1994

| | | How Men Voted | How Women Voted | GAP |
|---|---|---|---|---|
| 1978 | Democratic | 55% | 56% | |
| | Republican | 42 | 43 | 0 |
| 1982 | Democratic | 54 | 57 | |
| | Republican | 44 | 41 | 6 |
| 1986 | Democratic | 51 | 55 | |
| | Republican | 47 | 42 | 9 |
| 1990 | Democratic | 50 | 54 | |
| | Republican | 47 | 43 | 8 |
| 1994 | Democratic | 43 | 54 | |
| | Republican | 57 | 46 | 22 |

### Figure 1
### Women in State Legislatures

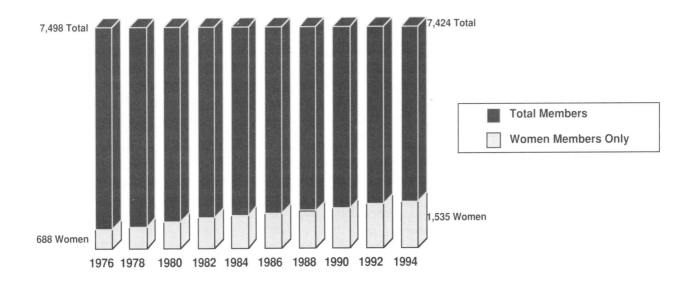

7,498 Total   7,424 Total   1,535 Women   688 Women

Total Members / Women Members Only

1976 1978 1980 1982 1984 1986 1988 1990 1992 1994

### Table 1
### Election Boxscore—Women in National Office

| | 1976 D | R | 1978 D | R | 1980 D | R | 1982 D | R | 1984 D | R | 1986 D | R | 1988 D | R | 1990 D | R | 1992 D | R | 1994 D | R |
|---|---|---|---|---|---|---|---|---|---|---|---|---|---|---|---|---|---|---|---|---|
| **House** | | | | | | | | | | | | | | | | | | | | |
| Total | 292 | 143 | 276 | 159 | 243 | 192 | 269 | 166 | 252 | 182 | 258 | 177 | 260 | 175 | 267 | 167 | 258 | 176 | 204 | 230 |
| Women | 13 | 5 | 11 | 5 | 10 | 9 | 12 | 9 | 11 | 11 | 13 | 11 | 14 | 11 | 20 | 9 | 35 | 12 | 31 | 17 |
| **Senate** | | | | | | | | | | | | | | | | | | | | |
| Total | 61 | 38 | 58 | 41 | 46 | 53 | 46 | 54 | 47 | 53 | 55 | 45 | 55 | 45 | 56 | 44 | 57 | 43 | 47 | 53 |
| Women | 0 | 0 | 1 | 1 | 0 | 2 | 0 | 2 | 0 | 2 | 1 | 1 | 1 | 1 | 1 | 1 | 5 | 1 | 5 | 3 |

## Table 3
## The Gender Factor:
## 1994 House Vote By Age

| | Voted Democratic | | Voted Republican | |
|---|---|---|---|---|
| | **Men** | **Women** | **Men** | **Women** |
| 18-24 | 40% | 58% | 60% | 42% |
| 25-29 | 46 | 58 | 54 | 42 |
| 30-39 | 42 | 53 | 58 | 47 |
| 40-49 | 42 | 55 | 58 | 45 |
| 50-64 | 42 | 52 | 58 | 47 |
| 65+ | 46 | 53 | 54 | 47 |

## Table 4
## The Gender Factor:
## 1994 House Vote By Education

| | Voted Democratic | | Voted Republican | |
|---|---|---|---|---|
| | **Men** | **Women** | **Men** | **Women** |
| HS Grad | 45% | 51% | 55% | 49% |
| Some College | 35 | 49 | 65 | 51 |
| College Grad | 37 | 53 | 63 | 47 |
| Post Grad | 50 | 67 | 50 | 33 |

## Table 5
## The Gender Factor:
## 1994 House Vote By Religious Preference

| | Voted Democratic | | Voted Republican | |
|---|---|---|---|---|
| | **Men** | **Women** | **Men** | **Women** |
| Protestant | 36% | 44% | 64% | 56% |
| Catholic | 40 | 56 | 60 | 44 |
| Jewish | 81 | 75 | 19 | 25 |
| None | 53 | 78 | 47 | 22 |

## Table 6
## The Gender Factor:
## Women Candidates in Senate Contests

| | | How Men Voted | How Women Voted | GAP |
|---|---|---|---|---|
| **Races with Republican Women** | | | | |
| ME | Olympia Snowe-R | 60% | 60% | |
| | Tom Andrews-D | 36 | 37 | 1 |
| NE | Jan Stoney-R | 49 | 41 | |
| | Bob Kerrey-D | 51 | 59 | 16 |
| NY | Bernadette Castro-R | 44 | 39 | |
| | D. P. Moynihan-D | 54 | 56 | 7 |
| TX | K. B. Hutchinson-R | 61 | 61 | |
| | Richard Fisher-D | 38 | 38 | 0 |
| **Races with Democratic Women** | | | | |
| CA | Dianne Feinstein-D | 41 | 52 | |
| | Michael Huffington-R | 52 | 38 | 25 |
| MN | Ann Wynia-D | 38 | 50 | |
| | Rod Grams-R | 54 | 45 | 21 |

Note: Data for Hawaii (Republican Maria Hustace ran), Rhode Island (Democrat Linda Kushner), and Vermont (Democrat Jan Backus ) not available.

## Table 7
## The Gender Factor:
## Women in Gubernatorial Contests

| | | How Men Voted | How Women Voted | GAP |
|---|---|---|---|---|
| **Races with Republican Women** | | | | |
| MD | Ellen Sauerbrey-R | 56% | 43% | |
| | Parris Glendening-D | 43 | 57 | 27 |
| ME | Susan Collins-R | 23 | 23 | |
| | Josepn Brennan-D | 31 | 36 | 5 |
| | Angus King-I | 38 | 34 | |
| **Races with Democratic Women** | | | | |
| CA | Kathleen Brown-D | 36 | 46 | |
| | Pete Wilson-R | 60 | 50 | 20 |
| IL | Dawn C. Netsch-D | 32 | 37 | |
| | Jim Edgar-R | 66 | 61 | 10 |
| TX | Ann Richards-D | 41 | 50 | |
| | George W. Bush-R | 58 | 49 | 18 |
| WY | Kathy Karpan-D | 36 | 44 | |
| | Jim Geringer-R | 62 | 55 | 15 |

Note: Data for Hawaii (Republican Patricia Saiki), and Iowa (Bonnie Campbell) not available.

# Summary Overview
## The 1994 Congressional Vote by Gender
### Percentage Voting Republican

|  | Women | Men | Gender Gap |
|---|---|---|---|
| **EVERYONE** | **46%** | **57%** | **22** |
| **By Age** | | | |
| 18-29 | 42 | 57 | 30 |
| 30-44 | 48 | 58 | 20 |
| 45-59 | 47 | 58 | 22 |
| 60+ | 46 | 55 | 18 |
| **By Education** | | | |
| Less than HS | 43 | 38 | 10 |
| HS Grad | 49 | 55 | 12 |
| Some College | 51 | 65 | 28 |
| College Grad | 47 | 63 | 32 |
| Post Grad | 33 | 50 | 34 |
| **By Race/Ethnicity** | | | |
| White | 53 | 63 | 20 |
| Black | 5 | 13 | 16 |
| Hispanic | 40 | 41 | 2 |
| **By Income** | | | |
| Less than $15,000 | 32 | 42 | 20 |
| $15,000-29,999 | 45 | 52 | 14 |
| $30,000-49,000 | 49 | 59 | 20 |
| $50,000-75,000 | 46 | 61 | 30 |
| $75,000-100,000 | 52 | 64 | 24 |
| $100,000+ | 59 | 65 | 12 |
| **By Party ID** | | | |
| Democrat | 9 | 13 | 8 |
| Republican | 91 | 92 | 2 |
| Independent | 52 | 63 | 22 |
| **By Ideology** | | | |
| Liberal | 12 | 26 | 28 |
| Moderate | 41 | 44 | 2 |
| Conservative | 76 | 83 | 14 |
| **By Denomination** | | | |
| Protestant | 56 | 64 | 16 |
| Catholic | 44 | 60 | 32 |
| Other Christian | 42 | 59 | 34 |
| Jewish | 25 | 19 | 12 |
| None | 22 | 47 | 50 |
| **By Union Membership** | | | |
| Union Household | 34 | 43 | 18 |

**Source**: VNS 1994 Exit Poll. VNS is the source for all succeeding "Summary Overview" tables in this chapter.

# The Education Factor

The 1994 vote of the educational strata showed a now-familiar pattern:  The GOP did best among the middling strata of postindustrial America—those with some college and bachelor's degrees, the Democrats best among those with relatively

little formal education and those
The latter relationship seems to
*telligentsia* in contemporary
lationship is significantly an over-
formal education tend to be the

with the most—graduate training.
derive from the position of the *in-*
American politics.  The former re-
lay of income:  those with little
poorest Americans.

In the essay that follows, Jim
the voting of the "some
publican of the educational strata
matic swing to the GOP, according
following).

Norman of *USA Today* examines
college"contingent—the most Re-
in 1994.  The group made a dra-
to both 1994 exit polls (Figure 1,

| How They Voted in House 1994 Races | R | D |
|---|---|---|
| <HS | 40% | 60% |
| HS | 52 | 48 |
| Some College | 58 | 42 |
| College Grad. | 55 | 45 |
| Post Grad. | 42 | 58 |

# The "Some College" Crowd: Who Are Those Guys Anyway?

## By Jim Norman

A word to election analysts and polling prognosticators as they expound on the keys to historic Republican gains in this year's elections: Don't forget the "some-college" crowd.

Much has been made of the Angry White Male's rumble to the right.  The Perot voters have been given their due for moving so overwhelmingly into the Republican column. Even gun owners and talk-show listeners have been cited as important players in the shift to a Republican majority in the House of Representatives after 40 years of Democratic control.

But what of that squishy "who-are-they-anyway?" group identified in most polls as "some college"?  Surely they deserve some mention.

Consider:

—Of all educational groups, they were the strongest supporters of Republican candidates in the Voter News Service exit poll, where they favored Republican candidates by a solid 58-42% margin.  This broke the trend of the past few House elections, when college graduates are the most likely to vote Republican.

—The Republican majority among those with some college was a major shift from the past three House elections. In all three, Democrats had won a majority.

—The some-college group represented almost three out of every ten voters in 1994, according to the VNS exit poll.

That's a large enough group so that their move into the Republican camp has a profound effect on the election.  If Democrats had been able to hold onto the some-college vote or had just been able to get an even split—they would have won a majority of the popular vote and possibly retained control of the House.

Any group large enough and volatile enough to swing the election deserves some attention, but post-election mentions of the some-college crowd have been mostly indirect— through references to the beleaguered middle-class—or by lumping them together with those who only went to high school.

It's not hard to see the reason for this.  Take almost any question on almost any poll, and see how the answers break down by educational level:  The odds are strong the "some-college" crowd will be smack in the middle of the opinion spectrum.  This discouraging lack of distinctiveness has caused them to be largely ignored in analyses of major political issues.  But below the surface blandness, this critical group does show characteristics that not only make it distinctive, but hint at why it swung so dramatically into the Republican camp this year.

—The some-college crowd is the youngest group.  Most college undergraduates fall into the 18-24 year old category, so it's no surprise that the some-college category is well represented in this age group.  But a study of early 1994 *USA Today*/CNN/Gallup polls show that the 18-24 year olds only account for 16% of those with some college—the majority

(57%) are in the prime wage-earning, family-raising years of 25-49.

—Many, if not a majority, of those wage earners are women. The combined 1994 Gallup polls show women represent 54% of those with some college. In the youngest category, 18-24 year olds, men and women split 50-50. But the proportion of women increases with age, accounting for 59% of those 50 and older. In poll after poll, these women wage earners have expressed concern about both their financial security and rising crime rates.

—More than any other educational group, the some-college group is squarely in the middle financially of the middle class; in some ways, they are the middle class. The Gallup polls showed slightly less than one-fourth making more than $50,000 a year, a quarter making less than $20,000, and half in the $20,000-$50,000 range. They make up a large proportion of the wage earners who feel it's getting harder and harder to make economic headway. Though they make decent wages, they feel vulnerable to the capricious swings of contemporary business cycles, downsizing, layoffs and restructuring. They are also the most desperate for a tax cut.

This young, majority-female, financially strapped group was solidly in the Democratic fold in 1992. Not only did they vote Democratic in House elections and the presidential race, they also overwhelmingly picked Democrats over Republicans to handle virtually all key issues in a December 1992 *USA Today*/CNN/Gallup poll.

But the movement away from Clinton and the Democrats started early in his administration. By late 1993, the Democrats were trailing on such high-profile issues as welfare, crime, taxes and the economy.

This year the months of August and September, when partisan battles raged in Congress over crime and health-care bills, were critical in pushing the some-college group into the Republican column. A look at *USA Today*/CNN/Gallup polls from June to November shows how their support on the House vote jumped from party to party before settling in the Republican camp in late September:

—June 11-12, 52% Democrat, 43% Republican
—July 15-17, 49% Republican, 42% Democrat
—August 8-9, 51% Democrat, 42% Republican
—August 15-16, 50% Republican, 40% Democrat
—September 6-7, 47% Republican, 46% Democrat
—September 23-35, 50% Republican, 43% Democrat
—October 7-9, 52% Republican, 43% Democrat
—October 18-19, 53% Republican, 38% Democrat
—October 22-25, 50% Republican, 45% Democrat
—November 2-6, 49% Republican, 40% Democrat

In the final month these pre-election polls clearly projected that the some-college voters would heavily favor Republicans, and the exit polls Nov. 8 confirmed they did.

The VNS exit poll also helped show how the some-college crowd's vote had shifted from 1992:

—They were more Republican and more conservative than in 1992. The shift was especially noticeable among conservatives; they were 30% of the some-college vote in 1992, 41% in 1994.

—They were more affluent and older in 1994, both reflecting trends among all voters from 1992 to 1994. Among the some-college group, 60% were 44 or younger in 1992, only 48% this year.

—The biggest shifts in voting occurred in the Midwest and the West: in the Midwest, some-college voters swung from voting 52% Democratic, 48% Republican in 1992 to 61% GOP, 39% Democrat this year. In the West, they went from 55-45% in favor of Democrats to 61-39% in favor of Republicans.

—The some-college group was nowhere near as likely to think the economy is in poor shape this year (31% in 1992, 11% now). But the "not good" category killed Democrats. Half were in this group, just as in 1992. Two years ago they favored Democrats 53-47%, this time Republicans by a whopping 63-37% margin.

—Though men shifted to the Republicans in greater numbers than women, the six-point shift by women left them favoring Republicans 51-49%—the only group of women on the educational scale to go Republican.

Post-election polls show the some-college group are pleased with the election's results and indicate a massive shift in attitudes on the parties from two years ago. After favoring Democrats by two-to-one margins in December 1992 to handle such key issues as the economy, the deficit, health care and unemployment, they now want Republicans in charge.

But Republicans have no reason to be complacent about securing the vote of this group. Though the some-college group favors Republicans over Democrats to handle major issues, they are not overly confident the Republicans can do the job. Furthermore, a late-November *USA Today*/CNN/Gallup poll shows they are more insistent than the general public that the Republicans take fast action on a host of issues:

—70% want tougher anti-crime laws to be passed within 100 days of the Republicans taking office.
—58% demand a vote on a tax cut in the same time span.
—55% want the House to act on a balanced-budget amendment in the first 100 days.

For this economically potent-but-pressured group, the message has been delivered. Having decided over the past two years that the Democrats were not the solution, the some-college crowd played a critical role in turning them out and replacing them with Republicans. Now, the November Gallup poll suggests, the some-college group has started the clock running on the GOP.

**Figure 1**

# The "Some College" Congressional Vote
# 1984-1994

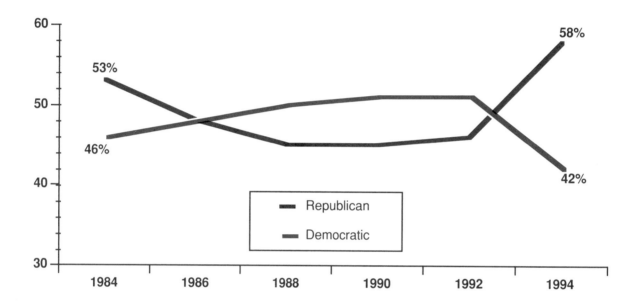

# Summary Overview

## The 1994 Congressional Vote by Education
### Percentage Voting Republican

|  | HS Graduate or less | Some College | College Graduate | Post Graduate |
|---|---|---|---|---|
| **EVERYONE** | **50%** | **58%** | **55%** | **42%** |
| **By Gender** | | | | |
| Male | 51 | 65 | 63 | 50 |
| Female | 48 | 51 | 47 | 33 |
| **By Age** | | | | |
| 18-29 | 45 | 58 | 52 | 40 |
| 30-44 | 58 | 57 | 53 | 37 |
| 45-59 | 49 | 58 | 57 | 41 |
| 60+ | 46 | 59 | 58 | 58 |
| **By Race/Ethnicity** | | | | |
| White | 56 | 64 | 61 | 47 |
| Black | 8 | 6 | 11 | 4 |
| **By Income** | | | | |
| Less than $15,000 | 37 | 45 | * | * |
| $15,000-29,999 | 47 | 52 | 44 | 36 |
| $30,000-49,999 | 51 | 59 | 51 | 43 |
| $50,000-74,999 | 65 | 63 | 57 | 37 |
| $75,000-99,999 | * | 62 | 71 | 43 |
| $100,00+ | * | * | 70 | 57 |
| **By Party ID** | | | | |
| Democrat | 10 | 11 | 11 | 11 |
| Republican | 92 | 91 | 92 | 84 |
| Independent | 61 | 66 | 58 | 47 |
| **By Ideology** | | | | |
| Liberal | 28 | 20 | 16 | 11 |
| Moderate | 37 | 48 | 46 | 38 |
| Conservative | 73 | 83 | 85 | 84 |
| **By Denomination** | | | | |
| Protestant | 57 | 66 | 62 | 53 |
| Catholic | 44 | 53 | 64 | 49 |
| Other Christian | 49 | 55 | 52 | 33 |
| Jewish | * | * | * | 23 |
| None | 43 | 56 | 25 | 24 |
| **By Union Membership** | | | | |
| Union Household | 41 | 40 | 41 | 33 |

*In this and all the summary tables that follow, the asterisk means "less than 1/2 of 1 percent."

# The Age Factor

Throughout much of the New Deal era, young people (for example, those under 30 years of age) were distinctly Democratic, while the oldest groups were the most Republican. This condition applied, analysis has shown, as long as the oldest group comprised persons who came of age politically prior to the Depression. Once the "New Deal Generation" had moved into the ranks of the elderly, the latter began appearing as the most Democratic age group. Many things changed, but some political

|  | | How They Voted in House 1994 Races | | |
|---|---|---|---|---|
|  | | | R | D |
| 18-29 yr. olds | | | 49% | 51% |
| 30-44 | | | 53 | 47 |
| 45-59 | | | 52 | 48 |
| 60+ | | | 50 | 50 |

loyalties were carried along as the continuum, those who came of age Reagan presidencies began showing group.

Important as these developments are of Republican and Democratic iden- to the vote of the age strata. As the ning of this chapter, and those which groups have differed little in the par- over the last decade. Those 18-29 publican group; they were in fact the 1994—though the age groups' differ- are tiny and not statistically significant.

cohort aged. At the other end of the politically during the Carter and up as the Republicans' best age

for understanding the age make-up tifiers, they do not provide a guide data in the master table at the begin- follow here, show, the various age tisan distribution of their House vote have not been a notably strong Re- Democrats' best age group in ences shown in the VNS exit poll

The above patterns reflect in part the fact that, in national voting of the past decade, Democratic candidates have tended to do relatively well among young independents who turn out to vote. And, in 1994, young Democrats were, according to the VNS data, more loyal to their party's congressional candidates than any other Democratic age group.

# Young Republicans?

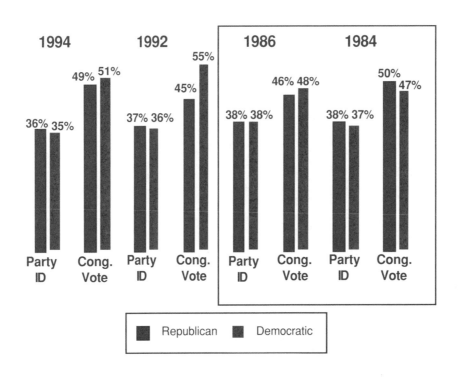

# Summary Overview

## The 1994 Congressional Vote by Age

### Percentage Voting Republican

|  | 18-29 | 30-44 | 45-59 | 60 and over |
|---|---|---|---|---|
| **EVERYONE** | 49% | 53% | 52% | 51% |
| **By Gender** | | | | |
| Male | 57 | 58 | 58 | 55 |
| Female | 42 | 48 | 47 | 46 |
| **By Education** | | | | |
| Less than HS | * | * | * | 41 |
| HS Grad | 48 | 60 | 50 | 49 |
| Some College | 58 | 57 | 58 | 59 |
| College Grad | 52 | 53 | 57 | 58 |
| Post Grad | 40 | 37 | 41 | 58 |
| **By Race/Ethnicity** | | | | |
| White | 58 | 61 | 58 | 54 |
| Black | 6 | 10 | 9 | 6 |
| Hispanic | 40 | 46 | 44 | * |
| **By Income** | | | | |
| Less than $15,000 | 37 | 41 | 33 | 37 |
| $15,000-29,999 | 46 | 44 | 50 | 49 |
| $30,000-49,999 | 53 | 54 | 52 | 55 |
| $50,000-74,999 | 49 | 55 | 53 | 55 |
| $75,000-99,999 | 59 | 62 | 55 | 62 |
| $100,000+ | 64 | 62 | 62 | 68 |
| **By Party ID** | | | | |
| Democrat | 6 | 11 | 13 | 12 |
| Republican | 90 | 93 | 90 | 92 |
| Independent | 54 | 55 | 60 | 60 |
| **By Ideology** | | | | |
| Liberal | 16 | 17 | 23 | 16 |
| Moderate | 45 | 43 | 40 | 43 |
| Conservative | 80 | 82 | 81 | 78 |
| **By Denomination** | | | | |
| Protestant | 60 | 60 | 59 | 60 |
| Catholic | 53 | 59 | 48 | 46 |
| Other Christian | 53 | 50 | 51 | * |
| None | 35 | 36 | 34 | * |
| **By Union Membership** | | | | |
| Union Household | 42 | 43 | 37 | 30 |

# Race and Ethnicity

African Americans remain, as my colleague Daryl Harris points out in the piece which follows, the great exception in the mix of ethnic-group voting in the United States. In the 1994 House contests, when the Republicans won support from 58% of

nonHispanic white voters, of 45% of
of Hispanic Americans, they managed
can Americans.

Just as slavery was a tragedy unique in
temporary social conditions have con-
in terms of partisan preference. As
nominated many more African-Ameri-
in any preceding election in this cen-
large majorities of the group as hostile

Americans of Asian ancestry, and 40%
to gain support from only 8% of Afri-

the US to African Americans, so continued to sustain a distinct group status
Harris points out, though the GOP
can candidates for federal office than
tury, the party is still perceived by
to its interests.

—ECL

### How They Voted in House 1994 Races

|  | R | D |
|---|---|---|
| Whites | 58% | 42% |
| Blacks | 8 | 92 |
| Hispanics | 40 | 60 |
| Asians | 45 | 55 |

# The 1994 Vote: The Race Factor

## By Daryl B. Harris

Presented elsewhere in this monograph are explanations for why critical portions of the electorate cast their ballots for Republican candidates in the 1994 midterm elections, resulting in the Republican party becoming the majority party in Congress for the first time in forty years. Reasons why the electorate granted Republican candidates the governing helm range from feelings of economic insecurity, dissatisfaction with the performance of an apparently cumbersome and liberal national government, and discontent with President Bill Clinton. Curiously absent from much of the post-election analyses by the media and others, however, were the sentiments of African-American voters, and the effect that race had on electoral outcomes.

Addressing these neglected, yet important matters, this essay examines the African-American and Latino vote in the 1994 elections. A profile of African-American sentiments is offered, suggesting that the African-American community was not in harmony with the so-called "angry electorate." This essay also discusses the performance of African-American candidates running for national offices. Here, the number of black Republican candidates who ran at the national level is a noteworthy issue.

### Bucking The Trend

Polling data show that general assumptions made about the entire electorate on such matters as how they voted, policy preferences, and their views about the role of government do not apply to all racial and ethnic groups, especially not to African-Americans. Whereas 58% of white voters cast ballots for Republican candidates in the November election, 92% of African-Americans backed Democrats. Clearly, the African-American contingent of the Demo-

cratic party's electoral coalition remains in tact. It is also important to note that 60% of Latinos voted for Democratic candidates in 1994, also bucking the Republican voting tide.

African-Americans' political preferences are shaped by their perceptions of racial group interests, the overall status of the black community, and the alternatives available to them within the limits of electoral politics. Together, the conservative drift of the country and the two-party system—which generates limited choices that tend toward the middle of the spectrum—obfuscate intragroup differences among African-Americans while emphasizing intergroup differences. What one gets in the narrow analytic context of electoral politics is a generally united black electorate indicating which candidates are more likely to advance their collective policy preferences.

Notwithstanding such limits, in the matter of President Clinton's job ratings, 1994 exit poll data show that while 54% of whites disapproved his performance, an astounding 75% of African-Americans approved it. With respect to the Democratic party, 49% of African-Americans felt that it does a good job of representing their interests, 39% that it does a poor job.

These data must, however, be viewed in light of analyses from National Black Election Study (NBES) data from 1984 and 1988 (Tate 1993; Dawson 1994).[1] These analyses of NBES data provide in-depth interpretations of African-American political attitudes. Dawson notes that in 1984 and 1988, nearly three-fourths of African-Americans believed that the Democratic party worked hard on their issue concerns. He also found that class divisions among African Americans did not significantly reshape black partisanship or affect evaluations of which party best advances their interests. Exit poll data from 1994 support this view, with 85% of black voters with incomes over $75,000 voting Democratic.

Tate observed from NBES data that although conservatism among African-Americans has increased over the past twenty years, going from 12% to 30%, African-Americans remain extremely liberal. Again, 1994 election exit-poll data confirm Tate's observation. For instance, when asked if they favored a more active or less active government, 65% of African-Americans (and 58% of Latinos) said they favored a more active government, while only 36% of whites indicated approval. Generally, African-Americans view the national government as an agent responsible for enhancing opportunities which they believe would otherwise be thwarted. By contrast, many white Americans have come to view the national government as intrusive, promoting the "special interests" of nonwhites and the poor at their expense.

## African-American Candidates In The 1994 Elections

Perhaps the most notable aspect of races where African-American candidates ran for major state-wide and federal office in 1994 was the number of challengers who ran as Republicans. Of the thirty African-American challengers running for national office, 23 (or 77%) were Republicans. This is remarkable insofar as the overwhelming portion of the African-American electorate identifies and votes Democratic. Not only did more black Republican candidates seek federal office, most (14 out of the 24 total, or 58%) challenged in districts that are majority non-white, thirteen of which were represented by African-American Democratic incumbents. African-American Republican candidates also ran in majority-white districts.

The fielding of African-American candidates by the GOP represents part of its strategy to make inroads in the black community. However, simply because these candidates possess African-American racial identity does not necessarily mean they can translate that into electoral mileage. As long as the African-American community views the Democratic Party as the party which, in general, best represents their collective interests, it will be difficult for most black Republican candidates to win office in minority districts. If the 1994 electoral results are indicative of African-American Republican candidates' ability to make inroads, then they have fallen far short. Only

two were victorious: incumbent Gary Franks of Connecticut and newcomer and one-time University of Oklahoma football star J.C. Watts. Both Franks and Watts represent districts that are overwhelmingly white. Franks represents the 5th district of Connecticut, with a black voting-age population of 4.4%, and Watts the 4th district of Oklahoma, with a black voting-age population of 6.5%.

In contrast to Republicans' overall success in unseating some powerful Democratic incumbents and in taking control of Congress, African-American Democratic candidates continued to have their way, at least in terms of the vote. Of the 40-member African-American delegation to the US Congress, 38 are Democrats. For the most part their seats are secure, owing to the Voting Rights Act of 1965 and its subsequent extensions. If any of these African-American Democrats are replaced in the near future, in all likelihood it would be by another African-American Democrat.

**Endnotes**

[1] Katherine Tate, *From Protest to Politics: The New Black Voters in American Politics* (Cambridge, MA: Harvard University Press, 1993); Michael C. Dawson, *Behind the Mule: Race and Class in African-American Politics* (Princeton, NJ: Princeton University Press, 1994).

## Table 1
## 1994 Black Major Party Nominees for Federal Office

| District | Democratic Candidate | Republican Candidate | Democratic Vote 1994 Total (000) | 1994 (%) | 1992 (%) | Republican Vote 1994 Total (000) | 1994 (%) | 1992 (%) |
|---|---|---|---|---|---|---|---|---|
| *US House of Representatives* | | | | | | | | |
| Al-7 | Earl Hilliard | Alfred Middleton | 114 | 77 | 80 | 35 | 23 | 17 |
| CA-9 | Ronald Dellums | Deborah Wright | 118 | 72 | 72 | 37 | 23 | 24 |
| CA-28 | Tommy Randle | • David Drier | 45 | 31 | 37 | 99 | 67 | 58 |
| CA-32 | Julian Dixon | • Ernie Farhat | 88 | 78 | 87 | 19 | 17 | 0 |
| CA-35 | Maxine Waters | Nate Truman | 60 | 78 | 83 | 17 | 22 | 14 |
| CA-37 | Walter Tucker | Unopposed | 59 | 78 | 86 | 0 | 0 | 0 |
| CT-3 | • Rosa DeLauro | Susan Johnson | 105 | 64 | 66 | 60 | 36 | 34 |
| CT-5 | • James Maloney | Gary Franks | 80 | 45 | 31 | 92 | 52 | 45 |
| D.C. | E. H. Norton | • Donald Saltz | 152 | 89 | 85 | 13 | 11 | 15 |
| FL-3 | Corrine Brown | Marc Little | 63 | 58 | 60 | 45 | 42 | 41 |
| FL-17 | Carrie Meek | Unopposed | * | 100 | 100 | * | 0 | 0 |
| FL-23 | Alcee Hastings | Unopposed | * | 100 | 65 | * | 0 | 31 |
| GA-2 | Sanford Bishop | • John Clayton | 65 | 66 | 64 | 33 | 34 | 36 |
| GA-5 | John Lewis | • Dale Dixon | 85 | 69 | 72 | 38 | 31 | 28 |
| GA-11 | Cynthia McKinney | • Woodrow Lovett | 72 | 66 | 73 | 38 | 34 | 27 |
| IL-1 | Bobby Rush | • William Kelly | 107 | 75 | 82 | 35 | 25 | 17 |
| IL-2 | Mel Reynolds | Unopposed | * | 100 | 85 | * | 0 | 14 |
| IL-7 | Cardiss Collins | Chuck Mobley | 87 | 79 | 83 | 23 | 21 | 16 |
| IN-10 | • Andrew Jacobs | Marvin Scott | 55 | 53 | 64 | 48 | 47 | 35 |
| LA-2 | William Jefferson | Unopposed | * | * | * | * | * | * |
| LA-4 | Cleo Fields | Unopposed | * | * | 74 | * | * | 0 |
| MD-4 | Albert Wynn | Michelle Dyson | 91 | 75 | 76 | 29 | 25 | 25 |
| MD-7 | Kweisi Mfume | • Kenneth Konder | 93 | 81 | 85 | 22 | 19 | 15 |
| MA-5 | • Martin Meehan | David Coleman | 141 | 70 | 58 | 61 | 30 | 37 |
| MA-9 | • Joe Moakley | Mike Murphy | 143 | 70 | 76 | 61 | 30 | 21 |
| MI-14 | John Conyes | • Richard Fournier | 130 | 82 | 84 | 26 | 17 | 16 |
| MI-15 | Barbara R. Collins | John Savage | 119 | 84 | 82 | 20 | 14 | 17 |
| MN-5 | • Martin Sabo | Dorothy LeGrand | 122 | 62 | 69 | 73 | 38 | 28 |
| MS-2 | Bennie Thompson | Bill Jordan | 66 | 53 | 78 | 49 | 39 | 22 |
| MO-1 | William Clay | • Donald Counts | 97 | 63 | 68 | 50 | 33 | 32 |
| MO-5 | • Karen McCarthy | Ron Freeman | 100 | 57 | 62 | 77 | 43 | 37 |
| NJ-10 | Donald Payne | • Jim Ford | 72 | 76 | 79 | 21 | 22 | 20 |
| NY-6 | Floyd Flake | • D.D. Bhagwandin | 66 | 80 | 81 | 16 | 20 | 19 |
| NY-10 | Edolphus Towns | Amelia S. Parker | 72 | 89 | 96 | 8 | 9 | 0 |
| NY-11 | Major Owens | • Gary Popkin | 59 | 89 | 95 | 7 | 10 | 0 |
| NY-15 | Charles Rangel | Unopposed | 74 | 96 | 95 | 0 | 0 | 0 |
| NY-17 | • Elliot Engel | Edward Marshall | 67 | 74 | 81 | 16 | 18 | 13 |
| NC-1 | Eva Clayton | • Ted Tyler | 67 | 61 | 68 | 42 | 39 | 31 |
| NC-12 | Mel Watt | • Joe Martino | 58 | 66 | 72 | 30 | 34 | 27 |
| OH-11 | Louis Stokes | • James Sykora | 113 | 77 | 78 | 33 | 23 | 20 |
| OK-4 | • David Perryman | J.C. Watts | 67 | 43 | 71 | 80 | 52 | 29 |
| OK-6 | Jeffrey Tollett | • Frank Lucas | 45 | 30 | 68 | 107 | 70 | 32 |
| PA-1 | • Tom Foglietta | Roger Gordon | 97 | 81 | 81 | 23 | 19 | 19 |
| PA-2 | Chaka Fattah | Lawrence Watson | 118 | 85 | 77 | 20 | 14 | 22 |
| SC-6 | James Clyburn | • Gary McLeod | 89 | 63 | 65 | 50 | 36 | 35 |
| TN-9 | Harold Ford | Rod Deberry | 95 | 58 | 67 | 69 | 42 | 28 |
| TX-10 | • Lloyd Doggett | A. Jo Baylor | 114 | 56 | 72 | 80 | 40 | 26 |
| TX-18 | Sheila J. Lee | Jerry Burley | 85 | 72 | 68 | 28 | 24 | 33 |
| TX-30 | Eddie B. Johnson | Lucy Cain | 73 | 73 | 74 | 26 | 26 | 25 |
| VA-3 | Robert Scott | • Tom Ward | 108 | 79 | 79 | 28 | 21 | 21 |
| *US Senate* | | | | | | | | |

•Indicates candidates not African-American.  *Indicates "data not available at the time of publication."
**Source**: David A. Bositis, *African-Americans and the Midterms* ( Washington DC:  The Joint Center for Political and Economic Studies, 1994).

# Summary Overview

## The 1994 Congressional Vote by Race and Ethnicity

### Percentage Voting Republican

|  | African-American | Hispanic | Non-Hispanic White |
|---|---|---|---|
| **EVERYONE** | **8%** | **41%** | **58%** |
| **By Gender** |  |  |  |
| Male | 13 | 41 | 63 |
| Female | 5 | 40 | 53 |
| **By Age** |  |  |  |
| 18-29 | 6 | 40 | 58 |
| 30-44 | 10 | 46 | 61 |
| 45-59 | 9 | 44 | 58 |
| 60+ | 6 | 25 | 54 |
| **By Education** |  |  |  |
| Less than HS/HS Grad | 9 | * | 44 |
| Some College | 6 | * | 64 |
| College Grad | 11 | * | 61 |
| Post Grad | 4 | * | 47 |
| **By Income** |  |  |  |
| Less than $15,000 | 5 | * | 44 |
| $15,000-29,999 | 7 | * | 55 |
| $30,000-49,999 | 8 | * | 60 |
| $50,000-74,999 | 13 | * | 58 |
| $75,000+ | 15 | * | 64 |
| **By Party ID** |  |  |  |
| Democrat | 1 | 6 | 14 |
| Republican | 83 | 91 | 92 |
| Independent | 19 | * | 60 |
| **By Ideology** |  |  |  |
| Liberal | 3 | * | 22 |
| Moderate | 6 | * | 48 |
| Conservative | 17 | * | 85 |
| **By Union Membership** |  |  |  |
| Union Household | 8 | * | 44 |

# The Region Factor

The South has had a long string of "first time evers" over the past quarter century. In the 1994 congressional balloting, for the first time ever, the southern electorate gave the GOP an electoral majority. And white Southerners were by a large margin more Republican than were white voters in any other part of the US. *America at the Polls 1994* discussed this long-unfolding southern realignment story with pollster Claibourne Darden.

### How They Voted in House 1994 Races

|          | R    | D    |
|----------|------|------|
| East     | 48%  | 52%  |
| Midwest  | 54   | 46   |
| South    | 52   | 48   |
| West     | 51   | 49   |

# The Great Southern Realignment, Take 10

### *A Conversation with Claibourne Darden*

**America at the Polls**: In the wake of the 1994 elections what's especially distinctive about the South?

**Claibourne Darden**: Politically the South has become the bedrock of Republican presidential support. It used to be the West and Midwest, but that's no longer the case. This has all come about fairly recently.

**ATTP**: Was there was a sharp shift this year, or are we seeing the next stage of a slow development?

**CD**: I'd say it was a significant acceleration of the change that has been going on for years. For generation after generation the South automatically voted Democratic in reaction to the Civil War and Reconstruction. The era of the "yellow dog Democrat" lasted up to the Kennedy years. After that, one started seeing the shift, primarily of southern white males, going over — at the presidential level — to the Republican candidates. Then the Republicans elected a senator or congressman, then a few more senators and congressmen, then governors and finally state legislators. But, when it comes to offices like county commissioner, sheriff, district attorney, school superintendent, and the like, Republicans have achieved relatively little penetration as of yet.

**ATTP**: Why it is taking so long for the Republicans to get down to the local level?

**CD**: When it comes down to the local elected offices, you have no grass root operations and no real training fields for *their* politicians. In 1994, Republicans did very well in several state legislatures, which reflects the beginnings of grass roots growth and successful expansion of party influence at the local level—continuing the trend toward Republican domination in the South.

**ATTP**: Some have suggested that the overall results understate the extent to which the South has become Republican because there are still a number of leftover Democratic incumbents hanging on. Do you think the South really is up for grabs in terms of the congressional vote at the moment?

**CD**: It depends on the district. There are still solid black districts that elect black Democrats, but you also have your white upper middle class districts that are going to elect white upper middle class Republicans. The middle-middle-class white districts — what we call the "Bubba" vote — are the ones that turned Republican.

**ATTP**: To what extent is what happened this year part of an anti-incumbent effort to "throw the rascals out" as oppposed to a movement to the Republicans as such.

**CD**: There was a slight anti-incumbency trend, but it was Democratic incumbents who really took the brunt of this development. For example, the only white Democratic congressman who won in Georgia was Nathan Deal, who walked away from Clinton from the day he went up there to Washington. He got re-elected by a landslide. It was primarily an anti-Democratic trend based upon dissatisfaction with a number of incumbent Democratic politicians, but primarily with Bill Clinton.

**ATTP:** For a long time there was a notion that southern politicians were shut out of the presidency and a hope in certain quarters that a southerner in the White House might restore Democratic fortunes. But, if anything, the situation grew worse with Carter, and now even more so with Clinton.

**CD:** When Jimmy Carter was president, things did not go well for him. Some people said he was 5'10" but the water was 6 feet deep. But Bill Clinton is making Jimmy Carter look good.

**ATTP:** What is Clinton's biggest problem — the issues, his general leadership, or his character?

**CD:** His character. His credibility is virtually non-existent among "middle-middle" class voters. Southerners, white southern males anyway, still hold on to a few chivalrous attitudes, such as, "a man's word is his bond," and so forth.

**ATTP:** Character can mean general credibility: Will he stick to his positions, can he be believed when he says he will do something or has done something. And then there is the more general moral/ethical dimension. People have talked about Clinton being weak in both areas. Would either be especially important in the South?

**CD:** Believability is the much more important of the two, although if it were not so, the morality issue would still be very significant. The last rung on the ladder is always the most important one, and the morality issue is one rung below believability, honesty and credibility. Would you lend Bill Clinton ten thousand dollars? A lot of people would say "no," and that's his problem.

**ATTP:** Is there any particular group that you think has been especially the focus of the change in the South?

**CD:** The answer is clearly white males. They were the first to go Republican. What caused the tremendous landslide was the white male "Bubba" vote. Females historically trail in such a change. Differences between men and women were especially strong among the middle-middle class voter.

**ATTP:** Are the predictions of the loss of the South for the Democrats, and the strong Republican identification of the region, premature?

**CD:** One thing you can count on in politics is that nothing is permanent. What is more critical and potentially very damaging is if racial parties get started in the South — a black party and a white party. This is what brought about the collapse of the Democratic party. The only salvation here is for the Republican party to honestly try to recruit a number of black citizens. But I have seen very little of this actually attempted.

**ATTP:** If the Republicans were to recruit black candidates more aggressively, would that cut into the "Bubba" vote?

**CD:** Only a little bit. Where's "Bubba" going? Compare the case of Mondale when he has given an ultimatum by NOW to choose a women vice president or face a walkout. Where were they going to walk to? You can't cultivate your core vote openly and expect to get the marginal vote you need to win elections. As soon as you get away from the middle of the middle class, you lose. But campaign after campaign you see politicians cultivating their pocket vote.

**ATTP:** You have identified the young white male vote as being especially crucial. Is that something you expect to continue over time?

**CD:** White males are going to be dominant. What we have seen for 15 years is young people leaning more and more Republican, and as they get older they carry that partisanship with them. In the 60s young people were Democratic. They've grown up now and are in their fifties. It's the ones just behind them who are Republican.

**ATTP:** Can this election be seen as a referendum on the role of government, and do you think the South has a distinctive view of that basic issue?

**CD:** Voters didn't like the fact that incumbents — and that means primarily Democrats — were socializing America. There is a laundry list of ways money can be flushed. I have a place in Georgia, and the federal government pays 75% of costs to build roads on my property. There are hundreds of examples like that, and the American public is fed up. Then there is the debacle of Hillary and health care reform, which are both separate and related issues. Clinton's pro-gay positions are extremely unpopular. He increases taxes while increasing spending, but tells the American people he is cutting spending. How can one believe him? It doesn't seem as if anybody is in control, which feeds back into the credibility question.

**ATTP:** Do you think 1994 will be a high water mark for Republican ascendancy, or just one stop along the road to greater Republican dominance?

**CD:** It depends on what Congress does, especially the House of Representatives. The ball is in the Republican court in the minds of voters. If they do even a few of the things they say they are going to do, they're still in the ballpark. But if they don't, the outcome is uncertain.

**ATTP:** What promises do you see as being especially crucial for them to keep?

**CD:** Reduce government spending; make government more efficient; reduce taxes, and spur the economy It used to be the case that if you had a good economy you could take it to the bank. Incumbents were very popular then and were re-elected. We have a reasonably good economy today, but incumbents nevertheless went down the tube. Among the ten problems Republicans say they are going to tackle, they have to nail five or six. They must start doing things right away, conveying to the American people very specifically that they mean business, that they are going to cut out government waste, and that they are going to keep their word. I can't tell you how many people asked me after the election, "I wonder if they are going to do what they said they would do?".

**ATTP**: Could Clinton have avoided this?

**CD**: Probably, if the President did have personal credibility, and assuming the economy stayed strong. In all the elections historically since 1932 or so, the White House party lost an average of about 28 seats each time, but that varied substantially. The Republicans in this election were going to gain seats anyway, but we're not talking about *a* 50-52 seat change for technical or historical reasons!

**ATTP**: Are there particular stories in individual states that you think are worthy of attention?

**CD**: Every race has its own anecdotes. On a national level, I am not so sure that many of them are significant. Some of the Republicans who lost ran a much better race then others who won. The Republicans who did well are the ones who set the agenda, and the agenda was Bill Clinton.

**ATTP**: What about Texas, where Richards was a relatively popular incumbent?

**CD**: It was part of that anti-Clinton trend. It went all the way down to the state house.

**ATTP**: Are there any special danger signals for the Republicans?

**CD**: I look at politics as a very slow moving pendulum. For forty years, the Democrats were too strong for the Republicans to beat; they had to lose for themselves, and that's what happened. Republicans may become too strong for the Democrats to beat, but they too can lose an election through their own mistakes. The religious right is the biggest danger the Republican party faces. Other issues, like recruiting blacks, are so far down the line it doesn't make any difference. The religious right, unless contained, will do exactly the same thing to the Republican party that the radical left did to the Democratic party. Any time you openly cultivate an extreme, you lose that marginal vote that you need. The religious right will perhaps not become dominant, but could muster enough votes in the primaries to force the Republican candidates away from middle America. And when this happens, you're reading Michael Dukakis's campaign manual.

**ATTP**: Do you think the religious right is a special threat in the South—a region noted for its religious conservatism?

**CD**: The potential damage probably will show up in the South before it's seen elsewhere. A number of Republican candidates already feel they are forced to support some religious right issues so that they can win in primaries. But if they adopt them firmly, this will be their undoing in a general election — the same fate the Democrats can expect if they espouse radical left causes in their primaries.

**ATTP**: Does that help to explain what happened to Ollie North in Virginia?

**CD**: His is a special case. He is a celebrity, and a lot of folks were for him, but many fell out with him over the issue of lying. That was their chief objection.

**ATTP**: Which goes back to the credibility issue. This is especially interesting considering the fact that both North and Robb had problems involving "character." Robb's problems tended to have more to do with questions of traditional morality.

**CD**: Yes, which we are more used to. We can accept those more easily than the credibility problem.

**ATTP**: We have spoken mostly about white voters, what about the black vote in the South?

**CD**: There are a lot of folks who didn't vote. In the South the black vote went down the tube. That accounted, as much as anything, for the Republican victories.

**ATTP**: What accounted for a falloff in black participation?

**CD**: Black turnout depends on who's running. If a candidate excites their interest, blacks come in from every direction. Turnout just goes through the roof. Without such interest, turnout is negligible.

**ATTP**: Did we see a substantially different turnout among black voters where there was a black candidate running?

**CD**: It's not just a question of a black candidate. I don't know of a contested race this year with a powerful black candidate running against a viable white candidate.

**ATTP**: If George Bush won the 1992 presidential election would we now be looking at a South with a Republican congressional majority?

**CD**: One has no reason to believe we would see anything even remotely like the 1994 election, if George Bush had been elected president. In fact, history teaches us we would have had a Democratic gain. So "thank you, George!" That's what the new Republicans ought to be saying.

# Summary Overview
## The 1994 Congessional Vote by Region
### PercentageVoting Republican

|  | East | South | Mid-West | West |
|---|---|---|---|---|
| **EVERYONE** | **48%** | **52%** | **54%** | **51%** |
| **By Gender** |  |  |  |  |
| Male | 54 | 59 | 59 | 56 |
| Female | 43 | 47 | 48 | 46 |
| **By Age** |  |  |  |  |
| 18-29 | 46 | 49 | 56 | 45 |
| 30-44 | 50 | 52 | 55 | 54 |
| 45-59 | 50 | 53 | 55 | 52 |
| 60+ | 46 | 54 | 50 | 50 |
| **By Education** |  |  |  |  |
| Less than HS | * | 45 | * | * |
| HS Grad or less | 52 | 49 | 57 | 50 |
| Some College | 49 | 58 | 61 | 61 |
| College Grad | 63 | 51 | 53 | 52 |
| Post Grad | 38 | 44 | 47 | 40 |
| **By Race/Ethnicity** |  |  |  |  |
| White | 52 | 65 | 56 | 57 |
| Black | 8 | 6 | 15 | 10 |
| Hispanic | * | 52 | * | 27 |
| Asian | * | * | * | 39 |
| **By Income** |  |  |  |  |
| Less than $15,000 | 32 | 33 | 39 | 44 |
| $15,000-29,999 | 42 | 48 | 50 | 48 |
| $30,000-49,000 | 49 | 53 | 58 | 55 |
| $50,000-75,000 | 51 | 55 | 57 | 52 |
| $75,000-100,000 | 59 | 68 | 57 | 51 |
| $100,000+ | 55 | 75 | 64 | 53 |
| **By Party ID** |  |  |  |  |
| Democrat | 15 | 11 | 9 | 7 |
| Republican | 88 | 93 | 91 | 93 |
| Independent | 54 | 59 | 61 | 49 |
| **By Ideology** |  |  |  |  |
| Liberal | 25 | 17 | 15 | 12 |
| Moderate | 42 | 38 | 46 | 44 |
| Conservative | 77 | 77 | 83 | 84 |
| **By Denomination** |  |  |  |  |
| Protestant | 58 | 58 | 61 | 61 |
| Catholic | 50 | 54 | 53 | 53 |
| Other Christian | 46 | 40 | 59 | 58 |
| Jewish | 28 | * | * | * |
| None | * | 29 | * | 33 |
| **By Union Membership** |  |  |  |  |
| Union Household | 46 | 30 | 39 | 34 |

# The Religious Factor

The "religious factor" looked much the same in the 1994 balloting as it had in other recent contests—and looked very different from patterns prevailing in earlier eras. Two stories emerge from an analysis of the data—one of the continuation of a trend which has seen Catholics leave their strong historic attachment to the Democratic party, the other involving a relative newcomer to the American politi- cal scene—a group often described as the "religious right."

Historically, Roman Catho- Democratic candidates. Over the changing. The shift was first evi- balloting, for the first time in US backed GOP *congressional nomi-* lic voters provided bedrock support for last quarter-century, though, this has been dent in presidential voting. In the 1994 history, a majority of Catholic voters *nees* (Table 2).

Exit poll data from both VNS further indication of how voters "religious right." When VNS themselves "part of the religious sponded affirmatively. When which applied, 15% of voters and Mitofsky International give the reader define themselves with respect to the asked respondents whether they consider right political movement," 19% re- asked later in the survey to check off any checked "Born-again Christian/Funda- mentalist." But when Mitofsky International gave a similar check-off list, 27% of voters chose "Born again/Evangelical Christian."

As the data on the next page indicate, respondents located by each of these cuts or definitions were heavily Republican in their 1994 congressional vote—not surprisingly, the more so in the case of the more restrictive definitions.

**How They Voted in House 1994 Races**

| | R | D |
|---|---|---|
| Protestant | 60% | 40% |
| Catholic | 52 | 48 |
| Jewish | 22 | 78 |
| Other Christian | 50 | 50 |
| None | 37 | 63 |

—Marc Maynard

## Vote by Catholics for President and Congress

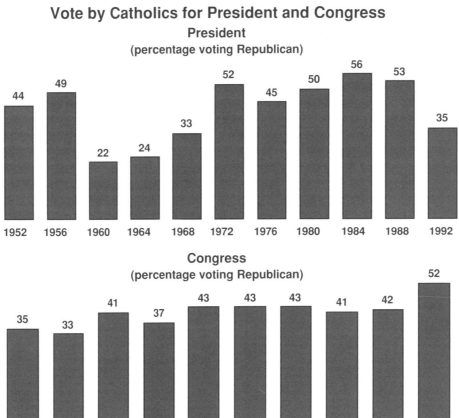

### President
### (percentage voting Republican)

| 1952 | 1956 | 1960 | 1964 | 1968 | 1972 | 1976 | 1980 | 1984 | 1988 | 1992 |
|---|---|---|---|---|---|---|---|---|---|---|
| 44 | 49 | 22 | 24 | 33 | 52 | 45 | 50 | 56 | 53 | 35 |

### Congress
### (percentage voting Republican)

| 1976 | 1978 | 1980 | 1982 | 1984 | 1986 | 1988 | 1990 | 1992 | 1994 |
|---|---|---|---|---|---|---|---|---|---|
| 35 | 33 | 41 | 37 | 43 | 43 | 43 | 41 | 42 | 52 |

**Source**: Pre-1976, Gallup Post-Election Surveys; 1976-1988, CBS News Exit Polls; 1990-1992, Voter Research Service Exit Polls; and 1994, Voter News Service Exit Poll.

## Tracking the "Religiosity Factor"

# How You Ask the Question Matters

**Question**: Do you consider yourself of **the religious right political movement?**

**House Vote 1994**

| Yes | All | Whites only |
|-----|-----|-------------|
| 19% | 61%R | 74%R |

Which of the following apply to you?...

**"Born again Christian/Fundamentalist"**

**House Vote 1994**

| Yes | All | Whites only |
|-----|-----|-------------|
| 15% | 69%R | 80%R |

**"Part of the religious right political movement"**

| Yes | House Vote 1994 |
|-----|-----------------|
| 6% | 85%R |

**Source**: Voter News Service, November 8, 1994.

**Question**: Do any of the following apply to you?

**" Born Again/Evangelical Christian"**

| Yes | House Vote 1994 |
|-----|-----------------|
| 27% | 61%R |

**White, Born Again, Attend Church Weekly**

| Yes | House Vote 1994 |
|-----|-----------------|
| 13% | 80%R |

**Source**: Mitofsky International, November 8, 1994.

## Things May Not Be as They're Commonly Presumed

Example: When the 15% of the 1994 VNS sample who checked "Born-again Christian/Fundamentalist" were asked whether they consider themselves of the "religious right political movement," they responded:

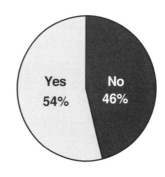

# Summary Overview

## The 1994 Congressional Vote by Religion
### Percentage Voting Republican

| | Catholic | Jewish | Protestant | Other Christian | None | Religious Right |
|---|---|---|---|---|---|---|
| **EVERYONE** | **52%** | **22%** | **60%** | **50%** | **37%** | **60%** |
| **By Gender** | | | | | | |
| Male | 60 | 19 | 64 | 59 | 47 | 67 |
| Female | 44 | 25 | 56 | 42 | 22 | 55 |
| **By Age** | | | | | | |
| 18-29 | 53 | * | 60 | 53 | 35 | 56 |
| 30-44 | 59 | * | 60 | 50 | 36 | 66 |
| 45-59 | 48 | * | 59 | 51 | 34 | 62 |
| 60+ | 46 | * | 60 | 43 | * | 57 |
| **By Education** | | | | | | |
| Less than HS | 28 | * | 48 | * | * | 34 |
| HS Grad | 48 | * | 60 | 52 | * | 60 |
| Some College | 53 | * | 66 | 55 | 56 | 66 |
| College Grad | 64 | * | 62 | 52 | 25 | 66 |
| Post Grad | 49 | * | 53 | 33 | 24 | 70 |
| **By Race/Ethnicity** | | | | | | |
| White | 55 | 21 | 65 | 67 | 38 | 74 |
| Black | * | * | 8 | 4 | * | 6 |
| Hispanic | 32 | * | * | * | * | * |
| **By Income** | | | | | | |
| Less than $15,000 | 36 | * | 45 | 38 | * | 40 |
| $15,000-29,999 | 40 | * | 58 | 44 | * | 53 |
| $30,000-49,000 | 54 | * | 58 | 51 | * | 69 |
| $50,000-75,000 | 58 | * | 60 | 56 | * | 71 |
| $75,000-100,000 | 68 | * | 62 | * | * | * |
| $100,000+ | 65 | * | 80 | * | * | * |
| **By Party ID** | | | | | | |
| Democrat | 11 | 11 | 14 | 6 | 8 | 10 |
| Republican | 90 | * | 91 | 94 | 87 | 95 |
| Independent | 62 | * | 64 | 54 | 44 | 66 |
| **By Ideology** | | | | | | |
| Liberal | 21 | * | 19 | 15 | 12 | 13 |
| Moderate | 44 | * | 48 | 38 | 38 | 38 |
| Conservative | 78 | * | 87 | 77 | * | 82 |
| **By Union Membership** | | | | | | |
| Union Household | 41 | * | 39 | 32 | * | 46 |

Note: The religious right are based on those who said they considered themselves to be "part of the religion right political movement" (19% of sample).

# As Independents Go...

In the 1994 elections, as in many elections in recent history, the independent voter played a major role in determining the results. Democratic identifiers strongly backed Democratic candidates, and Republicans strongly supported their party's nominees. In 1994 House races, independents backed Republican candidates by a 58% to 42% margin, according to VNS exit polls, thereby providing the margin for the party's victory.

A look at recent national elections indicates a strong tendency for independents to be arrayed behind the eventual winner. Table 1 shows House and presidential votes of independents since 1976. On only three occasions did independent voters not back the winning candidate: The 1976 presidential race, and the 1980 and 1984 House elections. In each of these instances independents gave majority backing for the GOP, while the nation as a whole voted Democratic.

Turning to key state races in 1994, a similar pattern is seen. In all but three of seventeen gubernatorial and senatorial races held in the ten most populous states, majorities of independent voters supported winning candidates. The three exceptions are the New York, Pennsylvania and Virginia senatorial contests (see Table 2).

## Table 1
### The Independent Vote for President
### 1976-1992

|      | 1976 | 1980 | 1984 | 1988 | 1992 |
|------|------|------|------|------|------|
| Dem. | 48%  | 31%  | 36%  | 43%  | 38%  |
| Rep. | 52   | 56   | 64   | 57   | 32   |

### The Independent Vote for Congress
### 1976-1994

|      | 1976 | 1978 | 1980 | 1982 | 1984 | 1986 | 1988 | 1990 | 1992 | 1994 |
|------|------|------|------|------|------|------|------|------|------|------|
| Dem. | 54%  | 51%  | 43%  | 50%  | 45%  | 49%  | 51%  | 51%  | 52%  | 42%  |
| Rep. | 44   | 45   | 54   | 46   | 52   | 45   | 43   | 45   | 43   | 58   |

## Table 2
### Vote of Independents in Gubernatorial and Senatorial Races in the Most Populous States

| State | Race | Independents' Vote | | Statewide Vote | |
|-------|------|------|------|------|------|
|       |      | Dem. | Rep. | Dem. | Rep. |
| California | Gov. | 37% | 54% | 40% | 55% |
|            | Sen. | 44  | 41  | 47  | 45  |
| Florida    | Gov. | 55  | 45  | 51  | 49  |
|            | Sen. | 24  | 76  | 70  | 30  |
| Illinois   | Gov. | 34  | 64  | 34  | 64  |
| Michigan   | Gov. | 34  | 66  | 39  | 61  |
|            | Sen. | 38  | 51  | 43  | 52  |
| New Jersey | Sen. | 47  | 47  | 50  | 47  |
| New York   | Gov. | 34  | 59  | 45  | 49  |
|            | **Sen.** | **48** | **49** | **55** | **42** |
| Ohio       | Gov. | 22  | 74  | 25  | 72  |
|            | Sen. | 36  | 51  | 39  | 53  |
| Pennsylvania | Gov. | 37 | 44 | 40 | 45 |
|            | **Sen.** | **50** | **45** | **47** | **49** |
| Texas      | Gov. | 42  | 57  | 46  | 54  |
|            | Sen. | 33  | 65  | 38  | 61  |
| Virginia   | **Sen.** | **40** | **43** | **46** | **43** |

**Source**: VNS 1994 Exit Poll.

# Chapter 5
# 1994 Vote: Key Races

The 1994 balloting saw big Republican gains all across the United States. This shift in national power has commanded most of the attention in post-election commentary.

Nonetheless, a many individual state and congressional district contests had their own individual drama and importance. In New York, three-term Governor Mario Cuomo—one of the Democrats' brightest lights nationally over the past decade—struggled for a fourth term against Republican George Pataki, who had not previously sought statewide office. The polls showed Cuomo's chances buoyed temporarily by the endorsement he received from the Republican mayor of New York City, Rudolph Giuliani, but the Governor's run fell short. Pataki brought the governorship back to the GOP for the first time since the Nelson Rockefeller era two decades ago.

The Texas gubernatorial race was, almost literally, a blood feud. Here, the son of a former president challenged an incumbent governor who had mocked his father in a famous speech to the 1992 Democratic National Convention. Were this not enough, the Governor was endorsed in her 1994 reelection bid by the man who, perhaps more than any other, had brought about the 1992 defeat of the challenger's father. When this family feud had played itself out, George W. Bush had defeated Ann Richards by a 7-point margin.

Other races had their own drama. In the Pennsylvania Senate contest, the Democratic incumbent, who had won election—and national recognition—in 1991 by campaigning on the need for a national health-care program, lost in 1994 to a Republican opponent who attacked him for his health-care stand. Across the country, in Washington's 5th congressional district, the Speaker of the US House of Representatives lost his reelection bid—the first sitting speaker to lose in 130 years.

Not all the state results were disappointments for the Democrats, of course. They retained their senate seat in California—despite record spending from a personal fortune by the GOP challenger. They retained the Maryland governorship in an extraordinarily interesting, hard fought, and close contest. And, a bit to the south in Virginia, incumbent Democratic Senator Charles Robb bested the Republican nominee, Oliver North, in a race in which negative judgments—of both major party contenders—dominated to an extent rarely seen in American politics.

In the pages which follow, *America at the Polls* surveys these seven key races closely.

—David Wilber

# Four Pollsters' Perspectives

**A Conversation With:**　　　**Micheline Blum, Texas**

**John Brennan, California**

**Scott Keeter, Virginia**

**Lee M. Miringoff, New York**

**America at the Polls:** How would each of you describe the mood or worries or whatever that most drove voters' decisions on November 8 in the states you were following most closely?

**John Brennan:**　　May I begin with California? It's interesting to talk about this state especially because of the impact of the immigration issue. Since I started working out here in early 1991, California has gone through two big shifts in outlook. When I first got out here the big problems in this state, as cited in the polls, were "growth" and "drought." But in the latter part of 1991, the state went into a drastic economic downturn, probably the worst since the Great Depression. Because of that, in 1992 the economy (as it did nationally) just dominated the election and helped Bill Clinton win this state by 13 percentage points over George Bush. In general, there was a huge swing toward the Democrats, we elected two female Democratic senators. This year, I think a lot of people were looking back at those 1992 results. This is the mistake we keep making—thinking that one election predicts the next. We are going to do it with the 1994 election, expecting it to predict 1996 and we will be wrong again.

　　Really what happened between 1992 and 1994 is that Californians changed drastically again. Somewhere in the summer to the fall of 1993, we started to see the immigration and the crime issues basically just come out of nowhere. They weren't even discussed in 1992. But by the time you get into the early part of 1994 and into the June primary, those issues were equal to if not greater than the economy as issues driving voters. Those were issues that Pete Wilson just took over. In our [*Los Angeles Times*] exit poll on November 8th, we found amazingly—even though this state is definitely not in good economic shape by any means, still lagging behind the rest of the nation in recovery—that voters were basically casting their ballot on the illegal immigration, crime, and tax issues. They were mentioned more than the economy, and immigration just dominated the landscape.

**Lee Miringoff:** In New York there were some carryovers from 1992. This year we saw again some of the same frustration on the part of the electorate—this would seem to be true nationally as well as in New York—that drove things two years ago. In a sense, Clinton was the beneficiary of that sentiment in 1992 and the victim of it in 1994. What he found this year is that people still care about the same issues—they just don't see politics as a way to articulate and resolve them. Here in New York, we picked up a lot of economic insecurity. I wonder, if in some ways California's Proposition 187, although an immigration issue, was still a kind of surrogate for economic insecurity.

**JB:** Yes, it is in part economic. But it's also more than that. One of the things that we were surprised by in our exit polling is that Proposition 187, and Pete Wilson as well, did very well among voters who said they were *better off* and those who said they were *worse off* financially than four years ago. Also, 187 swept income groups up and down the scale. This doesn't mean there wasn't an economic underpinning to it but it is a larger issue. There is now a politics of diminished expectations. It's partially economic but it also involves values and security. People just don't feel good about their lives.

**Micheline Blum:** They don't feel safe. That's part of what you are seeing both with crime and immigration. Immigration itself is less of an issue in Texas. Crime was the biggest one. George W. Bush—the former President's son—grabbed the issue and ran with it and handled it specifically in the terms Texans were looking for. We had done a poll early in the year about issues, and exactly what voters wanted done. Bush did his homework. He addressed those issues in the terms people were using.

　　On crime, they needed to feel that once a criminal was put away for a really serious offense, he was going to stay away. There were certain safety issues people wanted to hear about and Bush addressed them.

In general we saw in Texas some of what Lee and John were describing—an impatience and an "anti-whoever is in charge right now" that worked in Bill Clinton's favor last time, but in the Republicans' favor this time. In many ways elections across the US were the Republicans to lose—and the only Republicans who lost made some major misstep.

**Scott Keeter:** Virginia is a very good example of a state where it was the Republicans' to lose—and they lost. They did so by selecting a candidate who had many serious personal problems. (It sounds like I am talking about Chuck Robb, but I am not.) Oliver North was ultimately unelectable even with the tailwind Republican candidates had this year. Moreover, voter aversion to North by large segments of the electorate was so great that he provoked a decent turnout on the part of moderates and liberals—and this probably helped re-elect a couple of House Democrats who might otherwise have been swept away.

People who called themselves conservative voted overwhelmingly for North. The interesting number from the exit polls, though, was for people who called themselves moderates. In other states this year, moderates tended to go Republican. But in Virginia, according to the VNS exit poll, moderates voted 59% for Robb and only 28% for North. In our [Virginia Commonwealth University] last pre-election poll, we asked voters if they saw the candidates as liberal, moderate or conservative and then (if they said liberal or conservative) if they were extreme liberals or extreme conservatives. North was much more likely to be called an extremist than Robb.

**AATP:** Mickey, you said crime was a big issue of concern. Yet Ann Richards, the incumbent governor, had worked hard over her term to address voter concerns on this issue. Her prison-building program, for example, wasn't just window dressing. Why then didn't concerns on this issue work for her, rather than against her?

**MB:** There are many contradictions and reasons for what happened in Texas. You had two popular candidates, in particular a very popular governor who sort of did everything right... and still lost. She was pretty good on most of the issues. What's more, people in Texas think that everything is going in the right direction rather than the wrong track, unlike many other states. In the exit poll, nearly 70% of voters thought the condition of the Texas economy to be excellent or good. Richards had built more prisons and crime rates were down—but still when we asked in our polls, people still felt safer about crime with Bush. It's a puzzle that we have been trying to figure out.

Part of it may have to do with how they spoke on the issues. Richards talked more about building prisons. Perhaps many Texans didn't see that as having much effect on their lives. They wanted to know that once a crook was put away, he would stay away. Bush talked more about not releasing felons early. There also maybe a gender factor. In Texas, crime just may be a tough issue for a woman to win on.

**LM:** There was no bigger builder of prisons than Mario Cuomo, but that doesn't necessarily convert into being tough on crime.

**MB:** Right. You could be building all the prisons imaginable and it doesn't necessarily make people feel that you've dealt with the crime issue or make them feel safe.

**LM:** The New York situation was so different from Texas. Here, you had an electorate that had grown tired of Mario Cuomo, even fatigued by him, and a challenger who was totally unknown. As for the economy, New York has not really rebounded from the recession. Our polling showed the overwhelming majority of New Yorkers felt the economy was still in recession. All this produced a very grumpy electorate. It made seeking a fourth term too tall an order for Mario Cuomo.

**AATP:** Nationally, the Republicans made much of the role of government issue. The "Contract with America" was filled with proposals to scale back government taxing and spending. How big was this issue in the political outcomes in your states?

**JB:** It was an issue for us in the Senate race between Feinstein and Huffington. The lines were drawn on this. Huffington attempted to define himself as a very clearly anti-government candidate, and to depict Dianne Feinstein as the quintessential, pro-government incumbent. Even though she had only been in the Senate two years, his tag line on her was "a career politician who will do or say anything to be re-elected." In this anti-government environment Feinstein was still fighting as the strong representative of California—someone who goes to Washington to advocate California, make government work for California. Huffington basically said, "I want to go to Washington to get Washington off California's back."

When we asked questions in our pre-election polls about what kind of a senator voters were looking for—someone who is going to be a strong advocate in Washington for bringing things home to California, or an outsider who will go to Washington to get the federal government off California's back—we never got a majority picking the latter. The result was 48/33. In the long run, that helped Feinstein survive. Yes, there was an anti-government mood out there, but our exit polling found that her record basically held favor even in this Republican/anti-Clinton tide. There were enough people who still felt good about what she had done to have her squeeze out a two point victory. Many Californians still felt they wanted an advocate in Washington.

**LM:** The slogan Pataki used against Cuomo was "too liberal too long." In fact, it was much more the latter than the former that did Cuomo in. I don't think it was as much about ideology as it was about this huge political persona who dominated New York politics for so long, and this grumpy electorate who wanted to move in a different direction. In New York, Cuomo was caught up a bit in having lost a certain star quality—no longer being the future presidential candidate, or a Supreme Court candidate—that had fueled his popularity.

One of the things I am struck by is that the gap between running for office and governing is so great—and widening—as to make governing extremely difficult. More than being for government or against government, the electorate was looking for more results. They looked at Washington and Clinton, and saw them adrift. They looked at New York and they saw it still headed in the wrong direction. That inability to govern effectively, to get results, was really what brought Cuomo and a lot of other officeholders down.

**AATP:** Still, Cuomo's fellow Democratic incumbent, Pat Moynihan, won re-election to the Senate by a comfortable margin. Moynihan's opponent was not well known but, as you have pointed out, Lee, Cuomo's opponent was equally unknown. So why did these two races end so differently?

**LM:** Moynihan is an interesting figure in New York. He has extended his support beyond the traditional Democratic base of New York City into many of the up-state areas—which is where Cuomo got his clock cleaned. Cuomo lost the election in the up-state New York cities where Democrats did not show up, and his numbers just fell dramatically. Another part of why Moynihan did well was that the money spent against him was much less than that spent against Cuomo. The governor's race really over shadowed everything else.

The result of the Senate race and many of the others are why I don't call this an anti-incumbent election as such. Only one Democratic Senate incumbent who had served a full six-year term was ousted... Jim Sasser in Tennessee. What the Democrats couldn't

do was hold onto the open seats that had been held by the party. Senators didn't get hit like some of the chief executives did—as in Texas and New York.

Cuomo and Moynihan really had very different personas in New York. Cuomo had just come down from a very lofty perch, while Moynihan's popularity has been more constant. He hasn't been nearly as controversial, at least in terms of Republican/Democratic politics.

**AATP:** Mickey Blum, how did the argument about "big government" play out in Texas?

**MB:** As a general rule Texas definitely hates big government. In addition, Bush did speak to it. He talked about bringing the control of schools back to the local districts. He portrayed himself as a businessman and an outsider—the latter being somewhat amusing for the son of a former president. But I don't know that is in fact what won it for him. I suspect having the last name "Bush"—not being the outsider, but rather the popular son of an extremely popular president—was key. Texans are very conservative, and they do trust Republicans to spend less, and they do think of the Democrats as bringing them more government, but I don't know that they really tagged Ann Richards with that.

**SK:** I have been struck by polling, including that done by the Times Mirror organization, which indicates there has been a drop over the last couple of years of reasonable size—10 percentage points or more in some measures— in the proportion of individuals who want the government active in areas such as taking care of the needy. Given how balanced our politics has been over the last several elections, this is significant. The 1994 election played out this shift—modestly but significantly—in the center of gravity in our politics. When you combine this shift with the mobilization conservatives were able to achieve through talk radio, and things like the gun issue, you got something large enough to make

the difference in this election.

**JB:** That's an important point. I am still not convinced that the American people have walked away from the basic New Deal credo that government should do things to help people. What seems to be happening here is that there is skepticism about government's doing a good job, and concern that it is helping the wrong people. I also think there was a certain amount of scapegoating going on in this election. Will Senator Al D'Amato and all the Republican governors in the Northeast allow their middle-class entitlement called "Amtrak" to be cut? Is Bob Dole going to vote against farm supports? We have subsidies here in California on water—I don't think Pete Wilson will allow those to be touched. Recent polls show that as soon as you start talking about middle class entitlements, people say NO to cuts. People want government out of their lives and off their backs, but this means curbing welfare cheats, illegal immigrants, criminals watching color TV in prisons. It's those places where government should be cut. I agree that there has been the marginal, but important move which the Times Mirror research has picked up. But I always say about Californians that there are an awful lot of conservatives on the day after an earthquake who are looking around for those government loans. I am still not convinced that we are in for real middle-class entitlement cuts.

**AATP:** How big was the "Clinton factor" as such in this year's results?

**LM:** As for New York, it was not surprising that when Clinton was going nowhere else to campaign he was still coming to New York City. His numbers were still good here even when they were not so good in most other places. He did a lot of fundraising in New York City. From a national perspective, obviously the administration failed miserably to provide any kind of unifying theme and treated the races as local episodic events. If they had been in a campaign mode as they were in 1992, when the Contract for America was put out, they probably would have had Carville and others out there with a response before the ink had dried. The White House did not handle this election at all well.

I am struck by the findings of a late November CBS poll, which shows that most people think the economy is actually doing pretty well right now, but think that Clinton is doing badly handling the economy. Somewhere along the line you have to make an effort and respond, as they would have in a presidential campaign setting, to what was being asserted by the GOP. Instead, they just let it sit out there.

**SK:** On their face the Clinton numbers nationally are not ghastly. He has a fairly decent base of support. The problem is that the intensity of the people who dislike him is much greater than that of those who back him. That factored in the turnout: People who didn't like Clinton, or see him as a symbol of all things wrong in Washington, were much more likely to show up to vote than were Clinton partisans and much more likely to let their view on Clinton shape their vote in their state races.

**MB**: Texas is more anti-Clinton than the county at large, and has been since he was elected. George Bush did carry Texas in 1992. There was good reason for George W. Bush to try to nationalize this year's gubernatorial election, to link Richards to Clinton as often as he could, and to stress how she would try to get him re-elected in 1996. Bush ran advertisements saying that. It was an important message in Texas, because in some ways George W. Bush was trying to make this year's contest a rerun of 1992. In Texas a lot of people wanted to express some dissatisfaction with Clinton and have a chance to vote for a Bush.

There was also a Senate race in Texas—even though it was a rout, it wasn't talked about very much. When the exit polls looked at the top concerns of the Kay Baily Hutchison voters, you really did see the Clinton connection. Hutchison ran very strongly as an anti-Clinton candidate. It's not

that Richard Fisher was really a "pro-Clinton candidate" or anybody who was terribly tied to him, but Hutchison played the anti-Clinton card all the way through. That factor was most important to voters who were backing her. She ran away with her election, and her message also spilled over into the governor's race. It did help Bush's message.

**JB**: We were amazed when we did polling on Clinton earlier in the year, when Whitewater was getting attention, that Clinton's job ratings were rising in California. Clinton has always had a cache of goodwill here. We had him as high as 58% approval—which for Clinton is a good number.

Overall, though, Clinton has very low approval numbers for a President. I think there is a "character" drag that could be 5-6 points—he has had it since he was inaugurated. It's one of his major problems. Lately, he can't get above 43% or so in approval. In California, as I've said, he rode up into the high 50s and maintained an approval rating in the mid-50s through the spring of this year. But then he started to tumble in the fall. He was hanging around 50 at the time of the election.

What does this tell us about the Feinstein-Huffington race? We asked specifically in both the pre-election and the exit polling what Feinstein's "Clinton connection" did. We found that it hurt her more than it helped her: 26% of Huffington voters said that Feinstein's support for Clinton was a factor in their vote against Feinstein. That was the second most mentioned factor in the exit poll. The one larger number was the 32% who said their vote for Huffington owed most to Feinstein's being a taxer and spender. Now, 18% of Feinstein voters said that her connections to Clinton motivated them to back her. The tie was by no means only a negative. Still, when you add up those numbers, it's a net negative. Clinton got 46% of the vote here in 1992. We did not ask his job rating in the exit poll, but we asked his "re-elect" number: at this point it was 38%

for him, 51% against him, with 11% unsure. He is in trouble in California as he is in most of the country.

**AATP:** We have one last big question for you. After almost every election, it seems, we read accounts claiming that *voter turnout* was a main factor shaping the results. In a sense, this is always true. Had Party A, which lost by three points, gotten out a much higher proportion of its potential voters than it in fact did, and Party B's vote remained the same, Party A could have won the contest.

But realistically, this year, is there any indication that Republicans benefited from the turnout level and structure, or that higher turnout might well have led to different results?

**LM:** This election had a lot to do with the mobilization of the Republican base. When you had 30 seats in the House which were won by Republicans with 52% of the vote or less—difference in turnout or mobilization can easily make a big difference in terms of who wins.

Turnout was a big story this time. It reflects the inability of the Democrats to offer a unifying national alternative. When Clinton got on the campaign stump, he was doing it in the old style. He'd go into one state and campaign for one particular candidate, and then hop to another place. Meanwhile, there was no unifying theme. In a sense that was the inability of the Democrats to make a clear national statement about anything—which in politics you need to mobilize your core. You need to fuel your base, to energize it. The Republicans have the advantage in this off-year election of being much more unified and mobilized, and at least having the rallying point of a drifting administration in Washington, which didn't seem to be doing anything but lurching in one direction or another. That really fueled Republican mobilization and had a lot to do with what happened on November 8.

**JB:** In California at least, we did not have an increase in *Republicans* in this year's electorate. We did have a major increase in *conservatives*—a 10 point increase, though the party ID of the electorate that assembled this year is virtually the same as it was in 1992 and 1990. We also had a slight shift toward male voters. I see conservatives notably mobilized. It's kind of puzzling that there wasn't a higher Republican party ID. The California electorate tends to be almost at parity in party affiliation. This year we showed about 40% Republican, 40% Democratic, with the rest independents and others, and that is what we had in 1990 and 1992.

**MB**: We had both in Texas—an increase in the electorate in people calling themselves conservatives and in Republicans. I should note, though, that this may have nothing to do with turnout as such. There has been a realignment going on in Texas for years now—as more and more people start calling themselves Republicans. This has shown up both in exit polls and in pre-election surveys. It's not only true of those people who showed up on election day. It's true among all registered voters. So in fact, there is a realignment going on apart from mobilization.

I do think that there was a mobilization difference, however, in 1994. Ann Richards did not give her voters as much reason to turn out. Bush tried to nationalize the election and tie her to Clinton to help get his voters out, and he had success. Also, we asked in a late pre-election survey how upset respondents would be if the person who was not their candidate won. While neither side was going to be terribly upset—because, again, Texas was an

unusual case of two popular candidates—there certainly was some difference. Putting aside the people who weren't going to be upset at all no matter who was elected, you clearly saw that Bush was likely to win—because his side cared more. Richards and Bush were both popular, he was probably more popular and got higher marks on almost everything. Those who were more upset in general were more likely to show up and the exit poll findings suggest they did in fact show up in greater numbers on election day. Some of the Democrats and some of the women stayed home. In 1990, women had rallied behind Ann Richards, especially since she ran against someone [Clayton Williams] who was seen by many women as a threat. They didn't do that this time. They felt very comfortable with George W. Bush. He split the women's vote evenly with Richards. In fact, he won the white women's vote.

**LM**: Some things which we saw in New York, both in our final pre-election poll and in the results, might help clarify the turnout story. Ironically, Cuomo actually got more votes in defeat this time than he did when he won in 1990. There was an overall turnout increase statewide of about 10% in gubernatorial voting. So the perception that people were jumping from Cuomo is wrong. Actually, more people pulled his lever in 1994.

What's more, despite election-day reports that there were record turnouts upstate, New York City was actually a larger share of the statewide vote this time than four years ago. Upstate was actually 2% less of the share this year.

But, what we did see in the data was upstate Democrats falling out of the models in our pre-election polls. Then when we saw the actual numbers coming in, Cuomo was running 15 points weaker (than in 1990) in places like Buffalo, Syracuse and Rochester and in places where he actually carried upstate previously. Overall, we concluded that there was a decidedly Republican flavor to the pie this time around. New York City did not desert Cuomo, but the upstate Democratic areas did not deliver their usual Democratic vote.

**MB**: Was it just that upstate Democrats didn't show up, or that they voted Republican?

**LM**: We were seeing them falling out of "likely" voters as defined in our pre-election polls. They weren't prepared to go for Pataki, but they were tired of Cuomo.

**SK:** I think Mickey's comment earlier about who would be upset by the "other candidate" winning is a good concluding note here on the turnout or mobilization issue. This year, in most states, Republicans were more upset by the prospect of Democratic incumbents winning, than were Democrats about Republican incumbents being re-elected. In Virginia, though, things were different. Oliver North did a terrific job frightening Democrats, as well as many independents and some Republicans. He mobilized his own supporters extremely well, but he mobilized his opponents at least as well, if not better. In the process, he snatched away what otherwise had all the markings of an easy Republican victory.

# A look inside

# NEW YORK

"Too Liberal Too Long" is what Republican gubernatorial candidate George Pataki had to say about Democratic incumbent Mario Cuomo. On election day, New Yorkers agreed. Pataki defeated Cuomo, 49 to 45%, in the incumbent's fourth run for governor.

It was an election that came down to the wire—most pollsters judged the race too close to call. Pre-election polls showed each candidate in the lead at various points in the race and seemed to indicate that Cuomo was picking up steam as November 8 approached.

For Cuomo voters, the election was about the Governor's personal strengths and leadership abilities. An October 2 WCBS News/*New York Times* pre-election survey showed Cuomo receiving high marks in the areas of leadership, caring, and honesty. A Marist Institute for Public Opinion survey [September 1994] asked New Yorkers, "Since becoming New York's governor in 1983, do you think Mario Cuomo has generally been a good governor, or not?" Fifty-one percent said that Cuomo had been a good governor.

For the most part Pataki voters focused on Cuomo's long tenure. More than 60% of those responding to a WCBS/*New York Times* pre-election survey believed that Cuomo had been governor for too long. Of those who said they would vote for Pataki, 32% gave "time for a change" as their reason while 29% said they were voting for Pataki because they did not like Cuomo.

Cuomo's first run for political office was unsuccessful; he lost the 1974 primary for lieutenant governor. In 1977 Cuomo ran for mayor of New York City losing to Ed Koch, before being elected lieutenant governor in 1978. In 1982, Cuomo, the "underfinanced underdog," beat Koch in the Democratic gubernatorial primary and went on to win the race for governor, against Lew Lehrman, 51 to 47%.

Throughout his first two terms, Cuomo enjoyed great popularity, receiving approval ratings upwards of 70%. While governor, he was twice considered a serious contender for the Democratic Presidential nomination and once for a seat on the Supreme Court. Each time Cuomo took himself out of the running claiming that there was still much to be done in New York. As the national recession settled into the state, Cuomo's job ratings steadily declined. This year New Yorkers decided it was time for a change.

— Jennifer M. Necci

## Governor's Race — 1994*

| | Cuomo (D) | Pataki (R) |
|---|---|---|
| **ALL** | 45% | 49% |
| **By Gender** | | |
| Male | 42 | 53 |
| Female | 48 | 46 |
| **By Age** | | |
| 18-29 | 42 | 51 |
| 30-44 | 43 | 51 |
| 45-59 | 42 | 52 |
| 60+ | 54 | 42 |
| **By Education** | | |
| HS Grad or less | 35 | 60 |
| Some College | 42 | 53 |
| College Grad | 43 | 51 |
| Post Grad | 59 | 36 |
| **By Race** | | |
| White | 40 | 54 |
| Black | 89 | 9 |
| **By Income** | | |
| Less than $15,000 | 54 | 42 |
| $15,000-29,999 | 44 | 48 |
| $30,000-49,999 | 43 | 52 |
| $50,000-74,999 | 43 | 51 |
| $75,000-99,999 | 42 | 51 |
| $100,000+ | 58 | 38 |
| **By Party ID** | | |
| Democrat | 79 | 18 |
| Republican | 14 | 79 |
| Independent | 33 | 58 |
| **By Ideology** | | |
| Liberal | 68 | 28 |
| Moderate | 51 | 45 |
| Conservative | 22 | 71 |
| **By Denomination** | | |
| Protestant | 39 | 56 |
| Catholic | 39 | 56 |
| Other Christian | 36 | 53 |
| Jewish | 77 | 19 |

* Independent candidate Thomas Golisano received 4% of the vote.
Source: VNS 1994 Exit Poll.

# The New York Governorship:  An Electoral History

| Year | Total Vote | Candidate | Votes | Percent |
|------|-----------|-----------|-------|---------|
| 1982 | 5,254,891 | Mario Cuomo (D) | 2,675,213 | 50.7% |
|      |           | Lew Lehrman (R) | 2,494,827 | 47.4 |
| 1986 | 4,294,124 | Mario Cuomo (D) | 2,775,229 | 64.6 |
|      |           | Andrew O'Rourke (R) | 1,363,810 | 31.7 |
| 1990 | 4,056,896 | Mario Cuomo (D) | 2,157,087 | 53.2 |
|      |           | Pierre Rinfret (R) | 865,948 | 21.3 |
|      |           | Herbert London (C) | 827,614 | 20.4 |
| 1994 | 5,073,399 | Mario Cuomo (D) | 2,286,017 | 45.1 |
|      |           | George Pataki (R) | 2,477,986 | 48.8 |

**Source:** For 1982-90 see *America Votes*, Vol. 19 (Chevy Chase, Maryland: Elections Research Center, 1991); for 1994 see *Congressional Quarterly*, November 12, 1994.

# Mario Cuomo's Performance Ratings, May 1983-November 1984

**Question:** Would you rate the job Governor Mario Cuomo is doing in office as excellent, good, fair, or poor?

## New York State

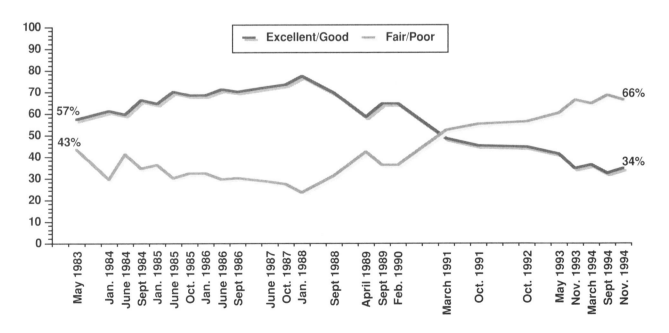

**Source:** Surveys by the Marist Institute for Public Opinion, May 1983-November 1994.

# The Upstate Vote Completely Deserted the Governor

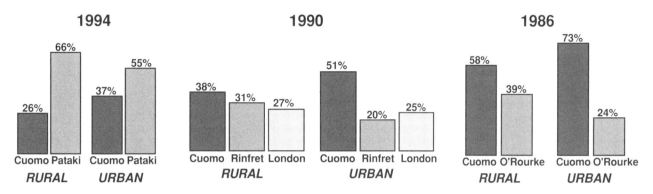

**Note:** Excludes the vote in the New York City metropolitan area.

# The Black Vote Stayed with Cuomo

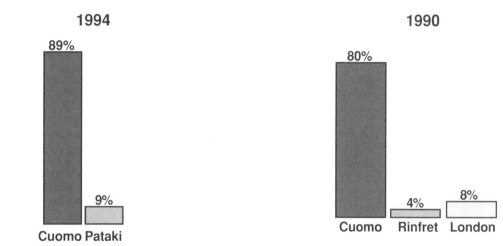

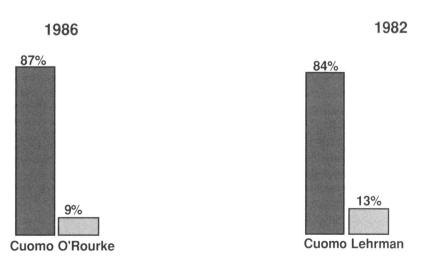

**Note:** Black vote estimated at 8%.

**Note:** Black vote estimated at 7%.

**Note:** Black vote estimated at 17%.

**Note:** Black vote estimated at 13%.

**Source:** VNS 1994 Exit Poll; Voter Research & Surveys 1990 Exit Poll; CBS News 1986 Exit Poll; CBS News 1982 Exit Poll.

# Traditional Democratic Support from Catholics Dropped Off in 1994

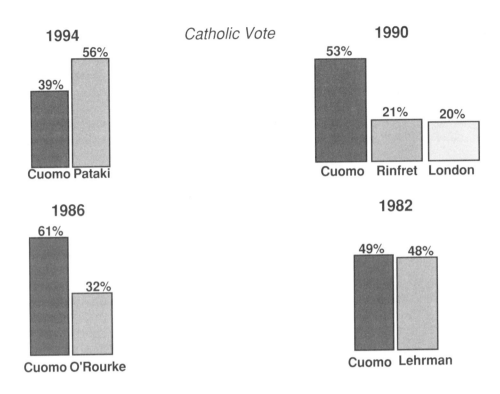

*Catholic Vote*

**Support for Cuomo from those identifying the death penalty or abortion as an important issue in deciding how to vote remained unchanged.**

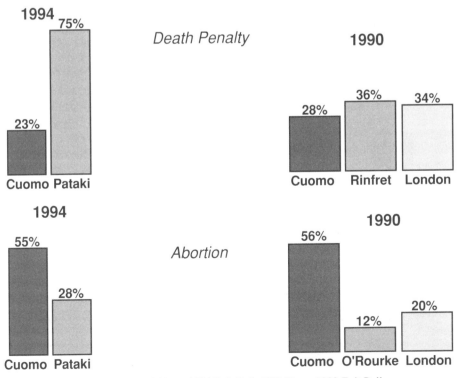

**Source:** VNS 1994 Exit Poll; VRS 1990 Exit Poll; CBS News 1986 Exit Poll; CBS News 1982 Exit Poll.

# On the Voters' Minds

**Question:** What do you consider to be the number one problem facing New York State?

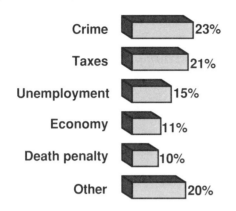

Crime 23%
Taxes 21%
Unemployment 15%
Economy 11%
Death penalty 10%
Other 20%

**Question:** In general, thinking about the way things are going in New York State, do you feel things are going in the right direction or that things are going in the wrong direction?

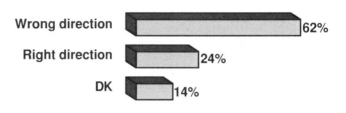

Wrong direction 62%
Right direction 24%
DK 14%

**Source:** Survey by the Marist Institute for Public Opinion, September 19-21, 1994.

**Question:** What is the main reason you are thinking of voting for Cuomo/Pataki?

## Cuomo Voters

Know him/Like him 37%
Good job/Leadership 27%
Political party 10%
Other 26%

## Pataki Voters

Lesser of 2 evils 10%
Economic plan 10%
Other 19%
Time for change 32%
Dislike Cuomo 29%

**Source:** Survey by the WCBS News/*New York Times*, October 4, 1994.

**Question:** Would you describe your support for (Cuomo/Pataki) as strongly favoring him, or do you like but with reservations, or do you support because you dislike the other candidates?

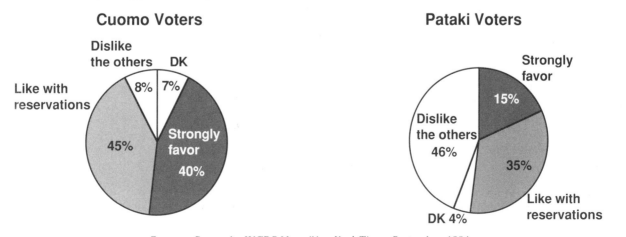

## Cuomo Voters

Dislike the others 8%
DK 7%
Like with reservations 45%
Strongly favor 40%

## Pataki Voters

Strongly favor 15%
Like with reservations 35%
Dislike the others 46%
DK 4%

**Source:** Survey by WCBS News/*New York Times*, September, 1994.

# A look inside

# TEXAS

Much has been made of the so-called angry voter and the impact of generalized public angst on electoral contests across the nation. But far from angry, voters in Texas arrived at the polls pleased with the condition of the state's economy and their own personal financial situation, and, according to pre-election polls, satisfied with the job done by their state's chief executive. All good signs, presumably, for an incumbent governor seeking re-election. But in Texas, it would not be enough. The Republican challenger, George W. Bush, was successful in his bid to unseat Ann Richards, the incumbent Democrat, taking the governorship by a margin of 53 to 46%.

It is likely that George W. Bush was the beneficiary of some of the 2,350,389 votes cast in his favor on election day simply because of the Bush name and his relationship to the past president, a favorite son in Texas who carried the state in his 1992 re-election bid. But history, and exit poll data, suggest that there was more to this Republican victory than a good family name.

Until the late 1970s, Texas had a continuous record of two and three term Democratic governors. But in 1978, Texas elected a Republican governor—something it had not done for more than one-hundred years. Since then, the governorship has changed hands, and parties, with each election.

In spite of the state's rich Democratic history, exit polls conducted in Texas since 1986 have continued to show an electorate nearly three times more likely to consider itself conservative than liberal. The same polls have documented a steady *increase* in the number of voters calling themselves Republican. In 1986, 40% of Texas voters identified themselves as Democrats compared with 28% who sided with the Republicans—a 12 point gap. In 1990, the Democratic edge had slipped to just 4 points. In 1994, party identification in Texas was 34 to 40%, a 6 point margin in *favor* of the Republicans.

Fueling this swing are young voters in Texas who—despite the likelihood that they've grown up in families that have characteristically voted Democratic—are being drawn to the Republican party. Party identification figures for 1986 showed the two youngest age groups, those 18-29 and 30-44, only slightly more Democratic than Republican, while in the higher age groups the Democrats held a commanding lead. In 1994, among 30-44 year old voters the Republican party holds an 8 point *lead* while the Democratic lead among the next highest age group—those 45-59—is now only 3 points. *Among 18-29 year old voters, the party identification figures are 51% Republican and 29% Democratic.*

It appears that the youngest voters in Texas may be the strongest group of Republican partisans yet. If this pattern continues, it signals a bright future for Republican candidates in a state with deep roots to the Democratic party. If, however, recent historic trends prevail, Texas may once again have a Democratic governor in 1998.

— John M. Barry

## Governor's Race — 1994

|  | Richards (D) | Bush (R) |
|---|---|---|
| **ALL** | 46% | 53% |
| **By Gender** | | |
| Male | 41 | 58 |
| Female | 50 | 49 |
| **By Age** | | |
| 18-29 | 41 | 59 |
| 30-44 | 44 | 54 |
| 45-59 | 48 | 52 |
| 60+ | 50 | 49 |
| **By Education** | | |
| HS Grad or Less | 56 | 44 |
| Some College | 41 | 59 |
| College Grad | 38 | 58 |
| Post Grad | 50 | 49 |
| **By Race/Ethnicity** | | |
| White | 36 | 63 |
| Black | 85 | 15 |
| Hispanic | 71 | 28 |
| **By Income** | | |
| Less than $15,000 | 63 | 37 |
| $15,000-29,999 | 49 | 51 |
| $30,000-49,999 | 44 | 56 |
| $50,000-74,999 | 45 | 54 |
| $75,000-99,999 | 39 | 61 |
| $100,000+ | 32 | 60 |
| **By Party ID** | | |
| Democrat | 90 | 10 |
| Republican | 11 | 87 |
| Independent/Other | 41 | 58 |
| **By Ideology** | | |
| Liberal | 82 | 18 |
| Moderate | 58 | 39 |
| Conservative | 20 | 80 |
| **By Denomination** | | |
| Protestant | 37 | 62 |
| Catholic | 54 | 42 |
| Other Christian | 40 | 60 |

**Source:** VNS 1994 Exit Poll.

# The Texas Governorship: An Electoral History

| Year | Total Vote | Candidate | Votes | Percent |
|------|-----------|-----------|-------|---------|
| 1974 | 1,654,984 | Dolph Briscoe (D) | 1,016,334 | 61.4% |
|      |           | Jim Granberry (R) | 514,725 | 31.1 |
| 1978 | 2,369,764 | John Hill (D) | 1,166,979 | 49.2 |
|      |           | William P. Clements (R) | 1,183,839 | 50.0 |
| 1982 | 3,191,091 | Mark White (D) | 1,697,870 | 53.2 |
|      |           | William P. Clements (R) | 1,465,937 | 45.9 |
| 1986 | 3,441,460 | Mark White (D) | 1,584,515 | 46.0 |
|      |           | William P. Clements (R) | 1,813,779 | 52.7 |
| 1990 | 3,892,746 | Ann Richards (D) | 1,925,670 | 49.5 |
|      |           | Clayton Williams (R) | 1,826,431 | 46.9 |
| 1994 | 4,393,219 | Ann Richards (D) | 2,014,304 | 45.9 |
|      |           | George W. Bush (R) | 2,350,389 | 53.5 |

## Fifty-Years of Texas Governors:  No Re-elections Since 1974

| Year | Governor | Party |
|------|----------|-------|
| 1944[1] | Coke Stevenson | Democrat |
| 1946 | Beauford Jester | Democrat |
| 1948 | Beauford Jester | Democrat |
| 1950 | Allan Shivers | Democrat |
| 1952 | Allan Shivers | Democrat |
| 1954 | Allan Shivers | Democrat |
| 1956 | Daniel Price | Democrat |
| 1958 | Daniel Price | Democrat |
| 1960 | Daniel Price | Democrat |
| 1962 | John Connally | Democrat |
| 1964 | John Connally | Democrat |
| 1966 | John Connally | Democrat |
| 1968 | Preston Smith | Democrat |
| 1970 | Preston Smith | Democrat |
| 1972 | Dolph Briscoe | Democrat |
| 1974[2] | Dolph Briscoe | Democrat |
| 1978[3] | William P. Clements | Republican |
| 1982 | Mark White | Democrat |
| 1986 | William P. Clements | Republican |
| 1990 | Ann Richards | Democrat |
| 1994 | George W. Bush | Republican |

1.  Stevenson won re-election.
2.  In 1974, the term of office for governor in Texas was increased from two to four years.
3.  In 1978, William P. Clements became only the second Republican elected Governor of Texas since the state's founding in 1845.  Edmund J. Davis, Republican, served as governor from 1870 until 1874.

**Source:** For 1944-82 see *Guide to US Elections*, Vol. 2 (Washington DC: Congressional Quarterly, 1985); for 1986-90 see *America Votes*, Vol. 19 (Chevy Chase, Maryland: Elections Research Center, 1991); for 1994 see *Congressional Quarterly*, November 12, 1994.

# In Texas, Big Republican Gains in Party Identification Since 1986

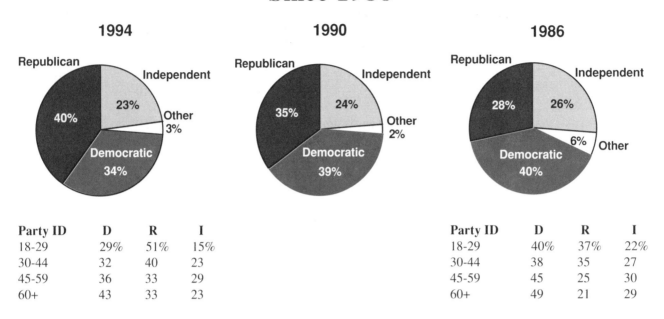

### 1994

Republican 40%
Independent 23%
Other 3%
Democratic 34%

### 1990

Republican 35%
Independent 24%
Other 2%
Democratic 39%

### 1986

Republican 28%
Independent 26%
Other 6%
Democratic 40%

| Party ID | D | R | I |
|---|---|---|---|
| 18-29 | 29% | 51% | 15% |
| 30-44 | 32 | 40 | 23 |
| 45-59 | 36 | 33 | 29 |
| 60+ | 43 | 33 | 23 |

| Party ID | D | R | I |
|---|---|---|---|
| 18-29 | 40% | 37% | 22% |
| 30-44 | 38 | 35 | 27 |
| 45-59 | 45 | 25 | 30 |
| 60+ | 49 | 21 | 29 |

## Conservatives Consistently Outnumber Liberals

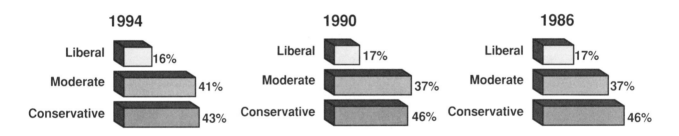

### 1994
Liberal 16%
Moderate 41%
Conservative 43%

### 1990
Liberal 17%
Moderate 37%
Conservative 46%

### 1986
Liberal 17%
Moderate 37%
Conservative 46%

# Support in Texas for Republican Candidates Highest Among the Young

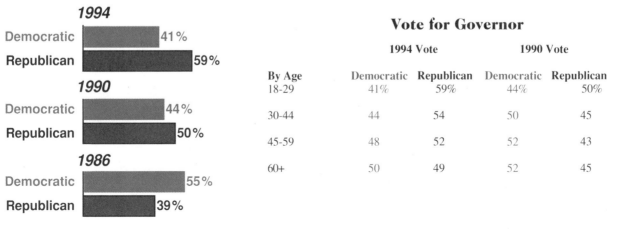

**18-29 Year Old Gubernatorial Vote**

### 1994
Democratic 41%
Republican 59%

### 1990
Democratic 44%
Republican 50%

### 1986
Democratic 55%
Republican 39%

### Vote for Governor

| By Age | 1994 Vote Democratic | 1994 Vote Republican | 1990 Vote Democratic | 1990 Vote Republican |
|---|---|---|---|---|
| 18-29 | 41% | 59% | 44% | 50% |
| 30-44 | 44 | 54 | 50 | 45 |
| 45-59 | 48 | 52 | 52 | 43 |
| 60+ | 50 | 49 | 52 | 45 |

**Source:** VNS 1994 Exit Poll; Voter Research & Surveys 1990 Exit Poll; CBS News 1986 Exit Poll.

# Independent Voters: Men More Consistently Than Women Back Republican Gubernatorial Candidates

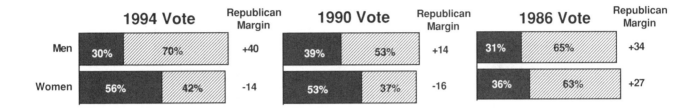

**Source:** VNS 1994 Exit Poll; VRS 1990 Exit Poll; CBS News 1986 Exit Poll.

# A Huge Gender Gap in 1994 Between the Most Highly Educated Men and Women

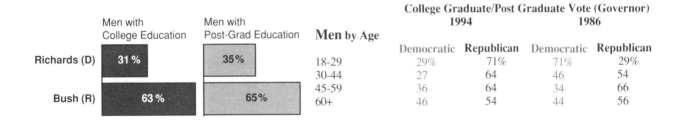

|  | College Graduate/Post Graduate Vote (Governor) | | | |
| --- | --- | --- | --- | --- |
| **Men by Age** | 1994 | | 1986 | |
|  | Democratic | Republican | Democratic | Republican |
| 18-29 | 29% | 71% | 71% | 29% |
| 30-44 | 27 | 64 | 46 | 54 |
| 45-59 | 36 | 64 | 34 | 66 |
| 60+ | 46 | 54 | 44 | 56 |

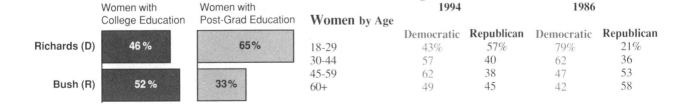

|  | College Graduate/Post Graduate Vote (Governor) | | | |
| --- | --- | --- | --- | --- |
| **Women by Age** | 1994 | | 1986 | |
|  | Democratic | Republican | Democratic | Republican |
| 18-29 | 43% | 57% | 79% | 21% |
| 30-44 | 57 | 40 | 62 | 36 |
| 45-59 | 62 | 38 | 47 | 53 |
| 60+ | 49 | 45 | 42 | 58 |

**Source:** VNS 1994 Exit Poll; VRS 1990 Exit Poll; CBS News 1986 Exit Poll.

# The Religious Factor in Texas Voting

**Protestants and "other Christians" voted for Bush. Catholics remained in the Democratic camp. However, white Catholics have been moving Republican since 1986, while Hispanic Catholics remained firmly Democratic.**

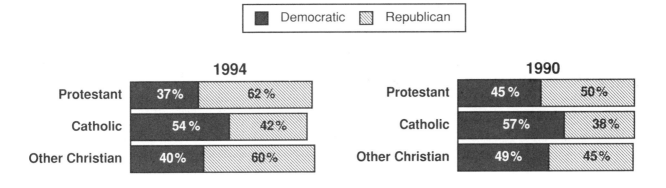

## Catholics Vote for Governor

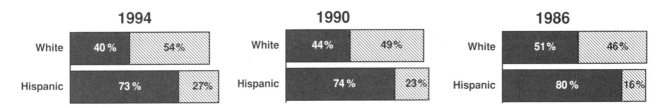

# Rating the Economy

**With the Texas economy sour in 1986, the electorate tossed out the Democratic incumbent in favor of the Republican challenger. In 1994, voters gave high marks to the state's economy but still forced the Democratic incumbent from office.**

**Question:** These days, is the condition of your state's economy: very good, fairly good, fairly bad, or very bad?

**Question:** Do you think the condition of Texas' economy is: excellent, good, not so good, or poor?

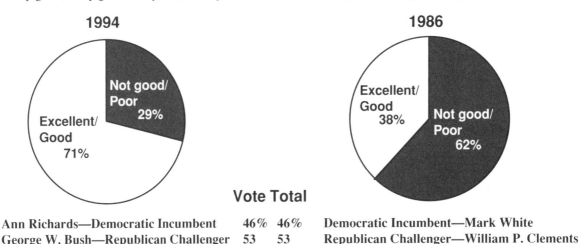

### Vote Total

| | | |
|---|---|---|
| Ann Richards—Democratic Incumbent | 46% | 46% | Democratic Incumbent—Mark White |
| George W. Bush—Republican Challenger | 53 | 53 | Republican Challenger—William P. Clements |

**Source:** VNS 1994 Exit Poll; VRS 1990 Exit Poll; CBS News 1986 Exit Poll.

# A look inside

# VIRGINIA

## Senate Race — 1994

|  | Rob (D) | North (R) | Coleman (I) |
|---|---|---|---|
| **ALL** | **46%** | **43%** | **11%** |
| **By Gender** | | | |
| Male | 40 | 48 | 11 |
| Female | 50 | 39 | 11 |
| **By Age** | | | |
| 18-29 | 38 | 49 | 14 |
| 30-44 | 43 | 44 | 13 |
| 45-59 | 47 | 41 | 11 |
| 60+ | 51 | 42 | 7 |
| **By Education** | | | |
| Less than HS | 45 | 44 | 11 |
| HS Grad | 40 | 49 | 11 |
| Some College | 42 | 46 | 13 |
| College Grad | 45 | 42 | 13 |
| Post Grad | 55 | 33 | 12 |
| **By Race** | | | |
| White | 37 | 51 | 13 |
| Black | 91 | 5 | 4 |
| **By Income** | | | |
| Less than $15,000 | 51 | 38 | 11 |
| $15,000-29,999 | 44 | 48 | 8 |
| $30,000-49,999 | 44 | 40 | 16 |
| $50,000-74,999 | 45 | 44 | 11 |
| $75,000-99,999 | 45 | 44 | 12 |
| $100,000+ | 41 | 44 | 15 |
| **By Party ID** | | | |
| Democrat | 90 | 5 | 5 |
| Republican | 12 | 75 | 13 |
| Independent | 41 | 43 | 17 |
| **By Ideology** | | | |
| Liberal | 78 | 11 | 10 |
| Moderate | 59 | 28 | 13 |
| Conservative | 17 | 71 | 12 |
| **By Denomination** | | | |
| Protestant | 43 | 45 | 12 |
| Catholic | 36 | 46 | 18 |
| Other Christian | 45 | 45 | 10 |
| None | 65 | 22 | 13 |
| Else | 58 | 33 | 9 |

The 1994 Virginia Senate contest between Democrat Chuck Robb and Republican Oliver North was one of the year's most heated and intense. Independent candidate Marshall Coleman received 11% of the vote but was never considered a serious contender. All the pre-election polls showed the race close. The polls also reflected strong dissatisfaction with both Robb and North. Many voters felt neither candidate could be counted on to be truthful. Both candidates had low favorability ratings.

Dissatisfaction with President Clinton, in combination with Robb's low ratings, pointed to a Republican victory. But North's weaknesses proved greater than Robb's. The opposition of many prominent Republicans—including Virginia's senior senator, John Warner, and Nancy Reagan— was perhaps decisive. To quote Virginia Commonwealth University pollster Scott Keeter, " (Robb) almost certainly wouldn't have gotten back (to Washington) if any Republican other than Oliver North had run against him."

Chuck Robb was elected Governor of Virginia in 1981. Although he was very popular he could not seek re-election at the end of his four-year term because Virginia law prohibits serving consecutive gubernatorial terms. Robb decided to run for the Senate in 1988, winning the seat in a landslide. However, his popularity steadily decreased over the next six years, in the face of continuing personal scandal. This set the stage for the intense race between two former marines, who were both disliked by many Virginians.

— Rob Persons

**Source:** VNS 1994 Exit Poll.

# Virginia Senate Seats:  An Electoral History

| Year | Total Vote | Candidate | Votes | Percent |
|---|---|---|---|---|
| 1978 | 1,222,256 | Andrew Miller (D) | 608,511 | 49.8% |
|  |  | John Warner (R) | 613,232 | 50.2 |
| 1982 | 1,415,622 | Richard Davis (D) | 690,839 | 48.8 |
|  |  | Paul Trible (R) | 724,571 | 51.2 |
| 1984 | 2,007,487 | Edythe Harrison (D) | 601,142 | 29.9 |
|  |  | John Warner (R) | 1,406,194 | 70.0 |
| 1988 | 2,068,897 | Charles Robb (D) | 1,474,086 | 71.2 |
|  |  | Maurice Dawkins (R) | 593,652 | 28.7 |
| 1990 | 1,083,690 | * |  |  |
|  |  | John Warner (R) | 876,782 | 80.9 |
| 1994 | 2,031,732 | Charles Robb (D) | 925,500 | 45.6 |
|  |  | Oliver North (R) | 873,954 | 43.0 |
|  |  | Marshall Coleman (I) | 232,278 | 11.4 |

* John Warner was unopposed in 1990.

**Note:**  Democrats won every post World War II Senate seat until 1970 when Harry Flood Byrd Jr., independent, was victorious receiving 53.5% of the vote.  He was re-elected as an independent in 1976.

**Source:**  For 1978-84 see *Guide to US Elections*, Vol. 2 (Washington DC: Congressional Quarterly, 1985); for 1988-90 see *America Votes*, Vol. 19 (Chevy Chase, Maryland: Elections Research Center, 1991); for 1994 see *Congressional Quarterly*, November 12, 1994.

**Chuck Robb had very positive job ratings as governor and for the first part of his term as senator.  But, his popularity steadily decreased year by year.**

**Question:**  Overall would you rate the job being done by the following persons as excellent, good, fair or poor?  If you don't know enough to judge, just tell me and we'll skip to the next one... Senator Chuck Robb

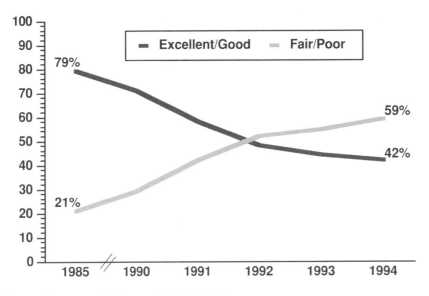

**Note:**  For 1985 the question text read, "Governor Chuck Robb."
**Source:**  Surveys by Virginia Commonwealth University, "Commonwealth Poll."

# On the Voters' Minds

**The pre-election polls showed Robb and North in a near dead heat through most of the race. Wilder withdrew from the race in mid-September and later endorsed Robb.**

**Question:** If the election for Senate were being held today and you had to decide right now, which candidate would you vote for?

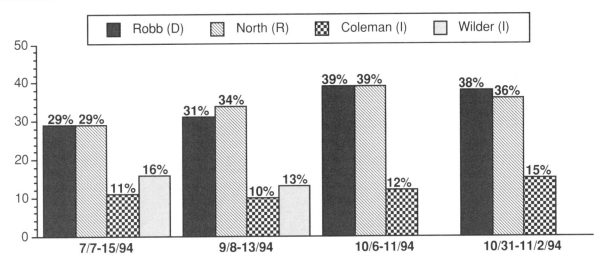

**Source:** Surveys by the Virginia Commonwealth University, "Commonwealth Poll."

**Question:** I am going to read you the name of each Senate candidate... please tell me if you generally view this person favorably, unfavorably, or if you have no opinion. What about...?

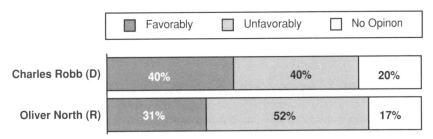

**Source:** Survey by the *Richmond Times-Dispatch*/Channel 12 News, October 31-November 3, 1994.

**Question:** As governor, Charles Robb socialized with suspected drug figures, despite warnings from the state's attorney general. How much influence, if any, does this have in your choice of candidates?

**Question:** Oliver North was convicted of felonies for his role in the Iran-Contra affair, but the convictions were either overturned or set aside. How much influence, if any, does this have in your choice of candidates?

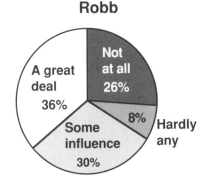
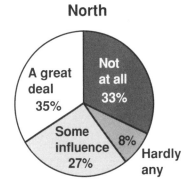

**Source:** Survey by the *Richmond Times-Dispatch*/Channel 12 News, October 17-20, 1994.

# North Did Best Among Young Men, Robb Did Best Among Middle-Age and Older Women

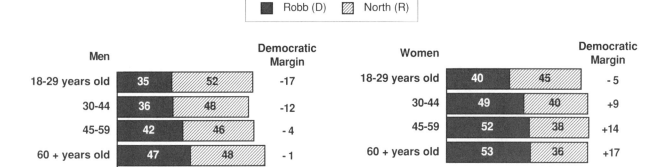

## Robb Gained His Biggest Margin Among College Educated Women

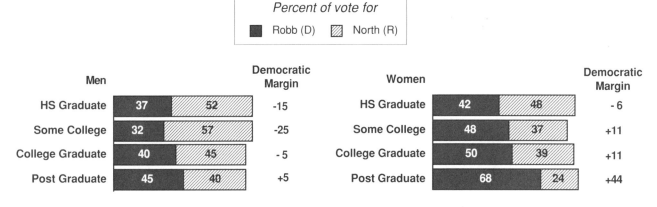

## The Issues That Mattered Most To People Were...

**Question:** Which 1 or 2 of these mattered most in your vote for US Senator?

|  | ALL | Robb Voters | North Voters |
|---|---|---|---|
| Honesty | 22% | 26% | 10% |
| Government spending | 22 | 19 | 26 |
| Clinton's performance as President | 20 | 17 | 27 |
| Economy/Jobs | 17 | 27 | 8 |
| Crime | 15 | 18 | 14 |
| Family values | 15 | 6 | 24 |
| Abortion | 14 | 14 | 16 |
| Time for a change | 11 | 3 | 19 |
| Foreign policy | 5 | 6 | 4 |

**Source:** VNS 1994 Exit Poll.

# A look inside

# WASHINGTON'S 5TH CD

Thomas S. Foley, who first won election by beating a 22-year veteran, was the first sitting Speaker to lose since Pennsylvania's Galusha Grow in 1862 (who had to contend both with the Republican losses of that Civil War year and a redrawn district as well). But 1994 was not the first difficult race for Foley: three times he has had less than 55% of the vote, and his margin was barely four points in 1980.

The election in Washington's fifth district *was* a referendum on Foley personally, and not simply on incumbency, or even Bill Clinton, although both played a role. On the Mitofsky International Exit Poll, voters split evenly on approval of Foley, and this correlated strongly with vote: 93% of those who approved voted for Foley; 96% of those who disapproved voted for George Nethercutt. That Foley himself was the issue is brought home by the fact that among the six in ten who said they were voting mainly for their candidate, Foley won three to two. But the one in three who said their vote was mainly *against* their candidate's opponent went even more strongly for Nethercutt.

More than half (52%) said their congressional vote had nothing to do with Bill Clinton, and this group went narrowly (54 to 46%) for the Speaker. The 19% who said they were voting to support Clinton went overwhelmingly (95%) for Foley; those against Clinton (28%) gave Nethercutt 92% of their ballots. Overall, attitudes were less favorable to Clinton than Foley, but the latter related more closely to vote.

Anti-incumbency as such cannot explain what happened either. On balance (61 to 29%), voters felt it was more important to have experienced people who know how government works than to have new faces in office. This went along with the VNS Exit Poll's finding that voters *disagreed* (by a similar margin) that government would work better if all new people were elected.

Experience worked strongly for Foley (96% of those who cited this as a factor voted for him), while almost all (99%) of those who said that it was time for a change went for Nethercutt, as did 93% of those who cited term limits as an issue in deciding how to vote. (However, this issue was named by fewer than one voter in five). Gun control worked modestly *for* Foley (he got 61% of the votes of those citing this as an issue), while he got only 31% of those citing the role of government.

Six of Washington's nine seats changed hands, moving from 8-1 Democratic to 7-2 Republican. Democrats retained only the 6th district (Olympic peninsula and part of Tacoma) and the 7th (Seattle), in both of which the Republicans fielded a different challenger this year. Jim McDermott won the Seventh handily while Norm Dicks was safely returned in the Sixth; but for both, the margin was reduced in 1994.

In the only re-match (the Fourth), Jay Inslee lost four points to transform a narrow Democratic victory to a clear Republican win for Richard Hastings. Maria Cantwell's (First) vote loss was on a par with Foley's, while Jolene Unsoeld (Third) lost more, and Mike Kreidler (Ninth) lost a smaller share of votes. Two Republicans faced a different Democrat. The Second's Jack Metcalf gained almost thirteen points to take what had been a Democratic seat, and Jennifer Dunn in the Eighth (the lone GOP incumbent) increased her vote share by some sixteen points.

— G. Donald Ferree, Jr.

## Congressional District 5—1994

|  | Foley (D) | Nethercutt (R) |
|---|---|---|
| **ALL** | 49% | 51% |
| **By Gender** | | |
| Male | 45 | 55 |
| Female | 53 | 47 |
| **By Age** | | |
| 18-29 | 45 | 55 |
| 30-39 | 45 | 55 |
| 40-49 | 55 | 45 |
| 45-59 | 47 | 53 |
| 60+ | 51 | 49 |
| **By Education** | | |
| HS Grad | 45 | 55 |
| Some College | 49 | 51 |
| College Grad | 45 | 55 |
| Post Grad | 57 | 43 |
| **By Income** | | |
| Less than $15,000 | 58 | 42 |
| $15,000-29,999 | 49 | 51 |
| $30,000-49,999 | 47 | 53 |
| $50,000-74,999 | 49 | 51 |
| $75,000-99,999 | 51 | 49 |
| $100,000+ | 37 | 63 |
| **By Party ID** | | |
| Democrat | 87 | 13 |
| Republican | 15 | 85 |
| Other | 47 | 53 |
| **By Ideology** | | |
| Liberal | 82 | 18 |
| Moderate | 59 | 41 |
| Conservative | 18 | 82 |
| **By Denomination** | | |
| Protestant | 45 | 55 |
| Catholic | 57 | 43 |
| Other Christian | 34 | 66 |
| None | 64 | 36 |
| **By Union Membership** | | |
| Union Household | 56 | 44 |

**Source:** Mitofsky International 1994 Exit Poll.

# The Washington 5th District: An Electoral History
## The Foley Era: Thirty Years Comes To An End

| Year | Total Vote | Candidates | Votes | Percent |
|------|-----------|-----------|-------|---------|
| 1964 | 158,714 | Thomas Foley (D) | 84,830 | 53.4% |
|      |         | Walt Horan (R) | 73,884 | 46.6 |
| 1966 | 131,881 | Thomas Foley (D) | 74,571 | 56.5 |
|      |         | Dorothy Powers (R) | 57,310 | 43.5 |
| 1968 | 155,750 | Thomas Foley (D) | 88,446 | 56.8 |
|      |         | Richard Bond (R) | 67,304 | 43.2 |
| 1970 | 131,565 | Thomas Foley (D) | 88,189 | 67.0 |
|      |         | George Gamble (R) | 43,376 | 33.0 |
| 1972 | 185,322 | Thomas Foley (D) | 150,580 | 81.3 |
|      |         | Clarice Privette (R) | 34,742 | 18.7 |
| 1974 | 136,698 | Thomas Foley (D) | 87,959 | 64.3 |
|      |         | Gary Gage (R) | 48,739 | 35.7 |
| 1976 | 207,571 | Thomas Foley (D) | 120,415 | 58.0 |
|      |         | Duane Alton (R) | 84,262 | 41.1 |
| 1978 | 160,849 | Thomas Foley (D) | 77,201 | 48.0 |
|      |         | Duane Alton (R) | 68,761 | 42.7 |
| 1980 | 232,235 | Thomas Foley (D) | 120,530 | 51.9 |
|      |         | John Sonneland (R) | 111,705 | 48.1 |
| 1982 | 170,365 | Thomas Foley (D) | 109,549 | 64.3 |
|      |         | John Sonneland (R) | 60,816 | 35.7 |
| 1984 | 222,426 | Thomas Foley (D) | 154,988 | 69.7 |
|      |         | Jack Hebner (R) | 67,438 | 30.3 |
| 1986 | 162,911 | Thomas Foley (D) | 121,732 | 74.7 |
|      |         | Floyd Wakefield (R) | 41,179 | 25.3 |
| 1988 | 210,311 | Thomas Foley (D) | 160,654 | 76.4 |
|      |         | Marlyn Derby (R) | 49,657 | 23.6 |
| 1990 | 160,199 | Thomas Foley (D) | 110,234 | 68.8 |
|      |         | Marlyn Derby (R) | 49,965 | 31.2 |
| 1992 | 246,408 | Thomas Foley (D) | 135,965 | 55.2 |
|      |         | John Sonneland (R) | 110,443 | 44.8 |
| 1994 | 216,131 | Thomas Foley (D) | 106,074 | 49.1 |
|      |         | George Nethercutt (R) | 110,057 | 50.9 |

**Source:** 1964-84: see *Guide to US Elections*, Vol. 2 (Washington DC: Congressional Quarterly, 1985); for 1986-94 data provided by Office of the Secretary of State, state of Washington.

# Massive Reversal in Two Year Period:
# Now 7 to 2 Republicans—Then 8 to 1 Democrats

| | Percent of Vote | 1994 Election Results | 1992 Election Results | Percent of Vote |
|---|---|---|---|---|
| CD-1 | 48.3% | Maria Cantwell (D) | **Maria Cantwell (D)** | 54.9% |
| | 51.7 | **Rick White (R)** | Gary Nelson (R) | 42.0 |
| CD-2 | 45.3 | Harriet Spanel (D) | **Al Swift (D)** | 52.1 |
| | 54.7 | **Jack Metcalf (R)** | Jack Metcalf (R) | 42.0 |
| CD-3 | 44.6 | Jolene Unsoeld (D) | **Jolene Unsoeld (D)** | 56.0 |
| | 52.0 | **Linda Smith (R)** | Pat Fiske (R) | 44.0 |
| CD-4 | 46.7 | Jay Inslee (D) | **Jay Inslee (D)** | 50.8 |
| | 53.3 | **Richard Hastings (R)** | Richard Hastings (R) | 49.2 |
| CD-5 | 49.1 | Thomas Foley (D) | **Thomas Foley (D)** | 55.2 |
| | 50.9 | **George Nethercutt (R)** | John Sonneland (R) | 44.8 |
| CD-6 | 58.3 | **Norm Dicks (D)** | **Norm Dicks (D)** | 64.2 |
| | 41.7 | Benjamin Gregg (R) | Lauri Phillips (R) | 28.0 |
| CD-7 | 75.1 | **Jim McDermott (D)** | **Jim McDermott (D)** | 78.4 |
| | 24.9 | Keith Harris (R) | Glenn Hampson (R) | 19.1 |
| CD-8 | 23.9 | Jim Wyrick (D) | George Tamblyn (D) | 33.9 |
| | 76.1 | **Jennifer Dunn (R)** | **Jennifer Dunn (R)** | 60.4 |
| CD-9 | 48.2 | Mike Kreidler (D) | **Mike Kreidler (D)** | 52.1 |
| | 51.8 | **Randy Tate (R)** | Pete von Reichbauer (R) | 43.2 |

**Source:** Office of the Secretary of State, state of Washington.

**In the fifth congressional district, Speaker of the House Tom Foley had stronger approval than Bill Clinton. Foley ratings are better than Clinton's in predicting the 5th district vote.**

**Question:** How do you feel about the way Thomas Foley is handling his job as congressman?

**Question:** How do you feel about the way Bill Clinton is handling his job as President?

## Washington 5th District Voters

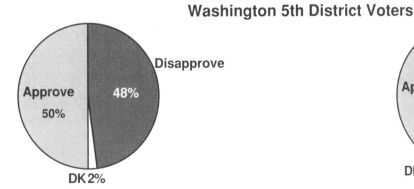

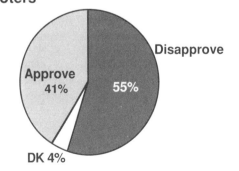

**Source:** Mitofsky International 1994 Exit Poll.

# Experience is a Plus, but if the Country is on the Wrong Track, You're Out of Office

**Question:** What is more important, having new faces in office [or] having experienced people who know how government works?

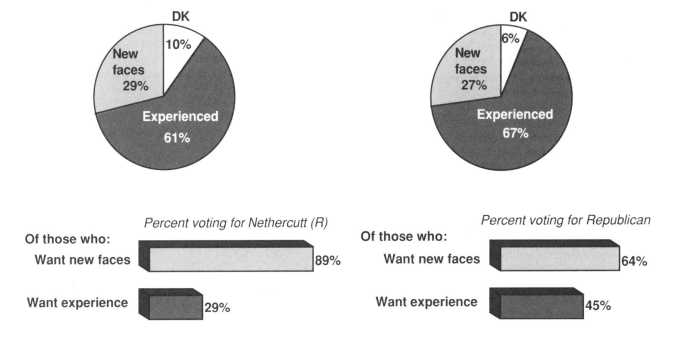

**Question:** Do you think that things in this country today are generally going in the right direction [or] seriously off on the wrong track?

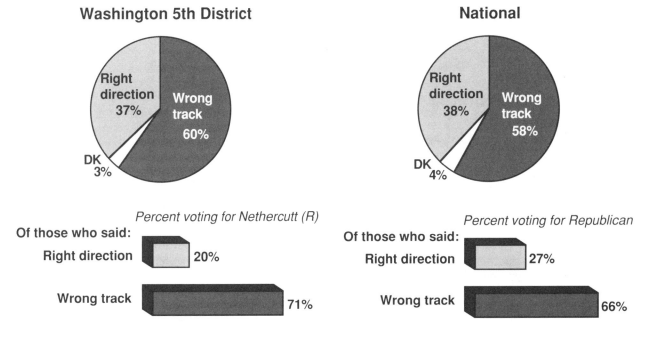

**Source:** Mitofsky International 1994 Exit Polls.

# After 30 Years of Service from Tom Foley—
# A Time for Change

**Question:** Would you say that your vote for US House of Representatives today was more a vote...?

**Question:** Which is more important to you? Electing a person to Congress who can do more for...?

## Washington 5th District

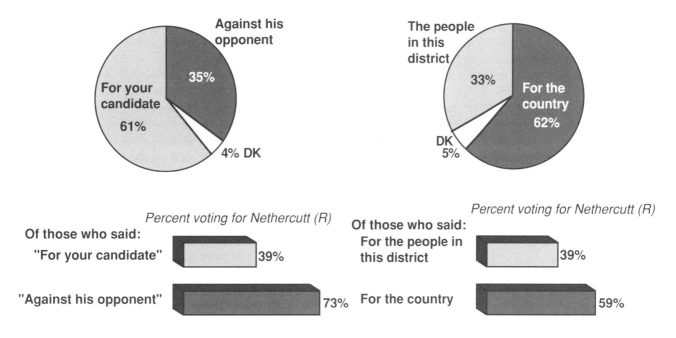

**Question:** Which two issues mattered most in deciding how you voted for US House?

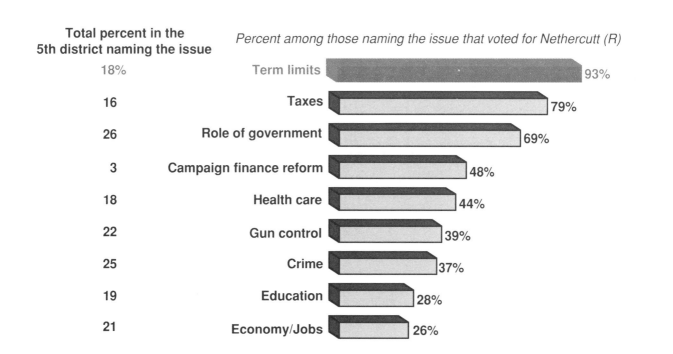

| Total percent in the 5th district naming the issue | Issue | Percent among those naming the issue that voted for Nethercutt (R) |
|---|---|---|
| 18% | Term limits | 93% |
| 16 | Taxes | 79% |
| 26 | Role of government | 69% |
| 3 | Campaign finance reform | 48% |
| 18 | Health care | 44% |
| 22 | Gun control | 39% |
| 25 | Crime | 37% |
| 19 | Education | 28% |
| 21 | Economy/Jobs | 26% |

**Source:** Mitofsky International 1994 Exit Poll.

# A look inside

# MARYLAND

Even traditionally liberal Maryland swayed with the national rightward shift in 1994. To say that Democrat Parris Glendening narrowly escaped defeat by Republican Ellen R. Sauerbrey in the governor's race is an understatement. The contest for the open seat vacated by retiring Governor William Schaefer (D) was decided by less than 6,000 votes. Not since 1966, when Spiro Agnew defeated George Mahoney in a racially divisive campaign, has a Republican been elected governor of Maryland. Democrats have had a lock on the Maryland State House for almost three decades, a hold that was not loosened even during the heyday of the Reagan-Bush years—that is, until this year.

The 1994 campaign for governor presented Maryland voters with a choice between ideological opposites. Sauerbrey campaigned on a vow to reduce the size of the government and cut personal income taxes by 24%. Pro-life, opposed to gun control, and in favor of an education voucher program, Sauerbrey was supported by the National Rifle Association and the Christian Coalition. Glendening—whom Sauerbrey nicknamed "Parris Spending"—unabashedly argued that government can be a positive force for citizens. He contended that her tax cut plan would destroy the education and social programs that Maryland citizens rely on. Gun-control advocates, labor, abortion rights and environmental groups rallied around Glendening. On election day, presented with a clear choice between ideological opposites, Maryland voters split down the middle - 50.2% for the Democrat, 49.8% for the Republican.

Sauerbrey came within a breath of victory despite being outspent (2:1) and notwithstanding the fact that among registered voters Democrats enjoy a 2:1 margin over Republicans (down from 3:1 in the 1970s). Her strongest support came from Republicans, men and whites, and she carried the Baltimore suburbs and the rural areas—21 out of 24 counties.

How did Glendening survive? He captured the votes of Democrats, women and blacks (who make up one quarter of Maryland voters). And Glendening, after a massive get-out-the-vote effort, carried three of the four most populous counties in the state—Baltimore City, Prince George's and Montgomery counties.

Glendening also prevailed on Sauerbrey's tax issue. Exit polls found that 76% of those people who ranked taxes as one of the most important issues cast their votes for the Democrat. Moreover, Sauerbrey's positions on taxes, gun control, education vouchers and abortion may have turned off undecided moderate voters. Consider, for example, that three out of four surveyed in a *Washington Post* pre-election poll were not opposed to the idea of increasing taxes for education. The poll also found majorities in favor of gun control and 56% opposed instituting a voucher program in Maryland.

With less than 6,000 votes separating the victor from the vanquished, Maryland now looks like a two-party system. Republican gains and Democratic staying power in 1994 seem particularly impressive when compared with 1986—a year when Schaefer (D) won all 24 counties. In terms of registered voters, the Democrats retain a strong homefield advantage. The field in 1994, however, looks quite different from the traditional liberal Democratic landscape. Governor Glendening takes the helm of a state that is torn over the proper role of government.

— Catherine P. Flavin

## Governor's Race—1994

| | Glendening (D) | Sauerbrey (R) |
|---|---|---|
| **ALL** | 50% | 50% |
| **By Gender** | | |
| Male | 44 | 56 |
| Female | 57 | 43 |
| **By Age** | | |
| 18-29 | 54 | 46 |
| 30-44 | 49 | 51 |
| 45-59 | 48 | 52 |
| 60+ | 54 | 46 |
| **By Education** | | |
| Less than HS | | |
| HS Grad | 51 | 49 |
| Some College | 43 | 57 |
| College Grad | 44 | 56 |
| Post Grad | 60 | 40 |
| **By Race** | | |
| White | 44 | 56 |
| Black | 90 | 10 |
| **By Income** | | |
| $15,000-29,999 | 58 | 42 |
| $30,000-49,999 | 51 | 49 |
| $50,000-74,999 | 50 | 50 |
| $75,000-99,999 | 51 | 49 |
| $100,000+ | 41 | 59 |
| **By Party ID** | | |
| Democrat | 81 | 19 |
| Republican | 13 | 87 |
| Independent | 43 | 57 |
| **By Ideology** | | |
| Liberal | 77 | 23 |
| Moderate | 61 | 39 |
| Conservative | 19 | 81 |
| **By Denomination** | | |
| Protestant | 49 | 51 |
| Catholic | 44 | 56 |
| Other Christian | 41 | 59 |
| Jewish | 79 | 21 |
| None | 55 | 45 |

**Source:** VNS 1994 Exit Poll.

# The Maryland Governorship: An Electoral History

| Year | Total Vote | Candidate | Votes | Percent |
|---|---|---|---|---|
| 1966 | 918,761 | George Mahoney (D) | 373,543 | 40.6% |
|  |  | Spiro Agnew (R) | 455,318 | 49.5 |
|  |  | Hyman Pressman (I) | 90,899 | 9.9 |
| 1970 | 973,099 | Marvin Mandel (D) | 639,579 | 65.7 |
|  |  | C. Stanley Blair (R) | 314,336 | 32.3 |
| 1974 | 949,097 | Marvin Mandel (D) | 602,648 | 63.5 |
|  |  | Louise Gore (R) | 346,449 | 36.5 |
| 1978 | 1,011,963 | Harry Hughes (D) | 718,328 | 71.0 |
|  |  | J. Glenn Beall (R) | 293,635 | 29.0 |
| 1982 | 1,139,149 | Harry Hughes (D) | 705,910 | 62.0 |
|  |  | Robert Pascal (R) | 432,826 | 38.0 |
| 1986 | 1,101,476 | William Schaefer (D) | 907,291 | 82.4 |
|  |  | Thomas Mooney (R) | 194,185 | 17.6 |
| 1990 | 1,111,088 | William Schaefer (D) | 664,015 | 59.8 |
|  |  | William Shepard (R) | 446,980 | 40.2 |
| 1994 | 1,410,299 | Parris Glendening (D) | 708,094 | 50.2 |
|  |  | Ellen Sauerbrey (R) | 702,101 | 49.8 |

**Source:** For 1966-82 see *Guide to US Elections*, Vol. 2 (Washington DC: Congressional Quarterly, 1985); for 1986-90 see *America Votes*, Vol. 19 (Chevy Chase, Maryland: Elections Research Center, 1991); for 1994 see *Congressional Quarterly*, November 12, 1994.

## Pre-election Tracking Showed a Close Race

**Question:** If the 1994 election for governor were held today, would you vote for the Democratic ticket of Parris Glendening and Kathleen Kennedy Townsend or the Republican ticket of Ellen Sauerbrey and Paul Rappaport (*Baltimore Sun*)?... As you may know, the candidates in November's election for governor in the State of Maryland include Parris N. Glendening, the Democrat and Ellen R. Sauerbrey, the Republican. Suppose the election were held today, for whom would you vote (*Washington Post*)?

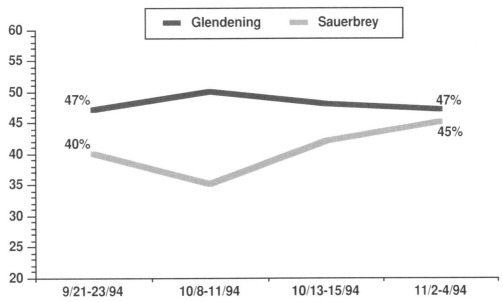

**Source:** All data except October 8-11 by Mason Dixon for *The Baltimore Sun*; October 8-11 survey by Chilton Research Services for *The Washington Post*.

# While the Democratic Party Keeps Winning, the Republicans Continue to Make Large Gains

|  | 1994 Vote | | | 1990 Vote | | | 1986 Vote | | |
|---|---|---|---|---|---|---|---|---|---|
|  | R | D | R Margin | R | D | R Margin | R | D | R Margin |
| TOTAL | 49.8% | 50.2% | - .4% | 40.2% | 59.8% | -19.6% | 17.6% | 82.4% | -64.8% |
| **Vote by County** | | | | | | | | | |
| Allegany | 57.1 | 42.8 | +14.3 | 33.4 | 66.6 | -33.2 | 25.1 | 74.9 | -49.8 |
| Anne Arundel | 60.4 | 39.6 | +20.8 | 51.0 | 49.0 | +2.0 | 16.8 | 83.2 | -66.4 |
| Baltimore City | 25.2 | 74.8 | -49.6 | 28.3 | 71.6 | -43.3 | 7.8 | 92.2 | -84.4 |
| Baltimore County | 56.8 | 43.2 | +13.6 | 46.9 | 53.1 | -6.2 | 14.6 | 85.4 | -70.8 |
| Calvert | 60.9 | 39.1 | +21.8 | 39.8 | 60.2 | -20.4 | 24.7 | 75.3 | -50.6 |
| Caroline | 66.9 | 33.1 | +33.8 | 69.1 | 30.9 | +38.2 | 19.7 | 80.3 | -60.6 |
| Carroll | 72.1 | 27.9 | +44.2 | 58.4 | 41.6 | +16.8 | 20.8 | 79.2 | -58.4 |
| Cecil | 63.8 | 36.2 | +27.6 | 49.3 | 50.6 | -1.3 | 19.9 | 80.1 | -60.2 |
| Charles | 61.0 | 39.0 | +22.0 | 35.1 | 64.8 | -29.7 | 21.0 | 79.0 | -58.0 |
| Dorchester | 60.8 | 39.2 | +21.6 | 67.2 | 32.8 | +34.4 | 11.8 | 88.2 | -76.4 |
| Frederick | 64.5 | 35.5 | +29.0 | 53.5 | 46.5 | +7.0 | 23.6 | 76.4 | -52.8 |
| Garrett | 77.1 | 22.9 | +54.2 | 60.5 | 39.5 | +21.0 | 38.9 | 61.1 | -22.2 |
| Harford | 64.8 | 35.2 | +29.6 | 48.5 | 51.5 | -3.0 | 16.3 | 83.7 | -67.4 |
| Howard | 53.6 | 46.4 | +7.2 | 38.1 | 61.9 | -23.8 | 17.9 | 82.1 | -64.2 |
| Kent | 57.8 | 42.2 | +15.6 | 57.4 | 42.6 | +14.8 | 15.8 | 84.2 | -68.4 |
| Montgomery | 41.4 | 58.6 | -17.2 | 29.9 | 70.1 | -40.2 | 24.5 | 75.5 | -51.0 |
| Prince George's | 31.6 | 68.4 | -36.8 | 21.1 | 78.8 | -57.7 | 18.7 | 81.3 | -62.6 |
| Queen Anne's | 65.1 | 34.9 | +30.2 | 69.3 | 30.7 | +38.6 | 18.2 | 81.8 | -63.6 |
| St. Mary's | 58.5 | 41.5 | +17.0 | 36.9 | 63.1 | -26.2 | 18.6 | 81.4 | -62.8 |
| Somerset | 63.3 | 36.7 | +26.6 | 52.5 | 47.5 | +5.0 | 14.7 | 85.3 | -70.6 |
| Talbot | 65.8 | 34.2 | +31.6 | 62.4 | 37.6 | +24.8 | 21.8 | 78.2 | -56.4 |
| Washington | 64.4 | 35.6 | +28.8 | 63.8 | 36.2 | +27.6 | 23.2 | 76.8 | -53.6 |
| Wicomico | 59.6 | 40.4 | +19.2 | 64.5 | 35.5 | +29.0 | 22.7 | 77.3 | -54.6 |
| Worcester | 62.1 | 37.9 | +24.2 | 48.1 | 51.9 | -3.8 | 18.7 | 81.3 | -62.6 |

**Source:** Data provided by the Maryland State Administrative Board of Election Laws.

# Sauerbrey Urged a Big Tax Cut... But Voters Stressing Taxes went Heavily for Glendening

**Question:** Which one or two of these issues mattered most in your vote for governor?

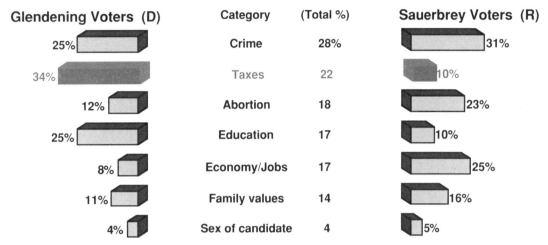

| Glendening Voters (D) | Category | (Total %) | Sauerbrey Voters (R) |
|---|---|---|---|
| 25% | Crime | 28% | 31% |
| 34% | Taxes | 22 | 10% |
| 12% | Abortion | 18 | 23% |
| 25% | Education | 17 | 10% |
| 8% | Economy/Jobs | 17 | 25% |
| 11% | Family values | 14 | 16% |
| 4% | Sex of candidate | 4 | 5% |

**Source:** VNS 1994 Exit Poll.

## While the Idea for a Tax Cut was Appealing, Voters were Not Convinced it was Possible

**Question:** Would you favor or oppose cutting the state income tax by 24%?

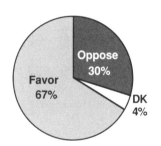

Oppose 30%
Favor 67%
DK 4%

**Question:** Suppose Sauerbrey is elected. Do you think she will be able to cut taxes by 24%, or not?

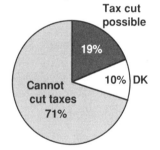

Tax cut possible 19%
10% DK
Cannot cut taxes 71%

**Source:** Survey by Chilton Research Services for *The Washington Post*, October 8-11, 1994.

**Where less than 6,000 votes decided the winner, the thought of jeopardizing essential government services with a 24% tax cut may have been enough to push voters away from Sauerbrey.**

**Question:** Do you believe it is possible to cut Maryland income taxes by 24% over the next four years without cutting essential government services?

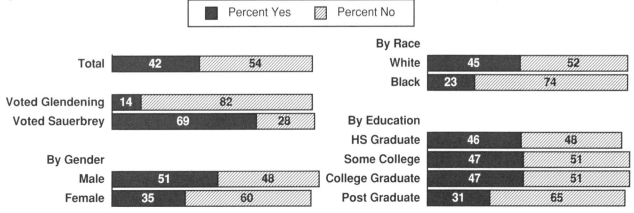

■ Percent Yes  ▨ Percent No

| | Percent Yes | Percent No |
|---|---|---|
| Total | 42 | 54 |
| Voted Glendening | 14 | 82 |
| Voted Sauerbrey | 69 | 28 |
| **By Gender** | | |
| Male | 51 | 48 |
| Female | 35 | 60 |
| **By Race** | | |
| White | 45 | 52 |
| Black | 23 | 74 |
| **By Education** | | |
| HS Graduate | 46 | 48 |
| Some College | 47 | 51 |
| College Graduate | 47 | 51 |
| Post Graduate | 31 | 65 |

**Source:** VNS 1994 Exit Poll.

# A look inside

# PENNSYLVANIA

Harris Wofford's bid for his first full term in the Senate was stopped short on November 8 by the GOP tide that swept the country. While Wofford's seat was just one of eight taken in the Senate by the Republicans this year, he had the dubious honor, along with Jim Sasser of Tennessee, of being one of only two sitting members to fall.

Perhaps better remembered as a 1960s civil rights activist or for his role in the founding of the Peace Corps, Wofford was appointed by Governor Robert Casey in 1990, until a special election could be held to fill the unexpired term of the late Senator John Heinz. Virtually unknown to voters in the state, the 65-year old Wofford ran for political office for the first time in that 1991 election, coming from behind to beat US Attorney General and former Governor Richard Thornburgh by a 55-45% margin. Although Pennsylvania is typically considered a "swing" state in presidential politics, its citizens had not elected a Democratic senator since 1962.

On its face, then, the outcome of the 1994 race marks a return to "politics as usual." But while Republican Rick Santorum will take his place in a long line of GOP senators, Pennsylvanians have broken their tradition of electing moderate Republicans to that office. Santorum, now the youngest member of the Senate at 36 years old, was considered by many to be too conservative to capture the seat held for 14 years by the moderate Republican John Heinz.

Hailed as "a spectacle of ideological conflict, presidential coattails and generational change," the Wofford-Santorum race pitted the aging liberal against the young conservative on such volatile issues as health care and abortion. Indeed, some believe that Wofford's loss resulted from the failure of Clinton's health care plan, an issue brought to the forefront of American politics by Wofford in his 1991 Senate bid. Others believe he suffered as a consequence of his position on the abortion issue. Governor Casey, a pro-life Democrat who originally appointed Wofford to the Senate, refused to campaign for the incumbent due to his pro-choice stance. While these two factors surely figured into the decision of some voters, economic issues, including taxes and jobs, also played a decisive role.

The final vote showed Wofford doing best among less than high school educated voters, union households, blacks, and those making less than $30,000 a year. Self-described moderates favored Wofford over Santorum by a 15-point margin, and independents were slightly more likely to vote for him as well. Santorum's base came from middle to high income families, whites, Protestants, high school and college graduates.

Geographically, a weak turnout in Philadelphia county, a long-time Democratic stronghold, combined with a high turnout in the predominantly conservative South Central and North Central regions of the state to make the race particularly tough for the incumbent senator. Vital to Wofford's victory in 1991 were the four suburban counties of Philadelphia. Traditionally considered solid Republican territory, Wofford won three of them that year. In 1994, however, these areas returned to the Republican fold.

As the Philadelphia suburbs go, so goes the nation.

—Regina M. Dougherty and Lois Timms-Ferrara

## Senate Race—1994

| | Wofford (D) | Santorum (R) |
|---|---|---|
| ALL | 47% | 49% |
| **By Gender** | | |
| Male | 45 | 51 |
| Female | 48 | 47 |
| **By Age** | | |
| 18-29 | 44 | 51 |
| 30-44 | 44 | 52 |
| 45-59 | 53 | 44 |
| 60+ | 45 | 50 |
| **By Education** | | |
| Less than HS | 57 | 38 |
| HS Grad | 43 | 52 |
| Some College | 47 | 47 |
| College Grad | 44 | 53 |
| Post Grad | 50 | 47 |
| **By Race** | | |
| White | 42 | 54 |
| Black | 91 | 5 |
| **By Income** | | |
| Less than $15,000 | 54 | 37 |
| $15,000-29,999 | 50 | 46 |
| $30,000-49,999 | 41 | 54 |
| $50,000-74,999 | 48 | 49 |
| $75,000-99,999 | 50 | 50 |
| $100,000+ | 38 | 60 |
| **By Party ID** | | |
| Democrat | 79 | 16 |
| Republican | 14 | 83 |
| Independent | 49 | 45 |
| **By Ideology** | | |
| Liberal | 80 | 18 |
| Moderate | 55 | 40 |
| Conservative | 19 | 76 |
| **By Denomination** | | |
| Protestant | 40 | 56 |
| Catholic | 48 | 48 |
| Other Christian | 46 | 46 |
| None | 61 | 37 |
| **By Union Membership** | | |
| Union Household | 54 | 44 |

**Source:** VNS 1994 Exit Poll.

# Pennsylvania Senate Seats:  An Electoral History

| Year | Total Vote | Candidate | Votes | Percent |
|---|---|---|---|---|
| 1976 | 4,546,353 | William Green (D) | 2,126,977 | 46.8% |
|  |  | H. John Heinz (R) | 2,381,891 | 52.4 |
| 1980 | 4,418,042 | Peter Flaherty (D) | 2,122,391 | 48.0 |
|  |  | Arlen Specter (R) | 2,230,404 | 50.5 |
| 1982 | 3,604,108 | Cyril Wecht (D) | 1,412,965 | 39.2 |
|  |  | H. John Heinz (R) | 2,136,418 | 59.3 |
| 1986 | 3,378,226 | Robert Edgar (D) | 1,448,219 | 42.9 |
|  |  | Arlen Specter (R) | 1,906,537 | 56.4 |
| 1988 | 4,366,598 | Joseph Vignola (D) | 1,416,764 | 32.4 |
|  |  | H. John Heinz (R) | 2,901,715 | 66.5 |
| 1991* | 3,382,746 | Harris Wofford (D) | 1,860,760 | 55.0 |
|  |  | Richard Thornburgh (R) | 1,521,986 | 45.0 |
| 1992 | 4,802,410 | Lynn Yeakel (D) | 2,224,966 | 46.3 |
|  |  | Arlen Specter (R) | 2,358,125 | 49.1 |
| 1994 | 3,503,878 | Harris Wofford (D) | 1,642,181 | 46.9 |
|  |  | Richard Santorum (R) | 1,732,526 | 49.4 |

# Fifty Years in Pennsylvania Senate Voting:  A Republican Ascendancy

| Year | Senator | Party |
|---|---|---|
| 1944 | Francis J. Myers | Democratic |
| 1946 | Edward Martin | Republican |
| 1950 | James H. Duff | Republican |
| 1952 | Edward Martin | Republican |
| 1956 | Joseph S. Clark | Democratic |
| 1958 | Hugh Scott | Republican |
| 1962 | Joseph S. Clark | Democratic |
| 1964 | Hugh Scott | Republican |
| 1968 | Richard S. Schweiker | Republican |
| 1970 | Hugh Scott | Republican |
| 1974 | Richard S. Schweiker | Republican |
| 1976 | H. John Heinz | Republican |
| 1980 | Arlen Specter | Republican |
| 1982 | H. John Heinz | Republican |
| 1986 | Arlen Specter | Republican |
| 1988 | H. John Heinz | Republican |
| 1991* | Harris Wofford | Democratic |
| 1992 | Arlen Specter | Republican |
| 1994 | Richard Santorum | Republican |

* Special election held November 5, 1991 to fill the unexpired term of the late Senator H. John Heinz.

**Source:** For 1944-82 see *Guide to US Elections*, Vol. 2 (Washington DC: Congressional Quarterly, 1985); for 1986-90 see *America Votes*, Vol. 19 (Chevy Chase, Maryland: Elections Research Center, 1991); for 1992 see *The Almanac of American Politics 1994* (New York: Macmillan Publishing Company, 1993); for 1994 see *Congressional Quarterly*, November 12, 1994.

# How the Race Unfolded: The Pre-Election Story— Close from the Start

**Question:** In the race for US Senate, who do you plan on voting for... Rick Santorum, Harris Wofford or haven't you made up your mind yet?

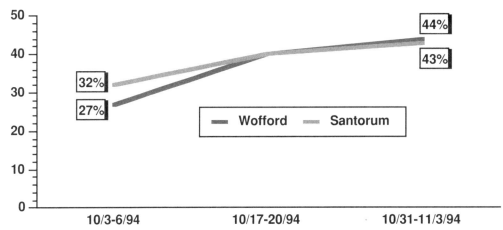

**Source**:   Surveys by Carnegie Mellon University for *The Pittsburgh Tribune Review* Publishing Company/Channel 11 News.

# Neither Candidate Got Great Marks

**Question:** I'd like to ask you a few questions about some people involved in state politics. Is your opinion of (Harris Wofford/ Rick Santorum) favorable, not favorable, undecided, or haven't you heard enough about (Harris Wofford/Rick Santorum) yet to have an opinion?

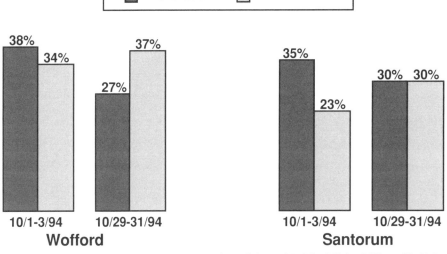

**Source**:   Surveys by The Keystone Poll conducted by the Center for Politics and Public Affairs, Millersville University.

**Question:** Now I'd like to ask you how much trust and confidence you have in some of the candidates for the senate: a lot, some, not much, or none.

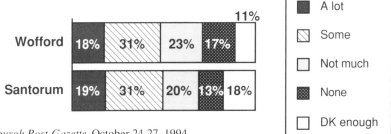

**Source**:   Survey by *Pittsburgh Post-Gazette*, October 24-27, 1994.

# When the Dust had Settled:  The Election Day Scenario

**Question:**  Which one or two of these mattered most in your vote for US Senate?

## Top 5 Responses

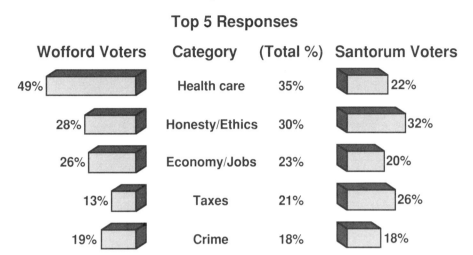

| Wofford Voters | Category | (Total %) | Santorum Voters |
|---|---|---|---|
| 49% | Health care | 35% | 22% |
| 28% | Honesty/Ethics | 30% | 32% |
| 26% | Economy/Jobs | 23% | 20% |
| 13% | Taxes | 21% | 26% |
| 19% | Crime | 18% | 18% |

# Salience of the Issues

## Health care mattered most...

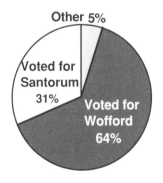

Other 5%
Voted for Santorum 31%
Voted for Wofford 64%

## Honesty/Ethics mattered most...

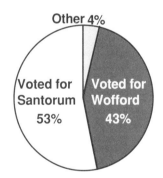

Other 4%
Voted for Santorum 53%
Voted for Wofford 43%

## Taxes mattered most...

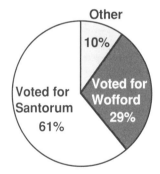

Other 10%
Voted for Santorum 61%
Voted for Wofford 29%

## The Clinton Factor

**Question:**  Do you think Harris Wofford agrees with Bill Clinton on issues...

| | Voted Santorum | Voted Wofford | Other |
|---|---|---|---|
| Too often (38%) | 84 | 12 | 4 |
| Right amount (33%) | 14 | 84 | 2 |
| Not enough (12%) | 27 | 60 | 13 |

**Source**:  VNS 1994 Exit Poll.

### The Philadelphia Story

Philadelphia voters in 1994 went overwhelmingly for Wofford:

| | |
|---|---|
| Wofford | 73% |
| Santorum | 23% |

But turnout was down from 1991:

| | 1991 | 1994 |
|---|---|---|
| Pennsylvania | 63.8% | 58.4% |
| Philadelphia County | 56.0 | 48.3 |

**Source:**  Pennsylvania Department of State

# Chapter 6
# 1994 Vote:
# Direct Democracy Ballot Issues

We examine here the many direct democracy measures—initiatives, referenda, and constitutional amendments—which appeared on state ballots in the past election. Direct democracy scholar Thomas E. Cronin leads with an article examining the patterns in referendum voting in this election and the ramifications of the growing popularity of returning the power back to the people. Following Cronin's commentary, we detail by policy area first the measures that passed and then those that failed. Term-limit votes are examined separately, because of their growing significance and an expected Supreme Court decision on their constitutionality. The chapter concludes with highlights from three direct-democracy measures voted on this past November: prohibiting illegal aliens from receiving public services in California; approving euthanasia in Oregon; and approving a higher cigarette tax in Arizona to pay for health care for the indigent.

—David Wilber

# Citizen-initiated Direct Democracy in the United States

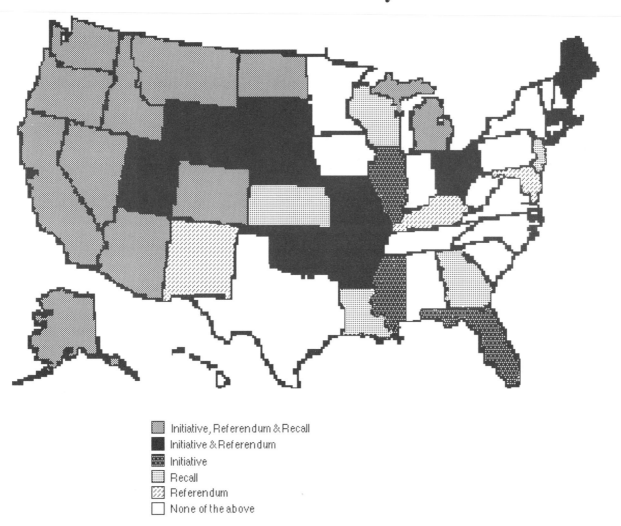

Initiative, Referendum & Recall
Initiative & Referendum
Initiative
Recall
Referendum
None of the above

**Note:** This map indicates states where citizen proposed direct democracy exists.
**Source:** Updated and adapted from Thomas E. Cronin, *Direct Democracy* (Massachusetts: Harvard University Press, 1989) p. 47.

# Direct Democracy—1994

## By Thomas E. Cronin

Voters in the November 8, 1994 elections voted on more ballot issues than in any year since 1932. Although there are exceptions, voters were generally in an anti-government, anti-politician, and conservative mood. Thus, term limits passed in several states, and in the District of Columbia. Californians protested against the federal government's failure either to control illegal immigration or to come to that state's aid in providing services for illegal aliens. Voters in three states adopted new campaign finance reforms. In several states, voters approved tougher punishment for criminals and called for more rights for crime victims. Oregon voters narrowly adopted a measure that will force public employees to contribute part of their salaries to their pension savings. And in New Mexico and Nevada, voters rejected proposed pay and expense allowance increases for state officials.

American voters generally respect the virtues of representative government, yet most yearn for at least an occasional opportunity to vote directly on public policy issues. Twenty-four states, plus the District of Columbia, now permit some form of citizen-initiative and referendum.

An *initiative* allows voters to propose a legislative measure or (depending on the state) a constitutional amendment by filing a petition bearing a required number of valid citizen signatures. The term *referendum* is usually used to describe the process in which a legislature refers a proposal or existing law to voters for their approval or rejection. However, a *popular or petition referendum* (a less frequently used device) refers an already enacted measure to the voters, allowing them to invalidate the law.

Voters in most states allowing direct democracy usually have to decide on just a handful of ballot issues. But voters in Oregon this November voted on 16 citizen-initiative measures as well as on two measures referred to them as referendum issues by the Oregon state legislature.

Although 1994 will understandably be remembered as the year the Republicans staged a major comeback at all levels of government and captured control of Congress for the first time in 40 years, it will also be remembered as a banner year for direct democracy and citizen voting on all kinds of social, fiscal and other policy issues.

## Highlights of the Direct Democracy Vote

### California's Proposition 187

The most publicized citizen initiative in the US was California's Proposition 187. Californians, by a 59 to 41% margin, voted to ban education, health and social services to illegal aliens. Proposition 187 also requires police to report people they suspect to be illegals to the State Department of Justice and the US Immigration and Naturalization Service.

A federal court issued a restraining order that prevented implementation of this citizen-initiated law, but it is clear that California voters sent an unmistakably loud message: namely, that they resent the national government's mandating state funding for programs for a large and growing illegal immigrant population, now estimated at about 1.5 million in California.

California's Republican Governor Pete Wilson championed Proposition 187 and urged voters to support it. They did so. His opponent, Democrat Kathleen Brown, opposed the measure, and was joined by Democratic US Senator Dianne Feinstein, President Bill Clinton, and two prominent national Republican leaders, Jack Kemp and William Bennett.

White voters approved the mea-

sure by a three-to-two margin. Older people and Republicans also favored this initiative by large margins. Hispanics overwhelmingly voted against it.

### Oregon's Measure 16

Another controversial and widely talked about initiative was Oregon's euthanasia measure. This "Death with Dignity Act" represents a legal acceptance of physician-assisted suicide that is the first of its kind in America. Passed by a narrow 51 to 49% margin, this carefully written initiative (modified from similar measures that failed in California and in the state of Washington) places the burden of decision on the terminally ill to ensure that it is *their* wish that will be carried out. It also offers legal protection for physicians involved in these cases.

A federal judge issued a temporary restraining order, saying he wanted to hear arguments about whether the law is constitutional.

Measure 16, as it was known in Oregon, requires that a physician determine that a patient has less than six months to live. It also requires a 15-day waiting period and a second physician's opinion. Once a patient has the approval of two doctors, and meets the waiting period requirement, the patient may choose when, where and with whom he will spend his last moments. Finally, the patient, not the physician, must place the fatal drug into his own mouth.

The Catholic church and other religious groups vigorously opposed Measure 16. But Oregon has a relatively small Catholic population and has the second-lowest percentage of church-goers in the nation (second only to Nevada).

Exit-poll data indicate that nearly 60% of males favored this euthanasia measure while female support was less than a majority. Younger people, under the age of 30, were quite favorable, but voters over the age of 60 were noticeably less supportive. Democrats and Republicans also differed, with

Democrats indicating much higher levels of support.

If upheld by the courts, this measure will very likely be pushed by advocates in several other states. It is likely to be promoted by various Right to Die committees and by the Hemlock Society, an international organization that supports assisted suicide.

### Other Issues of Interest

* Arizona voters, over the opposition of tobacco companies, voted to finance health services for poor people through an increase in cigarette taxes. Other states have tried similar measures and have failed. Colorado voters, for example, rejected a similar measure this year. Exit-poll data suggest that men and women in Arizona did not differ in their attitudes toward this cigarette tax measure. Data also show, however, that support for the tax was very much dependent upon the amount of formal education possessed by the respondent: More than two-thirds of those with advanced educational opportunities supported the tax increase, whereas two-thirds of those with only a high school education or less opposed it.

* In state after state, voters continued to support term limits for elected officials—usually by about a two-thirds majority.

* Two controversial anti-gay rights measures were narrowly defeated in Idaho and Oregon (a similar measure had been approved by Colorado voters in 1992). Opponents were well organized in Idaho and Oregon, and most state officials opposed these measures. The tourist industry in both states also rallied in opposition—no doubt in response to the losses suffered by Colorado's tourist industry when voters there decided to adopt limits on gay rights protections (this Colorado initiative has subsequently been overturned in the courts).

* In another controversial social issue, Wyoming voters decisively rejected a proposed law which would have prohibited abortion in all cases except

those in which "the mother's life is in danger or in cases of rape or incest."

* Casino gambling initiatives were defeated in Colorado, Florida, Massachusetts, Rhode Island, and Wyoming. However, citizens in New Mexico approved a lottery and video gambling. Missourians okayed slot machines on river boats. Georgians approved raffles by nonprofit organizations.

* Alaskans, by a 72 to 28% margin, affirmed the right of individuals "to keep and bear arms." Oregonians, by a narrow margin, banned the hunting of black bears with bait. Arizonians prohibited leg-hold traps and poison snares on public lands.

* Voters in North Dakota failed to repeal the mandatory seat belt statute.

* Voters in Alaska once again rejected the proposal to move their state capitol from Juneau to a more populated and central location near Anchorage.

## Votes on the Direct Democracy Process

In Colorado, voters soundly defeated the Douglas Bruce initiative (he is now a legend in Colorado for anti-government and anti-tax measures) to make the initiative and recall process

even easier to use. At the same time, Coloradans voted to limit all future initiatives to single issues. Voters in Florida, however, approved the principle that multiple issues can be covered in a ballot measure.

Voters in Rhode Island voted to cut the size of their state legislature and voters in California added provisions for the recall of state officials. In New Mexico the electorate overwhelmingly rejected a measure that would have eliminated recall elections of school board members.

Critics of direct democracy find fault in the process of citizens voting directly on laws. They do so for many reasons, but probably the chief reasons are: 1) they believe voters are inadequately prepared to cast votes on complicated matters, and 2) that this whole process undermines or, at the least, may weaken representative government and the legislative process.

Arguments for and against direct democracy could fill volumes. Here, I offer a small piece of evidence in support of direct democracy from the 1994 experience. Oregonians had to pass judgment on eighteen different measures. Many complained about the load and the responsibility. However, polls done this year in Oregon show, as

they have in other states in the past, that while voters often suggest that there are too many issues on the ballot or that the average voter is not well versed on many of the issues—the citizen-voter nonetheless wants to retain the voting option on the issues.

Perhaps a limit of six or seven issues per election should be prescribed to make ballot issue voting more rational and responsible. The states that regularly have the most issues on their ballots are, not surprisingly, those states that have the easiest signature requirements. States such as Oregon, North Dakota, and California regularly have several issues on their ballots, while Utah and Wyoming, with much higher levels of required signatures, have few issues on which to vote.

There are still twenty-six states which do not allow both citizen-initiatives and referendum. Apparently, these states seem to be in no rush to adopt direct democracy—although Mississippi did adopt the initiative in 1992 and New Jersey approved a state recall measure in 1993. However, in those states which do regularly use the tools of direct democracy in some form or another, it seems clear that the voters in those states have no desire to relinquish their powers.

**Source:** The data on the pages that follow were compiled from the November 8, 1994 election results by the Roper Center with the assistance of: Americans for Tax Reform, the Free Congress Foundation, the Public Affairs Research Institute of New Jersey, the National Conference of State Legislators, and *USA Today*.

# ELECTION RESULTS:
# Measures that Passed

## TAXING & SPENDING

| State | Subject Matter Covered on the Ballot | Percent Yes | No |
|-------|--------------------------------------|-----|-----|
| Alaska | Voters must approve costs to move legislature | 77% | 23% |
| Arizona | Relating to property tax exemption | 52 | 48 |
| Arkansas | Repeal the soft drink tax | 56 | 44 |
| Florida | Governmental revenue limits | 59 | 41 |
| Georgia | Homestead exemption for seniors | 79 | 21 |
| Massachusetts | Gas tax to fund repair of state's transportation systems | 74 | 26 |
| Michigan | Establish State Parks Endowment Fund—Divert funds | 71 | 29 |
| Montana | Limit sales and use tax to 4% | 54 | 46 |
| Nevada | Require a 2/3 vote in the legislature and a majority vote by referendum for any tax increase | 78 | 22 |
| North Dakota | Portion of oil extraction to go to education funds | 75 | 25 |
| Ohio | Repeal/Prohibit food and soft drink taxes | 66 | 34 |
| Oklahoma | Provide for a Permanent Common School Fund | 53 | 47 |
| Oklahoma | Taxes for public library systems | 52 | 48 |
| Rhode Island | Use gambling revenue for tax relief | 51 | 49 |
| Rhode Island | Reduce property taxes for education funding | 62 | 38 |
| South Carolina | Tax break for corporations | 58 | 42 |
| South Dakota | Taxation of private leases on state-owned lands | 58 | 42 |
| Utah | Changes to public school funding | 70 | 30 |

## BONDS

| State | Subject Matter Covered on the Ballot | Yes | No |
|-------|--------------------------------------|-----|-----|
| Maine | $9-million bond to remove state landfills | 57% | 43% |
| Maine | $20-million bond to protect drinking water | 51 | 49 |
| Maine | $15-million bond to create and retain jobs | 52 | 48 |
| Maine | $5-million bond to purchase up-to-date equipment for technical schools | 52 | 48 |
| Maine | $2-million bond for safety improvements at the Baxter School for the Deaf | 51 | 49 |
| New Jersey | $160-million bond to be sold to finance facilities for the disabled | 58 | 42 |
| New Mexico | $61.2-million bond issue for education | 52 | 48 |
| New Mexico | $2.5-million bond for libraries | 53 | 47 |
| New Mexico | $3.7-million bond for senior citizens facilities | 53 | 47 |
| Rhode Island | $56.5-million bond for transportation | 58 | 42 |
| Rhode Island | $29-million bond for education | 51 | 49 |
| W. Virginia | $300-million bond for infrastructure | 51 | 49 |

## GOVERNMENT

| State | Subject Matter Covered on the Ballot | Percent Yes | No |
|-------|--------------------------------------|------|-----|
| Florida | Change date on which legislature meets | 74% | 26% |
| Hawaii | Require senate approval of district court judges | 67 | 34 |
| Hawaii | Change list size for judicial nominees | 57 | 43 |
| Hawaii | Change terms of Judicial Selection Commission appointees | 64 | 36 |
| Hawaii | More Judicial Selection Commission changes | 55 | 45 |
| Hawaii | Limit on Board of Education's power | 63 | 37 |
| Idaho | Reapportionment of congressional districts | 64 | 36 |
| Idaho | Alternate forms of county government | 65 | 35 |
| Illinois | 3/5 vote needed for passage of a bill before May 31 | 69 | 31 |
| Kentucky | Require balanced budget for cities | 54 | 46 |
| Mississippi | Create a statewide grand jury | 82 | 19 |
| Missouri | Counties may adopt alternative forms of county government | 65 | 35 |
| Missouri | State officials' salaries set by citizens commission | 57 | 43 |
| Missouri | Property protection to require government reimbursement for lost revenue due to the acquisition of lands for park use | 65 | 35 |
| Montana | Protection of public pension funds and beneficiaries | 73 | 27 |
| Montana | Uniform time limit for gubernatorial action on bills | 70 | 30 |
| Nevada | Require meetings of legislative committees to be open to the public | 78 | 22 |
| New Mexico | Joint resolution to permit public support development | 53 | 47 |
| North Dakota | City meetings to be made public | 66 | 34 |
| Ohio | State tuition credits guaranteed by state | 60 | 40 |
| Oregon | Creates a vacancy if state legislator is convicted of a felony | 67 | 33 |
| Oregon | Public employees pay part of their salary toward pension | 50 | 50 |
| Rhode Island | Cut the size of the general assembly | 52 | 48 |
| Virginia | Prohibit pocket vetoes | 56 | 44 |

## ELECTORAL PROCESS

| California | Recall elections for state officers | 68% | 33% |
|-----------|-------------------------------------|-----|------|
| Colorado | Limits future citizen's initiatives to single subjects | 63 | 34 |
| Colorado | Defines how voters are informed on statewide ballot issues | 50 | 50 |
| Florida | Multiple subjects can be covered on initiatives and referenda | 58 | 42 |
| Missouri | Campaign finance reform | 74 | 26 |
| Montana | Lower the cap on campaign contributions and other revisions to campaign finance | 61 | 39 |
| Nevada | Defines and limits campaign contributions | 77 | 23 |
| New Mexico | Increase number of votes for judicial retention elections | 57 | 43 |
| Oregon | Change deadline for filling vacancies in general election | 88 | 12 |
| Oregon | Candidates may only use contributions from district residents | 53 | 47 |
| Oregon | Adopts contribution and spending limits, and other campaign finance law changes | 72 | 28 |
| Virginia | Revise voter registration laws to match federal laws, including allowing mail-in registration | 53 | 47 |

# SOCIAL ISSUES

| State | Subject Matter Covered on the Ballot | Percent Yes | No |
|---|---|---|---|
| Alaska | Individual right to keep and bear arms | 73% | 27% |
| Arizona | Increase state tax on tobacco products to finance health care for poor | 51 | 49 |
| California | Prohibit illegal aliens from receiving public services | 59 | 41 |
| Georgia | Raffles by nonprofits legal | 64 | 36 |
| Georgia | Regulations on serving alcoholic beverages at places where nudity is entertainment | 65 | 35 |
| Hawaii | State support for early childhood education—approval to issue bonds | 62 | 38 |
| Hawaii | State support for early childhood education—approval to use bonds | 53 | 47 |
| Massachusetts | Keep mandatory seat-belt law | 59 | 41 |
| Massachusetts | Retail stores can be open on holidays and before noon on Sundays | 53 | 47 |
| Missouri | Allow slot machine gambling on a riverboat | 54 | 46 |
| New Mexico | State lottery and video gambling | 54 | 46 |
| Oregon | Allow terminally ill adults to obtain prescriptions for lethal drugs | 51 | 49 |
| Rhode Island | Make state's casino law an amendment to the state constitution | 68 | 32 |
| South Dakota | Reauthorize the Video State Lottery System | 53 | 47 |
| South Dakota | Require the use of a safety belt in passenger vehicles | 51 | 49 |
| Vermont | Make Vermont constitution gender neutral | NA | NA |
| W. Virginia | Remove outdated language from the state constitution | 59 | 41 |
| Washington | Sales tax on cigarettes, liquor and soda to pay for violence reduction and anti-drug programs | 57 | 43 |

# CRIME/LEGAL SYSTEM

| State | Subject Matter | Yes | No |
|---|---|---|---|
| Alaska | Strengthen the rights of crime victims | 87% | 14% |
| California | Tougher sentences for repeat offenders | 72 | 28 |
| California | Expand no-bail provision | 79 | 21 |
| California | Establish commission on judicial performance | 64 | 36 |
| California | Elimination of justice courts | 61 | 39 |
| Colorado | No bail for violent offenders | 77 | 23 |
| Georgia | Setting up county courts | 56 | 44 |
| Georgia | Mandatory sentences for violent felons | 81 | 19 |
| Idaho | Guarantee the rights of victims of crimes | 79 | 21 |
| Illinois | Allow child witness testimony via closed circuit TV | 63 | 37 |
| Michigan | Amend state constitution to keep a criminal defendant who pleads guilty from getting an automatic appeal | 74 | 25 |
| Nevada | Extend jurisdiction of the Commission on Judicial Discipline | 56 | 44 |
| New Mexico | Grand jury petition requirements | 51 | 49 |
| Ohio | Increase victim's rights | 78 | 22 |
| Ohio | Simplified death penalty review | 70 | 30 |
| Oklahoma | Allow legislature to set minimum prison terms for felons | 81 | 19 |

NA = Not Available

## CRIME/LEGAL SYSTEM—continued

| State | Subject Matter Covered on the Ballot | Percent Yes | No |
|-------|--------------------------------------|-----|-----|
| Oregon | Legislature cannot reduce voter-approved criminal sentence without a 2/3 vote | 65% | 35% |
| Oregon | Sets mandatory sentences for listed felonies; covers those 15 years and older | 66 | 34 |
| Oregon | Requires state prison inmates to work full-time | 71 | 29 |
| Rhode Island | Establish a Judicial Selection Committee | 70 | 30 |
| Utah | Enhance the rights of crime victims | 69 | 31 |
| Vermont | Redefine how bail can be set for certain criminal charges; imprisonment for debt is prohibited | NA | NA |
| Virginia | Extend length of time for bringing civil child abuse lawsuits | 65 | 35 |
| Wyoming | Legislation to create life imprisonment without parole | 68 | 32 |

## MISCELLANEOUS

| Arizona | Prohibit the use of leg-hold traps and poison snares on public land | 59% | 41% |
|---------|---------------------------------------------------------------------|-----|-----|
| Florida | Limit marine net fishing | 72 | 28 |
| Georgia | Authorize the use of regional facilities | 69 | 31 |
| Massachusetts | Prohibit rent control | 51 | 49 |
| New Mexico | Student members to be appointed to the Board of Regents | 59 | 41 |
| North Dakota | Appointing students to State Board of Higher Education | 67 | 35 |
| Oklahoma | Allow wineries to make wine with grapes and fruit grown out of state | 56 | 44 |
| Oregon | Bans hunting of black bears with bait or hunting black bears or cougars with dogs | 52 | 48 |
| South Carolina | Involving the age of coroners | 82 | 18 |
| Washington | People other than dentists can make and sell false teeth | 58 | 42 |

NA = Not Available

# ELECTION RESULTS: Measures that Failed

## TAXING & SPENDING

| State | Subject Matter Covered on the Ballot | Percent Yes | No |
|---|---|---|---|
| California | Gasoline tax for passenger rail and mass transit buses | 20% | 80% |
| Massachusetts | A constitutional amendment proposing a graduated income tax | 30 | 70 |
| Massachusetts | Initiative petitions for graduated income tax | 29 | 71 |
| Missouri | Voter approval of tax increase | 22 | 78 |
| Montana | Property taxes based on acquisition value | 41 | 59 |
| Montana | Voter approval on new taxes | 47 | 53 |
| Montana | Requires a 2/3 vote of the legislature for any new or increased tax/fee | 49 | 51 |
| Montana | Replace the state's graduated income tax with a flat rate | 25 | 75 |
| Nevada | Authorize state agreements on public debt | 15 | 85 |
| Nevada | Reduction in taxes for companies relocating hazardous operations | 38 | 62 |
| Nevada | Allow certain tax exemptions on the sale of personal property | 32 | 68 |
| New Mexico | Allow counties to borrow funds for building repair and land | 48 | 52 |
| New Mexico | Increase the Severance Tax Permanent Fund | 45 | 55 |
| New Mexico | Increase the Land Grant Permanent Fund | 49 | 51 |
| Oregon | Bars new or increased taxes without voter approval | 45 | 55 |
| Oregon | State must maintain minimum state funding of schools and community colleges based on funds available from listed sources in the 93-95 biennium budget | 37 | 63 |
| Oregon | Replace state income, property and fuel taxes with a 2% sales tax | 24 | 76 |
| South Dakota | Change how the Permanent School Fund is invested | 44 | 56 |
| South Dakota | Property tax reform; tax levies cannot exceed 1% of property's assessed value | 49 | 51 |
| Wyoming | Authorize the investment of up to $500 million of state funds in Wyoming financial institutions | 37 | 63 |
| Wyoming | Invest 25% of state funds in shares of capital stock | 49 | 51 |

## BONDS

| State | Subject Matter | Yes | No |
|---|---|---|---|
| California | $1-billion bond for passenger trains | 35% | 65% |
| Maine | $5-million bond for academic improvement at the University of Maine | 41 | 59 |
| Maine | $21.3-million bond to improve transportation and road care | 46 | 54 |
| Rhode Island | $3.8-million bond for prison repair | 35 | 65 |
| Rhode Island | $4.5-million bond for historical preservation | 45 | 55 |
| Rhode Island | $5-million bond for the State House | 44 | 56 |

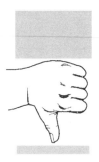

# GOVERNMENT

| State | Subject Matter Covered on the Ballot | Percent Yes | No |
|---|---|---|---|
| Alaska | Change capital from Juneau to Wasilla in January 1997 | 45% | 54% |
| Arizona | Create the office of Lieutenant Governor | 35 | 65 |
| Arizona | Legislative pay raise | 40 | 60 |
| Colorado | Government reform, including pay raises, campaign finance, recall, and a more powerful initiative | 24 | 76 |
| Hawaii | Board of Education nominated by governor, confirmed by senate | 42 | 58 |
| Michigan | Election of delegates to draft revisions to the state constitution in a convention | 28 | 72 |
| New Mexico | Give lawmakers a per diem and pay for other expenses | 46 | 54 |
| Oklahoma | Method for calling a convention for the state constitution | 48 | 52 |
| Oregon | Repeals prevailing wage-rate requirements for public workers | 38 | 62 |
| Rhode Island | Constitutional convention to revise the state constitution | 41 | 59 |
| South Dakota | Lower minimum age to hold office to 18 | 17 | 83 |

# ELECTORAL PROCESS

| State | Subject Matter | Yes | No |
|---|---|---|---|
| Colorado | Campaign finance reform to limit contributions | 46% | 54% |
| Massachusetts | Limit special interest spending on ballot questions | 41 | 59 |
| New Mexico | Eliminate recall elections of school board members | 29 | 71 |

# SOCIAL ISSUES

| State | Subject Matter | Yes | No |
|---|---|---|---|
| California | Establish a state-run health care system | 27% | 73% |
| California | Loosen regulations on smoking and tobacco products | 29 | 71 |
| Colorado | Legalize gambling in Manitou Springs and public airports | 7 | 93 |
| Colorado | State courts can interpret obscenity laws more broadly than the US Supreme Court | 37 | 63 |
| Colorado | Tobacco tax to pay for various health-care programs | 38 | 62 |
| Colorado | Permits the state to force biological parents/grandparents to pay delivery costs of babies born to mothers on welfare | 33 | 67 |
| Florida | Legalize casinos in limited areas | 38 | 62 |
| Georgia | State regulation on health-care providers | 41 | 59 |
| Idaho | Establish state policies regarding homosexuality | 50 | 50 |
| Minnesota | Allow off-track betting | 50 | 50 |
| New Mexico | Change voting age and other voter qualifications | 45 | 55 |
| North Dakota | Repeal the seat-belt law | 45 | 55 |
| Oklahoma | Entertainment tax to fund breast cancer research, prevention and treatment | 41 | 59 |

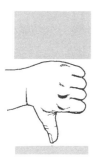

## SOCIAL ISSUES—continued

| State | Subject Matter Covered on the Ballot | Percent Yes | No |
|-------|--------------------------------------|-------------|-----|
| Oregon | Guarantee equal protection by listing prohibited grounds for discrimination | 43% | 57% |
| Oregon | Government cannot approve of or create classifications based on homosexuality | 48 | 52 |
| Oregon | Allow law regulating/prohibiting obscenity; No free speech protection for obscenity or child pornography | 46 | 54 |
| Rhode Island | Allow gambling in Providence | 23 | 77 |
| Rhode Island | Allow gambling in Pawtucket | 14 | 86 |
| Rhode Island | Allow gambling in Lincoln | 28 | 72 |
| Rhode Island | Allow gambling in Coventry | 15 | 85 |
| Rhode Island | Allow gambling in West Greenwich | 44 | 56 |
| South Dakota | Change voting age | 25 | 75 |
| Utah | Need to define what constitutes the non-sectarian study of religion in the state education system | 47 | 53 |
| Wyoming | Prohibit abortion unless mother's life is in danger or in cases of rape/incest | 39 | 61 |
| Wyoming | Establish procedures, gaming commission, penalties and taxes for local option gambling | 30 | 70 |

## CRIME/LEGAL SYSTEM

| State | Subject | Yes | No |
|-------|---------|-----|-----|
| Arizona | Enable legislature to limit damages on lawsuits | 39% | 61% |
| Arizona | Change time limits to sue | 38 | 62 |
| Nevada | Allows an increase in salary of supreme court and district judges | 16 | 84 |

## MISCELLANEOUS

| State | Subject | Yes | No |
|-------|---------|-----|-----|
| Arizona | Eliminate competitive bidding in exchanges of State Trust Land | 41% | 59% |
| Arizona | Establish guidelines for government taking private land | 40 | 60 |
| Colorado | Injured workers given more choices of medical treatment | 20 | 80 |
| Georgia | Tax break on blueberry plants | 46 | 54 |
| Maine | $10-million bond to improve fish hatcheries | 49 | 51 |
| Massachusetts | Re-establish college student fees for lobbyists | 49 | 51 |
| Michigan | Initiate a No-Fault Insurance Amendment | 39 | 61 |
| Nevada | Exemption of sales and use taxes on horses | 31 | 69 |
| New Mexico | Change name of state hospital | 42 | 58 |
| New Mexico | Change name of State Transportation Commission | 44 | 56 |
| Oregon | Amends chemical process mining laws | 42 | 58 |

# States Where Term Limits Have Passed on the Ballot

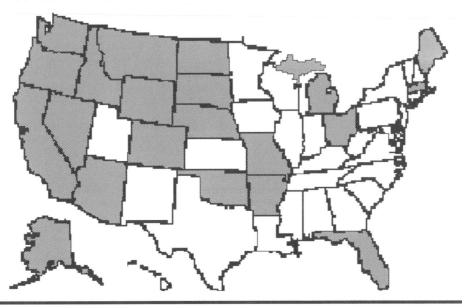

## When a Term-limit Measure Passed on the Ballot

| **1990** | **1992** | | **1994** | |
|---|---|---|---|---|
| California | Arizona | Nebraska | Alaska | Massachusetts |
| Colorada | Arkansas | North Dakota | Colorado | Nebraska |
| Oklahoma | California | Ohio | Idaho | Nevada |
| | Florida | Oregon | Maine | Oklahoma |
| | Michigan | South Dakota | | |
| | Missouri | Washington | | |
| | Montana | Wyoming | | |

**Question:** Do you think there should or should not be a limit on the number of terms to which a senator or member of Congress can be elected?

**Question:** Please tell me if you strongly favor, favor, strongly oppose, or oppose... Term limitations to limit the number of years members of Congress can serve?

**Question:** Now, thinking about the issue of term limitations for public office holders—a number of states have passed initiatives to limit the terms of their office holders. Most of the initiatives limit state representatives and statewide office holders to eight years and members of the US Congress and US Senators to six years. Do you approve or disapprove of this term-limit proposal? And do you strongly (approve/disapprove) or somewhat (approve/disapprove) of that?

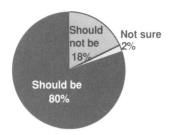

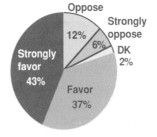

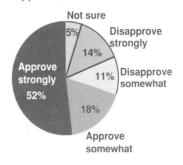

**Source:** Survey by Hart & Teeter Research Companies for NBC News/ *Wall Street Journal*, October 14-18, 1994.

**Source:** Survey by Princeton Survey Research Associates for the Times Mirror Center for the People and the Press, July 12-25, 1994.

**Source:** Survey by The Tarrance Group and Mellman & Lake, August 16-18, 1994.

# Term Limits:  Election Results

| State | Subject Matter Covered on the Ballot | Percent Yes | No |
|---|---|---|---|
| Alaska | Ban ballot listing of US Senators if they've served for 12 of the 18 preceding years and from the House if they've served six of the preceding 12 years.  Would not become effective until 24 other states have adopted similar measures. | 63% | 37% |
| Colorado | Limit US House members to three terms and US Senators to two terms.  Local officials, excluding judicial, to two terms. | 52 | 48 |
| Idaho | Ban US House candidates from running if they've served for more than six years in the last 11 years.  US Senate candidates would not be able to run if they've served 12 or more years in the previous 23 years.  Limits also would apply to state and local officials. | 59 | 41 |
| Maine | Ban US House candidates from running if they served for more than six years in the last 11 years.  US Senate candidates could not run if they served 12 years or more in the last 17 years. | 63 | 37 |
| Massachusetts | Limit terms for constitutional officers to two consecutive four-year terms, legislators and US House members limited to four consecutive two-year terms and US Senators to two consecutive six-year terms. | 52 | 48 |
| Nebraska | Limit US House members to three terms and US Senators to two terms.  The state legislature and local officials in towns with more than 5,000 residents would be limited to two terms. | 68 | 32 |
| Nevada | Limit US House members to six years and US Senators to 12 years.  Would not become effective until 24 other states have adopted similar measures. | 70 | 30 |
| Nevada | Limit terms of state legislature to 12 years and attorney general, judges, and other state constitutional posts to eight years. | 70 | 30 |
| Oklahoma | Limit US House members to six years and US Senators to 12 years.  Serving in both the House and the Senate for an 18 year total is allowed. | 67 | 33 |
| Utah | Establish 12-year term limits for US Senators and 8-year limits for all other congressional, state, and county offices, excluding judicial office.  Also, require run-off elections for federal, state and county offices when no candidate receives a majority vote for the office. | 35 | 65 |
| W. Virginia | Remove term limits on sheriffs. | 35 | 65 |

# Term Limits:  Exit Poll Results

**Question:** Should there be limits on the number of years a member of Congress can serve (or) No limits—they can continue to serve as long as they are re-elected (National)?...  How did you vote on Constitutional Amendment 17, which establishes stricter term limits for elected officials (Colorado)?...  How did you vote on Question 4, which establishes term limits for elected officials (Massachusetts)?

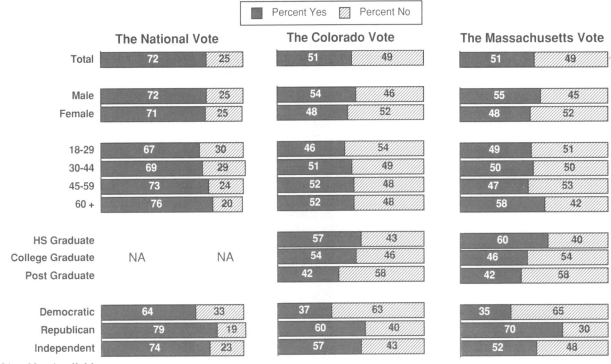

NA = Not Available
**Source:**  VNS 1994 Exit Poll.

# Prohibit Illegal Aliens from Receiving Public Services:
## CALIFORNIA

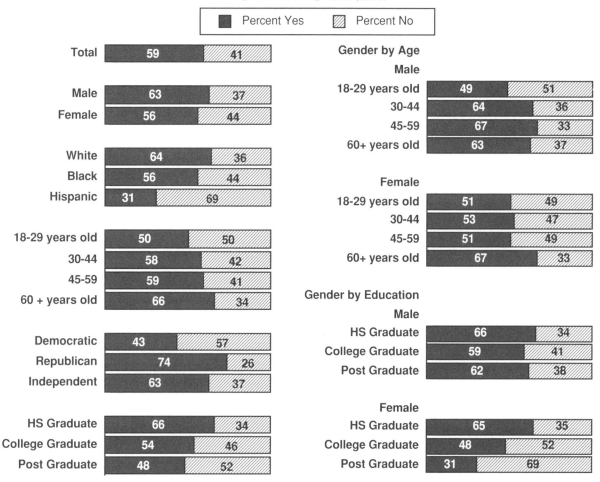

Source: VNS 1994 Exit Poll.

Question: Which of these statements do you agree with most regarding the illegal immigration initiative?

| | Total | Voted **For** | Voted **Against** |
| --- | --- | --- | --- |
| | | Proposition 187 | |
| It sends a message that needs to be sent | 50 | 77% | 12% |
| It will force the federal government to face the issue | 33 | 51 | 9 |
| It's poorly written/Doesn't solve the problem | 27 | 3 | 59 |
| It will stop immigrants from using state services | 21 | 33 | 3 |
| It would save the state millions of dollars | 20 | 33 | 3 |
| It would throw children out of school | 17 | 3 | 38 |
| It is racist/anti-Latino | 17 | 1 | 40 |
| It could create a health crisis | 12 | 2 | 25 |
| It would force cops to ID illegal immigrant criminals | 8 | 7 | 9 |
| It would cost the state billions in federal funds | 8 | 4 | 15 |
| None of the above | 4 | 2 | 5 |

Note: Multiple responses were allowed.
Source: *LA Times* 1994 Exit Poll.

# Euthanasia: Allow the Terminally Ill to Obtain Prescriptions for Lethal Drugs—OREGON

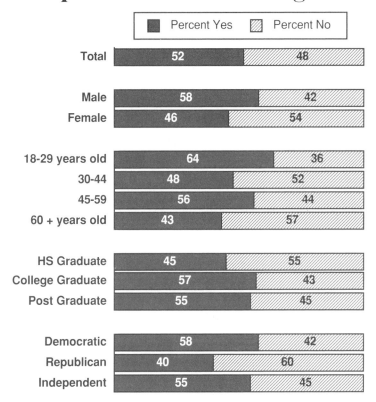

# Paying for Health Care for the Poor Through a Cigarette Tax — ARIZONA

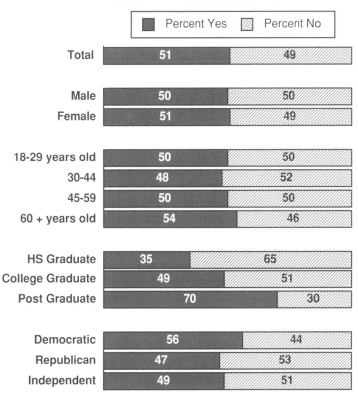

**Source:** VNS 1994 Exit Poll.

# Chapter 7
# 1994 Vote: The Money Story

## Challengers Do Not Need to Spend as Much as Incumbents to Win—They Need to Spend Enough to Be Known

### By Michael J. Malbin

The main story of the 1994 congressional elections is a story of change—change of party control, caused by a decidedly national and partisan tilt in the electorate's district-by-district judgments. Political scientists need to recognize change when it occurs, but we also should be disciplined enough to see if any underlying consistencies can help us make sense of what is new. This will be clear as we look at the role of money in the elections of 1994.

For years, if one wanted to make a prediction in the month or two before Election Day about whether an incumbent was facing a serious contest, the best single piece of financial information has been the amount of money raised by the challenger. That crucial fact is well understood by most election scholars. However, it has not been accepted in the legislative arena. Some of the most common proposals to reform campaign finance have been based on the assumption that mandated spending limits to equalize challengers and incumbents are needed to make elections more competitive. But it turns out that challengers do not need to spend as much as incumbents to win. *They need to spend enough to become known*; to bring their cases to the voters so the voters can make informed choices. If anyone had any reason to doubt this, the 1994 elections should drive the point home.

From 1984 through 1990, House challengers were severely underfunded—and almost all challengers lost. The picture began to reverse in 1992. During that year of redistricting—when incumbents were unsettled by the need to introduce themselves to new constituents, by Ross Perot's anti-politician presidential campaign, and by fourteen successful term limit state ballot initiatives—challenger funding in House races finally climbed back up to 1984 levels,

and 19 challengers defeated incumbents in the general election. (That compares to 14 successful challengers in 1990, 5 in 1988 and 6 in 1986.)

If 1992 was a financial turning point for challengers, 1994 was at least a temporary breakthrough: The average challenger spent roughly $225,000 as of November 28, 1994 (see page 131). That was one-third more than the average challenger spent in 1992, two-thirds more than in 1990 and almost double the average of 1988. Actually, to be more precise: the average Republican challenger went up more than 40% between 1992 and 1994 and the average Democrat stayed almost flat. Thirty-four Republican challengers were successful; none of the Democrats were.

The point is made even more dramatically if we focus on successful House challengers. The 34 Republican challengers who defeated Democratic incumbents spent an average of almost $650,000 through November 28 (see page 134). That is much more than successful challengers have spent in the past (except for a tiny handful who won in 1988). However, these successful 1994 challengers still ended up spending much *less* than the incumbents they beat—fully one-third less. (The *average* defeated incumbent spent almost $1 million in 1994!)

All of this tends to confirm (1) that money—or, more exactly, having the wherewithal to communicate—is essential to campaigning in contemporary congressional politics; but (2) money is not enough by itself to win. Having money means having the ability to be heard; it does not mean the voters will like what they hear. Incumbents who had worn out their welcome were heard—and rejected. So too were some challengers. Fred Overby of Georgia was the only Democratic challenger to spend more than $1 million in 1994. Of the $1.25 million his campaign reported through November, more than $800 thousand came from his own pocket. That turned out to be enough to earn him only 34% of the vote against the incumbent Republican, Mac Collins.

In some respects, this House race was a smaller version of the country's most-expensive-ever race for the US Senate: the contest between incumbent Dianne Feinstein and challenger Michael Huffington. Huffington put more than $28 million of his own money into an election in which he outspent the incumbent by better than two-to-one, only to lose by a narrow 2% margin. It is probably fair to say that money did everything money could do for Huffington. By the end of the campaign, he was well known to most Californians. At one point, he was even ahead in the polls. In the end, however, more spending did no more for him than it does for an embattled incumbent. The voters felt they knew enough to make a decision, and they decided against him.

The same thing happened to Oliver North in Virginia. North outspent the incumbent Charles Robb by almost four-to-one and still lost by nearly three percentage points to a Senator who proved to be only slightly less unpopular than he was. The North campaign is also a lesson in how not to misread financial records. The FEC reports that Oliver North spent almost $20 million on his campaign. But a closer look makes it clear that a lot of that money was spent on direct mail to raise small, individual contributions nationally. There is a world of difference between this kind of fundraising—in which it often costs a dollar to raise one—and writing a check to yourself, as Huffington did.

Direct mail is an option that is useful only to a candidate who is already well-known, or who has the sponsorship of an organization that can use "hot button" issues to keep the small checks flowing. Neither comes easily. Maybe that—combined with the low contribution limits that make it so hard to raise seed money—can help explain why more than *one-fifth* of the money raised by House challengers, and well over *one-third* of the money for Senate challengers, came from the candidates themselves (see page 136). These numbers are much higher than in the past. Challengers seem increasingly to be relying on their own funds to get started. In a democracy, one naturally feels uncomfortable about that. But one ought to feel at least as uncomfortable about what the situation would be like without self-funded challengers. Is the policy choice really between self-funding and no competition? Perhaps policy makers need to start thinking more systematically about the problem of seed money for new candidates.

Except for self-funding, it is too early to know whether there were important changes in the sources of funds in 1994. (Contributions from political action committees, parties and individuals are entered into the FEC computers months after the summary data we have been analyzing here.) Some post-election press accounts have suggested that business PACs gave more to Republican challengers and open-seat candidates than they have done for about the past decade.[1] There really is no way of knowing from present information whether business groups have turned aside from their very heavily pro-incumbent tilt of recent cycles. The detailed data of contributions through September 30 gives no hint of a major change (see page 137). However, September is too early for most PAC contributions to non-incumbents. Moreover, the gross indications we can glean from the overall numbers through November 28 do suggest that at least some shift may have occurred. This will require another look at the data in a few months.

Finally, we ought to take notice of the many sources of funds that are outside the direct control of the candidates. The most obvious of these are *independent expenditures*—spending that directly advocates the election or defeat of a candidate that legally must occur without consultation or coordination with the candidate (see page 138). The Supreme Court has ruled that these are constitutionally protected against federal spending limits, but reporting and disclosure may be required by law.

After any major election victory, it is normal to see supporters lining up to claim credit for having helped make the difference for the winner's success. This year, one of the most vocal interest groups on the day after the election was the National Rifle Association. According to reports filed through November 6, the NRA put more than $1.35 million into independent expenditures in 1994. Of this total, the NRA spent roughly $925 thousand (or two-thirds of its total) on behalf of just nine Senate Republicans during the final month of the campaign—an average of more than $100,000 per race. That figure represents 80% of the total independent spending from all sources on behalf of all Senate Republicans in 1993-94. The NRA's full spending budget of $1.35 million also represents almost one-third of the entire nation's independent spending on all congressional races in 1994.

The NRA was proportionally a much larger piece of the independent spending picture in 1994 than it had been in the past. However, this was not because the group changed its own spending patterns. Rather, the NRA's proportion grew as independent spending from other sources dropped. In 1992, independent spending for Congress amounted to $6.2 million. Based on FEC reports filed through November 6, the figure for 1994 was only $3.5 million. That is a major drop, but three committees account for most of the difference. The National Association of Realtors and the American Medical Association decided for tactical reasons to rely on direct contributions in 1994, rather than to use independent expenditures. The two committees each spent about $1 million independently in 1992. In addition, the National Right to Life Committee spent about $250 thousand this year—a $615 thousand drop from the $865 thousand it spent on congressional races in 1992 (which came on top of the $800 thousand it spent on behalf of President Bush). These three committees account for almost all (96%) of the difference between 1992 and 1994.

Even this does not complete the financial picture, however. The activities that we describe with the words "independent spending" are fully disclosed, and therefore knowable. Much less well known are the undisclosed millions that influence elections in a more indirect way. Who knows, for example, how much was spent in 1994 on: (1) get-out-the-vote drives sponsored by labor unions and dozens of other organizations; (2) the Christian Coalition's "report cards" that tell whether a candidate's issue positions agree with the organization's; or (3) television and other advertising bought by US Term Limits during the campaign to persuade Washington's fifth congressional district voters to write to their incumbent member, former House Speaker Thomas Foley, in his official capacity as their representative, to urge him to drop his lawsuit against the state's term limits? None of these activities need explicitly urge people to vote for specific candidates; none were reported as independent expenditures.

One lesson from these activities is that large, politically sophisticated interest groups are resilient organizations, fully able to adapt to complex regulatory environments. But that is "old news." We could have said the same thing about every election since 1974, when the FEC came into existence. What made the 1994 election new was the return of the challenger as well as the potential resurgence of partisanship. It will be interesting to see whether these two phenomena continue to be linked in the future.

**Endnote:**

[1] Peter Stone, "The GOP's New Gold Mine," *National Journal*, 12/3/94, p.2869; Jennifer Babson and Kelly St. John, "Momentum Helps GOP Collect Record Amount From PACs," *Congressional Quarterly*, 12/3/94, pp. 3456-59.

**Note:** The data in this chapter were obtained from published Federal Election Commission (FEC) reports and, in some instances, derived from an on-line FEC computer database, by the Rockefeller Institute of Government at the State University of New York. As this publication went to press, complete 1993-94 general election figures were not available. Instead, for 1993-94, the data are through November 28.

Where averages are reported herein it is important to consider that in some cases the number of candidates may have been small, particularly in the Senate, and thus distort measures of central tendency including means.

For the data contained herein we have used the following definitions regarding challenger and open-seat elections. Cases in which an incumbent lost in the primary have been classified as open-seat elections. In FEC publications, only if the incumbent does not run are the seats classified as open. The FEC classifies elections where an incumbent loses in the primary as challenger seats in the general election. Here challengers are only those running against an incumbent in the general election.

The Roper Center would like to express appreciation to the American Enterprise Institute for much of the 1984-92 FEC data which was published in AEI's *Vital Statistics on Congress 1993-1994*, editors: Norman J. Ornstein; Thomas E. Mann; and Michael J. Malbin. In many instances we have relied heavily on this publication as a source document.

# Total Campaign Expenditures for Congressional Candidates, 1984-1994

*(in millions of dollars)*

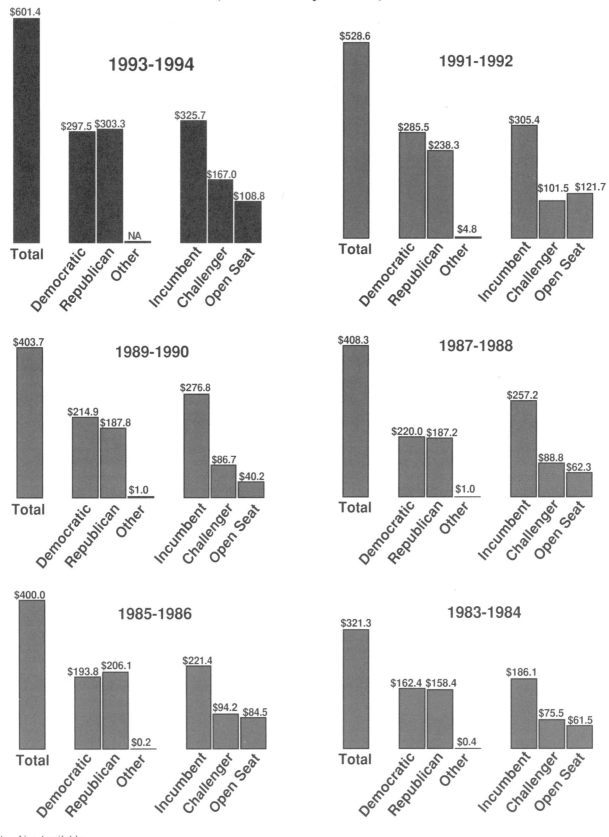

NA = Not Available

**Note:** Includes expenditures for the primary and general election by general election candidates.

# Campaign Expenditures for Congressional Candidates, 1984-1994

### *(net dollars)*

**HOUSE:**

| | 1994 | 1992 | 1990 | 1988 | 1986 | 1984 |
|---|---|---|---|---|---|---|
| **All Candidates** | | | | | | |
| Total expenditures | $330,644,138 | $331,557,602 | $237,680,795[*] | $222,258,024 | $210,230,941 | $176,882,849 |
| Average expenditure | 420,132[*] | 409,836[*] | 325,145[*] | 273,380 | 259,544 | 241,313 |
| Democratic average | 468,731 | 463,863 | 355,862 | 286,851 | 264,558 | 237,732 |
| Republican average | 372,500 | 354,311 | 290,910 | 258,330 | 253,954 | 245,591 |
| **Incumbents** | | | | | | |
| Incumbent average | 540,746[*] | 594,729[*] | 422,124 | 378,544 | 334,386 | 279,044 |
| Democratic average | 599,490 | 621,405 | 427,178 | 358,260 | 311,071 | 279,203 |
| Republican average | 455,527 | 553,774 | 414,222 | 409,217 | 368,629 | 278,781 |
| **Challengers** | | | | | | |
| Challenger average | 225,503 | 167,891 | 134,465[*] | 119,621 | 124,815 | 161,994 |
| Democratic average | 169,121 | 146,732 | 131,194 | 143,785 | 143,525 | 124,508 |
| Republican average | 257,806 | 180,774 | 133,889 | 100,440 | 109,703 | 190,960 |
| **Open Seats** | | | | | | |
| Open-seat average | 543,464 | 439,795 | 543,129 | 465,466 | 431,213 | 361,696 |
| Democratic average | 536,739 | 478,930 | 547,541 | 446,959 | 417,033 | 350,804 |
| Republican average | 550,322 | 398,797 | 538,037 | 484,684 | 446,775 | 372,589 |

**SENATE:**

| | 1994 | 1992 | 1990 | 1988 | 1986 | 1984 |
|---|---|---|---|---|---|---|
| **All Candidates** | | | | | | |
| Total expenditures | $270,780,834 | $199,512,653 | $173,674,925 | $184,977,565 | $189,676,464 | $141,962,276 |
| Average expenditure | 3,868,298 | 2,891,488 | 2,592,163 | 2,802,690 | 2,789,360 | 2,327,250 |
| Democratic average | 3,318,508 | 2,819,654 | 2,468,527 | 2,938,533 | 2,377,390 | 2,160,637 |
| Republican average | 4,418,087 | 2,965,434 | 2,719,546 | 2,666,848 | 3,201,329 | 2,499,417 |
| **Incumbents** | | | | | | |
| Incumbent average | 4,581,199 | 3,850,323 | 3,582,136 | 3,748,126 | 3,307,430 | 2,539,929 |
| Democratic average | 5,025,825 | 2,847,515 | 3,618,244 | 3,457,145 | 2,712,796 | 1,755,004 |
| Republican average | 3,869,798 | 5,103,833 | 3,541,212 | 4,111,852 | 3,604,747 | 3,128,622 |
| **Challengers** | | | | | | |
| Challenger average | 3,803,230 | 1,826,251 | 1,705,098 | 1,820,058 | 1,976,286 | 1,241,434 |
| Democratic average | 1,242,484 | 2,546,025 | 1,401,259 | 2,160,770 | 2,026,641 | 1,515,412 |
| Republican average | 5,403,697 | 1,209,301 | 1,988,680 | 1,547,489 | 1,875,575 | 830,466 |
| **Open Seats** | | | | | | |
| Open-seat average | 2,932,537 | 3,004,464 | 1,599,792 | 2,886,383 | 3,358,295 | 4,976,051 |
| Democratic average | 2,589,970 | 3,177,861 | 934,046 | 3,197,528 | 2,848,080 | 5,797,131 |
| Republican average | 3,275,104 | 2,831,067 | 2,265,538 | 2,575,237 | 3,868,511 | 4,154,971 |

[*] Includes independent Bernard Sanders, VT.
**Note:** Averages calculated using a mean. Includes expenditures for the primary and general election by general election candidates.

# Number of Candidates in the House Who Spent: $200,000; $500,000; or $1,000,000,  1984-1994

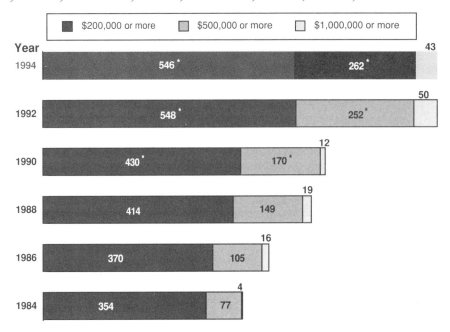

| ■ $200,000 or more | ■ $500,000 or more | □ $1,000,000 or more |

**Year**

- **1994:** 546* | 262* | 43
- **1992:** 548* | 252* | 50
- **1990:** 430* | 170* | 12
- **1988:** 414 | 149 | 19
- **1986:** 370 | 105 | 16
- **1984:** 354 | 77 | 4

# Number of House Incumbents, Challengers and Open-Seat Candidates Spending: $200,000; $500,000; or $1,000,000 in 1990 and 1994

|  | $200,000 or more | | $500,000 or more | | $1,000,000 or more | |
|---|---|---|---|---|---|---|
|  | 1994 | 1990 | 1994 | 1990 | 1994 | 1990 |
| **Incumbents** | | | | | | |
| Democratic | 204 | 195 | 113 | 76 | 28 | 7 |
| Republican | 130 | 124 | 56 | 48 | 4 | 2 |
| **Challengers** | | | | | | |
| Democratic | 34 | 24 | 6 | 5 | 1 | 1 |
| Republican | 84 | 36 | 35 | 12 | 6 | 0 |
| **Open Seats** | | | | | | |
| Democratic | 47 | 26 | 23 | 15 | 3 | 1 |
| Republican | 46 | 24 | 28 | 13 | 1 | 1 |

**Expenditures of House Challengers Who Won, 1984-1994**

**(average net dollars)**

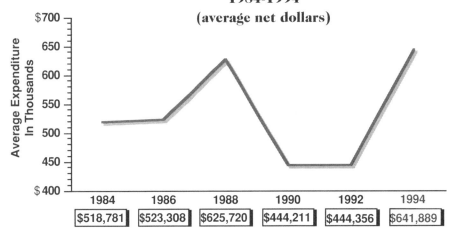

| 1984 | 1986 | 1988 | 1990 | 1992 | 1994 |
|---|---|---|---|---|---|
| $518,781 | $523,308 | $625,720 | $444,211 | $444,356 | $641,889 |

\* Includes independent Bernard Sanders, VT.

**Note:** Averages calculated using a mean. Includes expenditures for the primary and general election by general election candidates.

# House Expenditures by Election Margin, 1994
## *(average net dollars)*

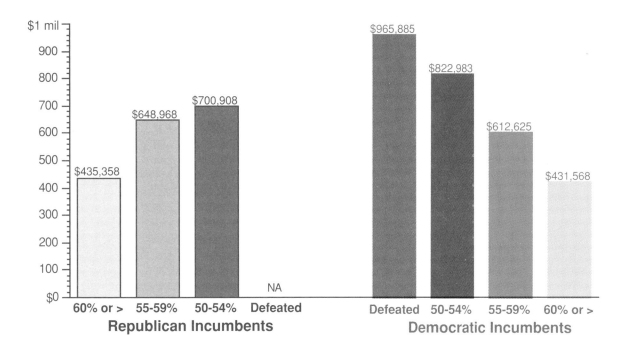

**Republican Incumbents**

- 60% or > : $435,358
- 55-59% : $648,968
- 50-54% : $700,908
- Defeated : NA

**Democratic Incumbents**

- Defeated : $965,885
- 50-54% : $822,983
- 55-59% : $612,625
- 60% or > : $431,568

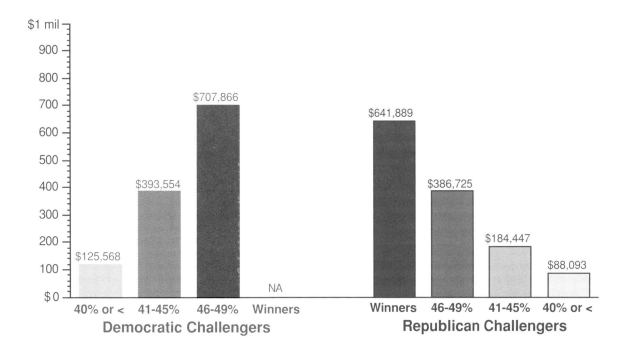

**Democratic Challengers**

- 40% or < : $125,568
- 41-45% : $393,554
- 46-49% : $707,866
- Winners : NA

**Republican Challengers**

- Winners : $641,889
- 46-49% : $386,725
- 41-45% : $184,447
- 40% or < : $88,093

NA = Not Applicable
**Note:** Averages calculated using a mean. Includes expenditures for the primary and general election by general election candidates.
**Source:** Data provided by the Rockefeller Institute of Government.

# Expenditures of Incumbents and Challengers by Election Outcome, 1984-1994
*(average net dollars)*

**HOUSE:**

| | 1994 | 1992 | 1990 | 1988 | 1986 | 1984 |
|---|---|---|---|---|---|---|
| **Incumbent won with more than 60%*** | | | | | | |
| Democratic Incumbent | $431,568 | $494,885 | $374,552 | $343,772 | $280,029 | $219,506 |
| Republican Challenger | 88,093 | 93,346 | 70,109 | 75,553 | 106,062 | 69,693 |
| | | | | | | |
| Republican Incumbent | 435,358 | 485,010 | 342,200 | 359,697 | 265,544 | 250,945 |
| Democratic Challenger | 125,568 | 79,808 | 43,088 | 87,597 | 72,459 | 73,835 |
| **Incumbent won with less than 60%** | | | | | | |
| Democratic Incumbent | 711,794 | 835,238 | 640,623 | 691,035 | 494,098 | 421,834 |
| Republican Challenger | 281,833 | 284,831 | 273,237 | 341,951 | 297,775 | 285,401 |
| | | | | | | |
| Republican Incumbent | 660,098 | 698,912 | 580,499 | 712,765 | 663,042 | 495,455 |
| Democratic Challenger | 460,907 | 275,058 | 213,907 | 445,871 | 354,759 | 386,819 |
| **Incumbent was defeated** | | | | | | |
| Democratic Incumbent | 965,885 | 950,861 | 589,795 | 935,494 | 528,101 | 483,204 |
| Republican Challenger | 641,889 | 487,033 | 334,444 | 349,438 | 326,375 | 577,044 |
| | | | | | | |
| Republican Incumbent | NA | 753,505 | 732,812 | 969,806 | 568,946 | 375,824 |
| Democratic Challenger | NA | 351,898 | 526,537 | 809,908 | 562,694 | 329,427 |

**SENATE:**

| | 1994 | 1992 | 1990 | 1988 | 1986 | 1984 |
|---|---|---|---|---|---|---|
| **Incumbent won with more than 60%*** | | | | | | |
| Democratic Incumbent | $1,694,421 | $2,662,706 | $2,441,681 | $2,355,863 | $1,722,633 | $1,620,869 |
| Republican Challenger | 152,447 | 767,720 | 1,253,086 | 469,702 | 209,065 | 508,264 |
| | | | | | | |
| Republican Incumbent | 4,408,974 | 2,781,370 | 2,180,738 | 3,619,881 | 2,346,358 | 1,606,604 |
| Democratic Challenger | 1,335,096 | 600,946 | 449,666 | 835,294 | 155,853 | 322,263 |
| **Incumbent won with less than 60%** | | | | | | |
| Democratic Incumbent | 5,860,581 | 2,829,340 | 5,299,049 | 6,829,053 | 6,178,367 | 1,833,432 |
| Republican Challenger | 6,614,861 | 1,158,645 | 2,829,360 | 4,360,469 | 6,219,961 | 996,804 |
| | | | | | | |
| Republican Incumbent | 2,611,717 | 6,307,257 | 5,252,478 | 5,641,766 | 4,233,941 | 8,068,429 |
| Democratic Challenger | 1,026,390 | 3,017,307 | 2,927,948 | 3,209,075 | 2,283,767 | 4,028,715 |
| **Incumbent was defeated** | | | | | | |
| Democratic Incumbent | 5,431,777 | 3,715,500 | NA | 1,338,622 | NA | 2,380,239 |
| Republican Challenger | 6,619,164 | 3,076,938 | NA | 1,075,631 | NA | 1,776,128 |
| | | | | | | |
| Republican Incumbent | NA | 6,138,484 | 7,229,154 | 2,993,042 | 3,842,246 | 4,090,013 |
| Democratic Challenger | NA | 5,022,338 | 1,380,560 | 2,996,572 | 2,919,779 | 3,711,199 |

\* Percentage of vote received by the two leading candidates.

NA = Not Applicable

**Note:**     Averages calculated using a mean. Includes expenditures for the primary and general election by general election candidates.

# Expenditures of Open House and Senate Seats by Election Outcome, 1984-1994
## *(average net dollars)*

**HOUSE:**

|  | 1994 | 1992 | 1990 | 1988 | 1986 | 1984 |
|---|---|---|---|---|---|---|
| Democratic, won with 60% or more | $522,734 | $394,815 | $534,671 | $397,458 | $545,144 | $290,693 |
| Republican, lost | 56,708 | 115,532 | 306,472 | 99,363 | 150,100 | 136,668 |
|  |  |  |  |  |  |  |
| Democratic, won with less than 60% | 681,479 | 659,396 | 652,727 | 737,714 | 503,662 | 511,049 |
| Republican, lost | 653,538 | 447,588 | 507,989 | 693,525 | 426,255 | 248,180 |
|  |  |  |  |  |  |  |
| Republican, won with 60% or more | 593,080 | 881,581 | 807,721 | 832,787 | 622,267 | 422,366 |
| Democratic, lost | 409,743 | 291,258 | 562,183 | 278,276 | 190,574 | 116,232 |
|  |  |  |  |  |  |  |
| Republican, won with less than 60% | 504,431 | 451,637 | 578,230 | 607,450 | 515,478 | 455,736 |
| Democratic, lost | 573,528 | 476,583 | 436,366 | 506,283 | 458,474 | 393,262 |

**SENATE:**

|  | 1994 | 1992 | 1990 | 1988 | 1986 | 1984 |
|---|---|---|---|---|---|---|
| Democratic, won with 60% or more | NA | $1,124,512 | NA | $2,881,666 | $2,057,422 | $3,180,975 |
| Republican, lost | NA | 498,107 | NA | 282,229 | 1,699,175 | 1,777,581 |
|  |  |  |  |  |  |  |
| Democratic, won with less than 60% | NA | 5,015,484 | NA | 7,491,600 | 3,242,445 | NA |
| Republican, lost | NA | 3,827,641 | NA | 2,908,101 | 2,580,921 | NA |
|  |  |  |  |  |  |  |
| Republican, won with 60% or more | $2,664,339 | NA | $1,536,352 | 876,877 | 2,408,766 | 7,063,519 |
| Democratic, lost | 2,708,969 | NA | 432,613 | 549,908 | 531,698 | 2,666,291 |
|  |  |  |  |  |  |  |
| Republican, won with less than 60% | 3,763,717 | 2,279,956 | 3,723,911 | 3,812,824 | 5,376,255 | 9,509,724 |
| Democratic, lost | 2,746,885 | 1,412,146 | 1,936,914 | 2,753,999 | 4,377,661 | 5,880,512 |

NA = Not Applicable
**Note:** Averages calculated using a mean.

# Money Raised and Where It Came From

| | Net Receipts (in millions) | | Individual Contributions | | PAC/Other Committee Contributions | | Candidate Contributions | | Candidate Loans | | Other Loans | |
|---|---|---|---|---|---|---|---|---|---|---|---|---|
| | 1994 | 1990 | 1994 | 1990 | 1994 | 1990 | 1994 | 1990 | 1994 | 1990 | 1994 | 1990 |
| **HOUSE:** | $344.8 | $249.5 | 52% | 45% | 37% | 41% | 1% | 1% | 7% | 5% | *% | *% |
| **Democratic** | 185.2 | 143.3 | 45 | 40 | 46 | 48 | 1 | * | 5 | 5 | * | * |
| Incumbents | 137.2 | 111.9 | 43 | 38 | 51 | 53 | * | * | 1 | 2 | * | * |
| Challengers | 20.4 | 14.6 | 50 | 47 | 25 | 29 | 4 | 3 | 16 | 15 | * | * |
| Open Seats | 27.6 | 16.9 | 51 | 44 | 31 | 34 | 1 | 1 | 14 | 16 | * | 1 |
| **Republican** | 159.6 | 106.2 | 60 | 52 | 31 | 33 | 1 | 2 | 9 | 6 | * | * |
| Incumbents | 80.5 | 70.0 | 59 | 51 | 36 | 41 | * | * | 1 | * | * | * |
| Challengers | 51.1 | 22.3 | 62 | 55 | 11 | 10 | 5 | 9 | 17 | 16 | * | 1 |
| Open Seats | 28.0 | 13.9 | 58 | 56 | 22 | 28 | 1 | * | 15 | 15 | * | 0 |
| **SENATE:** | $263.1 | 178.2 | 59 | 65 | 16 | 23 | 8 | 1 | 12 | 4 | * | 1 |
| **Democratic** | 111.7 | 85.6 | 60 | 67 | 19 | 23 | 6 | 2 | 9 | 3 | 1 | 1 |
| Incumbents | 78.5 | 63.5 | 59 | 68 | 20 | 26 | 8 | 0 | 6 | 0 | 1 | 0 |
| Challengers | 10.2 | 19.3 | 45 | 64 | 15 | 14 | 1 | 8 | 35 | 8 | * | 4 |
| Open Seats | 23.1 | 2.8 | 68 | 55 | 20 | 19 | * | 1 | 3 | 22 | * | 1 |
| **Republican** | 151.4 | 92.6 | 58 | 64 | 13 | 23 | 10 | * | 15 | 5 | * | * |
| Incumbents | 33.0 | 55.2 | 67 | 69 | 27 | 23 | * | 0 | * | 0 | * | * |
| Challengers | 87.4 | 30.0 | 51 | 57 | 3 | 18 | 18 | 1 | 26 | 16 | * | 1 |
| Open Seats | 30.9 | 7.4 | 69 | 46 | 24 | 38 | * | 0 | 1 | 0 | * | 0 |

\* less than 0.5%

**Note:** Major party candidates only. For 1990, the PAC/Other committee contribution figures refer to monies contributed to campaigns as reported by the PAC's making contributions. However, for 1994 these figures are monies reported by the campaigns that are comprised mostly of PAC funds, but also include monies from other candidate committees and some unregistered entities.

    The percentages do not sum to 100 because not all receipts are listed. These include such items as contributions from parties, transfers from other candidate committees, interest earned on campaign funds and deposits on items including phone banks where deposits are returned to the candidate when services are canceled.

# Political Party Contributions and Expenditures for Congress, 1984-1994
## Through 20 days prior to the General Election

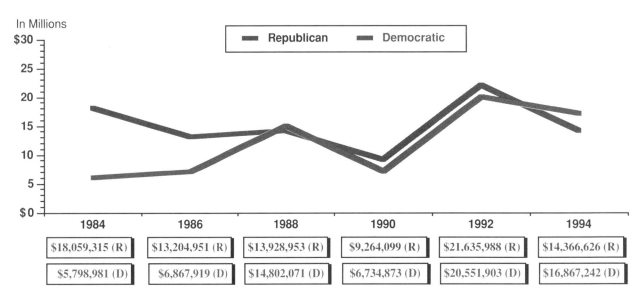

# Political Action Committee
# Contributions to Congressional Candidates
## Through September 30

| | Total Contributions | | Labor Contributions | | Corporate Contributions | | Trade/ Membership/ Health Contributions | | Non- Connected Contributions | | Other Contributions | |
|---|---|---|---|---|---|---|---|---|---|---|---|---|
| | 1994 | 1990 | 1994 | 1990 | 1994 | 1990 | 1994 | 1990 | 1994 | 1990 | 1994 | 1990 |
| **HOUSE:** | | | | | | | | | | | | |
| **Amount Contributed** (in millions of dollars) | $96.9 | $86.9 | $24.5 | $21.9 | $33.0 | $29.1 | $28.3 | $26.5 | $7.4 | $5.8 | $3.6 | $3.4 |
| **Percent Distribution** | | | | | | | | | | | | |
| **Incumbents** | | | | | | | | | | | | |
| Democratic | 60% | 60% | 75% | 75% | 56% | 53% | 54% | 56% | 55% | 55% | 65% | 65% |
| Republican | 26 | 29 | 4 | 6 | 36 | 40 | 33 | 35 | 22 | 25 | 27 | 29 |
| **Challengers** | | | | | | | | | | | | |
| Democratic | 4 | 3 | 10 | 10 | 1 | * | 2 | 1 | 4 | 5 | 1 | 1 |
| Republican | 2 | 2 | * | * | 3 | 2 | 3 | 2 | 7 | 4 | 2 | 2 |
| **Open Seats** | | | | | | | | | | | | |
| Democratic | 5 | 4 | 11 | 9 | 2 | 2 | 4 | 3 | 7 | 8 | 3 | 2 |
| Republican | 3 | 2 | * | * | 3 | 3 | 4 | 3 | 6 | 3 | 3 | 2 |

| | Total Contributions | | Labor Contributions | | Corporate Contributions | | Trade/ Membership/ Health Contributions | | Non- Connected Contributions | | Other Contributions | |
|---|---|---|---|---|---|---|---|---|---|---|---|---|
| | 1994 | 1990 | 1994 | 1990 | 1994 | 1990 | 1994 | 1990 | 1994 | 1990 | 1994 | 1990 |
| **SENATE:** | | | | | | | | | | | | |
| **Amount Contributed** (in millions of dollars) | $34.6 | $35.5 | $5.3 | $5.1 | $15.5 | $15.6 | $8.5 | $8.7 | $4.1 | $4.8 | $1.3 | $1.3 |
| **Precent Distribution** | | | | | | | | | | | | |
| **Incumbents** | | | | | | | | | | | | |
| Democratic | 40% | 43% | 56% | 64% | 34% | 34% | 37% | 38% | 42% | 54% | 49% | 52% |
| Republican | 29 | 32 | 3 | 6 | 36 | 40 | 35 | 36 | 27 | 24 | 27 | 29 |
| **Challengers** | | | | | | | | | | | | |
| Democratic | 4 | 6 | 20 | 25 | * | 1 | 1 | 4 | 2 | 7 | * | 3 |
| Republican | 5 | 12 | * | 1 | 6 | 17 | 5 | 13 | 7 | 7 | 4 | 10 |
| **Open Seats** | | | | | | | | | | | | |
| Democratic | 9 | 1 | 21 | 4 | 5 | * | 6 | 1 | 11 | 3 | 9 | * |
| Republican | 14 | 7 | * | * | 18 | 8 | 16 | 9 | 11 | 6 | 10 | 6 |

* Less than 0.5%

**Note:** For 1990, financial figures are for all contributions in the two-year election cycle as of September 30. For 1994, financial figures are for most contributions in the two-year election cycle as of September 30. As we went to print not all data through September 30, 1994 were available, however, we do not expect the distributions reported here will vary substantially from the final figures through September. Those in the "other" category refer to cooperatives and corporations without stock.

# Independent Expenditures for Congressional Elections, 1984-1994

## *(net dollars)*

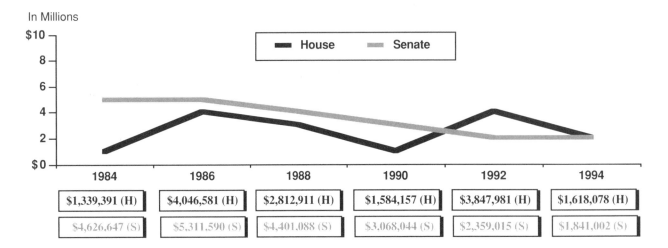

In Millions

| | 1984 | 1986 | 1988 | 1990 | 1992 | 1994 |
|---|---|---|---|---|---|---|
| | $1,339,391 (H) | $4,046,581 (H) | $2,812,911 (H) | $1,584,157 (H) | $3,847,981 (H) | $1,618,078 (H) |
| | $4,626,647 (S) | $5,311,590 (S) | $4,401,088 (S) | $3,068,044 (S) | $2,359,015 (S) | $1,841,002 (S) |

| | 1994 | | 1992 | | 1990 | |
|---|---|---|---|---|---|---|
| | **House** | **Senate** | **House** | **Senate** | **House** | **Senate** |
| **Total** | $1,618,078 | $1,841,002 | $3,847,981 | $2,359,015 | $1,584,157 | $3,068,044 |
| For Democrats | 429,933 | 164,896 | 1,393,989 | 1,129,490 | 709,292 | 780,832 |
| Against Democrats | 489,197 | 209,796 | 421,826 | 155,179 | 130,695 | 266,230 |
| For Republicans | 668,052 | 1,159,686 | 1,577,109 | 865,014 | 669,726 | 1,436,553 |
| Against Republicans | 30,896 | 306,624 | 455,057 | 209,332 | 74,444 | 584,429 |

| | 1988 | | 1986 | | 1984 | |
|---|---|---|---|---|---|---|
| | **House** | **Senate** | **House** | **Senate** | **House** | **Senate** |
| **Total** | $2,812,911 | $4,401,088 | $4,046,581 | $5,311,590 | $1,339,391 | $4,626,647 |
| For Democrats | 1,465,554 | 831,064 | 2,385,685 | 988,382 | 560,727 | 326,031 |
| Against Democrats | 278,723 | 617,066 | 227,286 | 632,412 | 118,171 | 410,428 |
| For Republicans | 919,929 | 2,809,517 | 1,313,578 | 3,342,790 | 633,646 | 1,807,981 |
| Against Republicans | 148,705 | 143,441 | 120,032 | 348,006 | 26,847 | 2,082,207 |

**Note:**  An independent expenditure is an expenditure by a person advocating the election or defeat of a candidate that is not made in conjunction with the candidate or his/her election committee. Independent expenditures are for all those reported as of November 6, 1994.

# Chapter 8
## "How I Won:"
### Conversations with
### Congressman John Hostettler (R-IN) and
### Congressman Tim Holden (D-PA)

Voters in 1994 expressed their displeasure with business as usual in the nation's capital. Fear of an angry electorate had rendered the Republicans—for the first time this century—the party with the most uncontested House seats on election day. And when the voters were actually given the chance to speak, the Democratic advantage of 78 seats in the House vanished, and the party of Lincoln held a 26 seat edge. A number of longtime Democratic incumbents found themselves out of a job on November 9, while others, many of whom had never before sought elective office, spent the latter part of the month preparing to begin work in Washington. Still, the majority of Democratic incumbents were successful in their bids for re-election and the Democratic party goes into the new year with control of more than 200 seats in the House.

Many of the 1994 congressional races received national attention, including Tom Foley's in Washington and Dan Rostenkowski's in Illinois. The loss suffered by both of these long-time incumbents will be studied by political scientists and election analysts for years to come. But many other races, while farther from the national spotlight, are equally instructive for studying the American electorate. We offer two examples here.

In the eighth congressional district in Indiana, the Republican challenger, engineer-turned-candidate John Hostettler, was successful in his first bid for political office, defeating Frank McCloskey by a margin of 52 to 48%. McCloskey, the incumbent Democrat, had represented the district since 1982.

In Pennsylvania, Democratic Congressman Tim Holden won a second term as the state's representative from the sixth district. Holden managed to hold on to his seat when he defeated Republican challenger Fred Levering by a healthy fourteen-point margin.

What follows are interviews conducted shortly after election day with each of these congressional representatives—one who rode the Republican tide and one who stood against it. The perspectives of these partisans on the 1994 election speak far beyond their own congressional districts and provide important insight into understanding the substance and meaning of the voters' behavior as they rendered their verdict on the 103rd Congress.

—John M. Barry and Regina M. Dougherty

# Interview with John Hostettler, Republican Congressman, Eighth Congressional District, State of Indiana

**America at The Polls:** Frank McCloskey has been involved in politics in the 8th congressional district for quite some time, first as mayor of Bloomington and then as congressman for more than ten years. He ran in a number of very close races but always seemed able to ride the tide and come out on top. In 1994, he wasn't so fortunate. On November 8, the voters of the 8th district elected *you* to be their congressional representative. Was your victory just another in the Republican tide that seems to have swept the country this year, or was your victory really more related to local issues and to people who wanted to see change?

**John Hostettler:** I think the notion of the Republican tide is a little over-emphasized because, as you know, we still have over 200 Democrats in the House. I think what really happened was that we had districts where there were notably conservative candidates challenging historically liberal incumbents. I know this was the case in our 8th district. I think voters were sending a message to Washington and to the White House that principles of liberalism are not well received in America—that they have failed us greatly. In our district, we gave a clear and distinct alternative to the liberal policies of Frank McCloskey, and emphasized a much more conservative message and philosophy. Throughout the campaign we offered our conservative agenda as a distinct alternative. We also wanted to be perceived as the outsider, coming in to reorganize the congress as an institution of integrity, an institution that can be trusted. That was the message that the folks in the 8th district sent to Washington.

**AATP:** Your district has historically supported more Democratic candidates than Republicans. Along comes a Republican candidate, who has the endorsement of some very conservative groups, and he wins! How do you explain that?

**JH:** The 8th district is, as a matter of fact, a very conservative district. Even on the Indiana University campus—a traditionally liberal stronghold—we found more conservatives this year. We did fairly well there. I am not sure that conservatives will overcome the liberal majority there but they are much stronger than they have been in the past 14-16 years. As far as the district is concerned, it is conservative, and although Congressman McCloskey has won in the past six elections, we did succeed in challenging his voting record. Through our excellent organization we got his voting record out and gave the voters a distinct

alternative. They chose the conservative message over the liberal message.

**AATP:** Did Mr. McCloskey's association with the Clinton administration and Clinton policies hurt him this year?

**JH:** I think it hurt him significantly. He was bold in his support of President Clinton and his policies. He voted for the tax increase of 1993 and for a crime bill that not only included a great number of "pork barrel" projects but also a gun ban. The semi-automatic rifle ban did not go over well in an area that is very supportive of the Second Amendment. He was also hurt by his support of the Clinton position on the issue of homosexuals in the military. Previously these kinds of bills would never have made it past the President's desk. Now his liberal agenda was actually manifest in legislation. The folks in the 8th district were able to make that determination, and they chose not to go the liberal route.

**AATP:** How would you summarize your message to the voters?

**JH:** My message is one of very limited government, self-determination and much more locally concentrated decision making. It is one that says Washington doesn't have all the answers, and that we are not going to solve the problems of our country by throwing more tax dollars around. The answers are local—that is the message we put out. The second point of our message is that we need to restore integrity and trust in our government. We had a congressman who some years ago had bounced 65 House bank checks. While there were other members of congress with similar problems, he was then one of only five members to vote to not disclose the records of the House bank. I think the bounced checks issue didn't hurt him so much as the fact that he voted to cover it up. There was a definite perception of lack of integrity in government. We offered to help restore that.

**AATP:** Are there one or two issues in the 8th district that you think were better addressed by you than by Frank McCloskey?

**JH:** The overriding themes were liberalism versus conservatism, big government versus small government. If there were specific issues that did not play well in this district, they were higher taxes and gun control. On the issue of higher taxes, people are increasingly anxious about the need to keep more of what they earn. We have better control over what we can afford to spend than the federal government has. On gun control, people in my district who like their Second Amendment rights as much as I do, didn't like those rights trodden upon by the Brady bill. Even though Indiana has a longer waiting period for gun purchase than is required by the federal government, we still saw that bill as an intrusion of the federal government into states' rights. Many of the counties with traditionally strong-willed labor constituencies take their Second Amendment rights very seriously. These have traditionally been Democratic voters, but they joined the Republican camp this year. That surprised a lot of people, including me.

**AATP:** Can you tell me about campaign spending?

**JH:** We were out-spent by about 1 1/2 to 1. Congressman McCloskey poured a lot of money into overhead while we prudently made very wise use of our money. He was able to start five weeks out and we, only four, but through a tremendous network of volunteers, we were able to channel our money not into consultants' fees or hired staff salaries, but into actual media programs to get our message out. This is the only way to defeat a 12-year incumbent. We were out-spent, but our spending was more effective.

**AATP:** But the source of your money was very different, wasn't it?

**JH:** Yes. We were able to raise about $290,000 from individuals. We received no special interest PAC money. We did receive some money from the Republican National Committee and the state Republican party but most of our support came from individual contributions. We had a lot of people who thought we couldn't run a campaign without PAC money. As a matter of fact, Frank McCloskey in the past decade has taken more special interest PAC money from labor unions

than any other legislator in the nation, so the Democrats naturally felt that we could not win without PAC money. I just decided in the primary that I wasn't going to take any special interest PAC money for this election, and that we were going to ask the people to help us in our campaign. I could not be everywhere, but there were so many people working for me—and they had a goal. Like our peer base, the Republican county structure was also very strong. Both were key to our victory.

**AATP:** Did turnout play any role at all in your victory?

**JH:** I believe so. I know that some people went out to vote for the first time in 16-20 years. As a matter of fact, I know one lady who voted for the first time in 70 years, so I think that while the turnout was not heavy it was a little bit better than in other off-year elections. I think that the people who came out and voted, voted for the alternative to the liberal policies that Mr. McCloskey represented. I think that we were able to win over conservative Democrats as well in this election.

**AATP:** David Wilhelm, the chairman of the Democratic National Committee, called you one of the principal candidates of the radical right, while McCloskey's voting record would rank him among the most liberal of Indiana's congressional delegation. Did the voters perceive this as a contest of liberalism versus conservatism?

**JH:** I believe so. Because of the extent to which Frank McCloskey was actually on the left, it was necessary for the national Democratic party machinery to portray me as equally far on the right—to demonize me and to cause some moderate to liberal Republicans to have concern. It obviously didn't work. We found out early on in the campaign that our Republican base was secure. The attempt by the opposition to label me part of the so-called "radical right" didn't work. I think that the voters saw through that, especially the Republicans, and then later, the conservative Democrats. It was a strat-

egy which they saw as necessary, because we said from the beginning that we were going to expose Frank McCloskey's liberal voting record. Because I did not have a voting record to attack, they had to demonize me in another way. If you examine the rest of the candidates there on the so-called "top 10 hit list," you'll find their opponents similarly liberal, I believe.

**AATP:** You came from outside the political world. Did you have any trouble defining a political persona?

**JH:** I would say to some extent I did actually, because I had never held political office—had never even run for a political office. People did not know about my political beliefs. They learned a lot of that initially from what other people were saying—for example, from David Wilhelm and those folks. But after our organization was established we had over a thousand volunteers in the district who were putting out our message as well. So between the media, my presentations, and the organization, we were able to put the picture before the voters that this is a conservative candidate who wants a smaller federal government, who believes that Washington has some problems and who wants to go there to help change those things. You know, I have three small children, and I mentioned this in every presentation I gave, saying that if I go to Washington and become part of the problem I am trying to solve then *my* children's future is in trouble. So I think that the people understood that I was looking to the future, and not just to the next election.

**AATP:** It sounds as if the role-of-government question was really central to the race between McCloskey and Hostettler. Is that right?

**JH:** Exactly. I think the public's perception is that a huge federal bureaucracy is not going to solve our problems. We have had over 30 years of the "great society." People can see what's happening around them and they can definitely see that what's coming out of Washington is not solving that problem. People are desirous to have decision-making put back in their hands and that's what we want to do. I am so glad to hear folks like Newt Gingrich talking about that: We are going to empower citizens, and they will once again determine where they want that power to reside—with the federal government, with the states, or in local communities.

**AATP:** Two years ago, Indiana had seven Democratic representatives and three Republicans. On November 8, the balance shifted, so that now the Republicans have the advantage, with six seats to the Democrats' four. That is a dramatic six-seat swing in the state of Indiana. What do you think the voters of Indiana were saying?

**JH:** They were speaking out against the liberalism of the White House. The people of Indiana were voting for a conservative voice to answer the liberal voice of the Clinton administration. And listen to what you're already hearing from the Democratic party, from President Clinton and the newly elected party leaders. For some reason, families and family values are now a priority for them, and they are going to try to come up with big-government solutions to problems facing families. I don't think they are going to work, but the word that they keep repeating over and over again is "families." I think that voters of Indiana said that the best way we can empower families is to get the federal government off their backs, to allow them to keep more of what they earn, and to allow the private sector to expand and employ the bread winners. That is the message that came from Indiana and from all over the country.

---

### INDIANA'S EIGHTH DISTRICT
### And The Winner is... Hostettler

**The People:** Population 1990: 554,347; 42% rural; 14% age 65+; 96% White; 3% Black; 1% Asian; 1% Hispanic origin. Voting age population: 421,666; 3% Black. Households: 58% married couple families; 27% married couple families with children; 37% college educated; median household income: $25,242; per capita income: $12,153; median gross rent: $341; median house value: $48,800.

| 1992 Presidential Vote | | 1988 Presidential Vote | |
|---|---|---|---|
| Clinton (D) | 103,844 (42%) | Bush (R) | 129,324 (57%) |
| Bush (R) | 97,062 (40%) | Dukakis (D) | 98,539 (43%) |
| Perot (I) | 43,177 (18%) | | |

**Election Results**

| 1994 General | John Hostettler (R) | 93,167 (52%) |
|---|---|---|
| | Francis X. McCloskey (D) | 84,751 (48%) |
| 1992 General | Francis X. McCloskey (D) | 125,244 (53%) |
| | Richard Mourdock (R) | 108,054 (45%) |
| | Others | 5,099 (2%) |

Source: Almanac of American Politics, 1993-94, *Congressional Quarterly*, November 12, 1994.

# Interview with Tim Holden, Democratic Congressman, Sixth Congressional District, State of Pennsylvania

**AATP**: Looking back to your victory in 1992, by most indicators your district should have gone Republican. Bush beat Clinton in the district and Dick Thornburgh carried it in his losing bid for the Senate. This time around, the tide was even less favorable for Democrats in the Keystone state—your district chose Republican Rick Santorum for Senate and Tom Ridge for Governor. In an election where many Democrats did not fare well, you beat your Republican challenger handily. In general, what do you think accounted for your win this year?

**Tim Holden**: You're absolutely right about the performance of the district—its Democratic performance has been poor as far back as we can trace it. I think Lyndon Johnson was the last Democratic Presidential candidate to win it. Now, how do I account for the win? Well, I think we had a good message—one that was about staying in touch with the district and about independence. I've made it a point to go home every weekend during the past two years, so I've kept in touch with my constituency and been accessible. Also, being independent—having a voting record that showed an independent streak—helped us fight off the swing that was coming. Now, we also had some fortunate breaks, too. The first person that was going to run against me—the poor guy had a nervous breakdown. As a result, there was a period of about four to six weeks where I didn't have an opponent. There were four Republicans fighting for it. So the opposition got a late start.

**AATP**: What about the role of campaign spending in your election?

**TH**: I out-spent my opponent by a margin of about two-to-one, but two years ago, I was out-spent two-to-one. I mean, you need money to be competitive, but there comes a point in time when you're spending too much. You know, I have $17,000 left. I probably should have $50,000 left. I spent money on things at the end that I really didn't have to. But I had it, and I didn't want to take any chances. Obviously, you need a certain amount of money to be competitive, and I think in my district, that's around $175,000.

**AATP**: Your district has been described as "culturally conservative." If that's so, how did you manage to escape the "liberal Democrat" label?

**TH**: How do I escape the liberal label? By not being liberal. I vote very conservatively. I think I probably have the most conservative voting record in the Pennsylvania Democratic delegation, and probably more conservative than Joe McDade and Tom Ridge.

**AATP**: You appear to vote more conservatively than most Northeastern Democrats.

**TH**: Yes. And a lot of Republicans, too.

**AATP**: Some have characterized the results of congressional voting this year as a backlash against traditional liberal values. Would you agree?

**TH**: Absolutely. People do see things in government that upset them. And I think the Republicans did an excellent job of painting Democrats as being a party of the giveaway programs of the past. And there's no doubt that we deserve some of that. But there's a lot of things that we need to hold onto to help working families. Social programs are easy to attack because of waste and abuse, but if you look at the other end of it, there are people that really need to be taken care of.

**AATP**: As far as you can see, are traditional, liberal Democrats a dying breed? And if so, what should the Democratic party do about it?

**TH**: The President ran as a moderate Democrat. But he's not serving as a moderate Democrat. I think that the President has catered to the liberal wing of our party. You know, a lot of these men and women are my friends, but the country has moved to the center, and maybe even right of center. And the Democratic party will not, in my opinion, gain the majority back in the House if it continues to espouse liberal values. We have to send out a middle-of-the-road message, we have to govern for the middle-of-the-road. I think the middle ground is where most of the country is and I think that the leaders of the Republican party right now are far, far right of center. I don't think that's where the country wants to be. The problem is that Democrats are painted as being too far to the left. So I think that what we have to do is move to the middle, and when we gain control again, we have to govern from the middle. We can't go back to taking on issues such as gays in the military and some of the other things that we just got painted with.

**AATP**: Governing from the middle presumably means the Democrats leave some issues behind and concentrate on others. Can you be specific?

**TH**: The perfect example is the crime bill. I voted for the crime bill, and I believe my margin of victory would have been bigger if I *hadn't*. Just because the guns are in there. If you would have taken the crime bill out—or the guns out of the crime bill —I don't think we would have lost control of the House. That was an issue that middle America cared about. Certainly gays in the military was another issue that was brought up by the administration and by the liberal end of our party, and that certainly didn't sell to the American people. On the other hand, we did so many things to help this economy. I mean, no question—we raised taxes on the wealthiest Americans. But we reduced unemployment. Reduced the deficit by 45%. In the district I represent, unemployment was down in one county from 10.2 to 6.8 and in another county from 6.8 to 4.8. No one talked about that. They talked about gays and guns, really. We shouldn't take on issues that are outside of the mainstream. We need to emphasize economic issues, continue to reduce the deficit, and things like that.

The Democratic party has to help the middle class. I'm not saying we can necessarily have a middle-class tax cut unless we find a way to pay for it that's not going to put the burden back on the middle class or the elderly. But I think we can do things to help education—we can invest in education for middle-class kids. If we take middle-class values, such as education for middle-class kids, and things like that, I think that will send the right message. Take family medical leave. I mean, I haven't heard anybody complain about that. Things like that will appeal to the majority of Democrats and middle class Republicans as well.

**AATP**: Where does health care fit in?

**TH**: I was not in favor of the President's plan. I was not in favor of Gephardt's plan or Mitchell's plan. I think we should do things in an incremental form. I think if we had taken a moderate approach there, we could have won the American people's backing on health-care reform.

**AATP**: Many Democrats this time around were attacked by their opponents for their association with President Clinton. I understand that your opponent, for example, tried to link you to Clinton on the health-care issue. Overall, did your ties to the President help or hurt you in the sixth district, or wasn't it really a factor in the race?

**TH**: I don't know. I mean, Levering ran commercials calling me "Bill Clinton's boy." But again, I think that we had a message of independence, and every time I had a public forum when he would bring that up I'd say, "Just off the top of my head, here are examples of instances where I disagreed with the President." I had the voting record to back it up. I think my voting percentage with the President was around 62%. So it was easy to fend that off. Well, not easy. But I did have the record to show my independence.

**AATP**: In spite of a national swing toward Republican candidates, there seems to have been a good number of Democrats in Pennsylvania who were able to hold on to their seats. What are the voters of Pennsylvania saying in 1994?

**TH**: I think Pennsylvanians are overall pretty conservative. Even Democratic Pennsylvanians. And I think our congressional delegation reflects it, except for a colleague in Philadelphia and a colleague in Pittsburgh who have more liberal voting records, and have more liberal constituencies. But I think the reason that our delegation didn't lose any numbers is that we had attractive candidates who had either a conservative voting record or had a platform that was not out-of-touch with the mainstream. They were not too far off to the left.

**AATP**: And at the national level: were the American people trying to send a message to the President and to Congress?

**TH**: People were trying to send a message about what they would like the government to do, and that is, in my opinion, to govern from the middle. Not to be over-intrusive, but not to forget either that you have an obligation to take care of some people. The public's perception was that Democrats were out of touch and too liberal.

**AATP**: The Democrats certainly had the upper hand in the House for a number of years, and now the Republicans are going to get their turn at it. What are you expecting to see?

**TH**: The Democrats sat in the majority for forty years and the Republicans had no responsibility to govern. They could just throw snowballs and say "no" to everything. Now they have the responsibility to govern. They've promised to deliver on the "Contract with America." And I'm going to vote for a lot of things in it. But some of the things I'm not going to vote for. Now the Democrats are going to have an opportunity to point out—from the minority side–what exactly is in that contract. And the Republicans are going to be the ones getting hit with the snowballs on many issues.

**AATP**: When you just mentioned the Contract with America you said there were some things in there you liked, and some things in there that you didn't like. What aspects of the Contract with America do Democrats need to embrace in order to do as you've suggested and move closer to the center? And what things should they still just outright reject?

**TH**: Well, you know, the line-item veto. I think we have to do that. Now forty-eight governors have it. There's no doubt that a lot of bills down here just get padded with pure pork and I think the chief executive should have the ability to line item that out and force us to override the veto to put it back in. I think the welfare reform—we have to do that. It's not working for the taxpayers. It's not even working for the recipients. A lot of the things on legal and tort reform that the Republicans are asking for in the Contract I think are good. We need not only malpractice reform, but we need product liability reform. I think those are things that we need to do.

The balanced budget amendment sounds great. Sounds like motherhood, apple pie and baseball. But how are you going to pay for it? You know, if we say we're going to have a total balanced budget amendment, and if we spend more than we take in, we're going to go into total sequestration of all funds. You're going to hurt veterans, you're going to hurt seniors, you're going to hurt education for kids and I'm not going to be for that.

---

### PENNSYLVANIA'S SIXTH DISTRICT
### And The Winner is... Holden

**The People:** Population 1990: 565,923; 44% rural; 17% age 65+; 92% White; 2% Black; 1% Asian; 2% Other; 3% Hispanic origin. Voting age population: 435,058; 2% Black; 2% Hispanic origin. Households: 59% married couple families; 25% married couple families with children; 28% college educated; median household income: $28,766; per capita income: $13,349; median gross rent: $367; median house value: $65,900.

| **1992 Presidential Vote** | | **1988 Presidential Vote** | |
|---|---|---|---|
| Bush (R) | 90,140 (41%) | Bush (R) | 117,434 (62%) |
| Clinton (D) | 78,776 (36%) | Dukakis (D) | 73,464 (38%) |
| Perot (I) | 50,333 (23% | | |

**Election Results**

| 1994 General | Tim Holden (D) | 89,184 (57%) |
|---|---|---|
| | Fred Levering (R) | 67,308 (43%) |
| 1992 General | Tim Holden (D) | 108,312 (52%) |
| | John E. Jones III (R) | 99,694 (48%) |

Source: Almanac of American Politics, 1993-94, *Congressional Quarterly*, November 12, 1994.

# Contributors

## EDITOR

**Everett C. Ladd** is executive director of the Roper Center(and its host institution, the Institute for Social Inquiry—ISI), and professor of political science at the University of Connecticut.

## PRODUCTION AND DESIGN

**Lynn A. Zayachkiwsky** is administrative assistant to the director, and production manager of Roper Center and ISI publications.

**Melanie Chebro** is administrative assistant at the Roper Center, and associate manager of Roper Center and ISI publications.

**Maud Sabourin** is responsible for machine-readable dataset production and documentation at the Roper Center and ISI.

## SENIOR DATA ANALYSTS

**John M. Barry** is associate director of the Roper Center and ISI.

**G. Donald Ferree, Jr.** is director of Roper Center and ISI polling.

**Marc G. Maynard** is senior research librarian at the Roper Center and ISI, and manages the Center's on-line information system (POLL).

**George Pettinico** is research librarian at the Roper Center and ISI.

**Lois Timms-Ferrara** is senior research librarian at the Roper Center and ISI, and manages the Center's user services department.

**David Wilber** is senior research librarian at the Roper Center and ISI, and assistant managing editor of The Public Perspective.

## DATA ANALYSTS

**Rob Persons** is research librarian at the Roper Center and ISI.

**Marianne Simonoff** is research assistant to the director of the Roper Center.

**Regina M. Dougherty** is a doctoral student in political science at the University of Connecticut, and a graduate assistant at the Roper Center.

**Catherine P. Flavin** is a doctoral student in political science at the University of Connecticut, and a graduate assistant at the Roper Center.

**Jennifer M. Necci** is a doctoral student in political science at the University of Connecticut, and a graduate assistant at the Roper Center.

# ARTICLES AND INTERVIEWS

***Micheline Blum*** is president of Blum & Weprin Associates, a full-service public opinion research company based in Manhattan. She co-founded the firm in 1990. From 1979 to 1989, she was manager of polling and election operations at NBC News, New York .

***Karlyn H. Bowman*** is resident fellow at the American Enterprise Institute for Public Policy Research and edits the Opinion Pulse section of the Institute's magazine, *The American Enterprise*. She writes frequently about American politics, including gender issues.

***John Brennan*** is director of the *Los Angeles Times* Poll, a position he has held since 1991. Before moving to California, he spent seven years at ABC News in New York where he held the position of senior polling associate.

***Thomas E. Cronin*** is a political scientist who serves as president of Whitman College in Walla Walla, Washington. He is author of *Direct Democracy: The Politics of Initiative, Referendum and Recall* (Harvard University Press, 1989) and other books on American politics.

***Claibourne Darden*** is president of Darden Research Corporation, an Atlanta-based polling concern which helps develop political strategy for both Democratic and Republican clients.

***Daryl Harris*** is associate professor of political science at the University of Connecticut. He writes on African-American politics and urban politics.

***Tim Holden*** is a Democratic congressman who has represented the Sixth District in Pennsylvania since 1992.

**John Hostettler** is a first-term Republican congressman from the Eighth District in Indiana.

**Scott Keeter** is associate professor of political science and director of the Commonwealth Poll at Virginia Commonwealth University. He is co-author of *What Americans Know About Politics and Why It Matters* (Yale University Press, forthcoming).

**Michael J. Malbin** is professor of political science at the State University of New York, Albany, and director for the Center for Legislative Studies at SUNY's Rockefeller Institute of Government. He is co-editor of *Limiting Legislative Terms* (Congressional Quarterly, 1992), and co-editor of *Vital Statistics on Congress* (Congressional Quarterly, 1994).

**Lee M. Miringoff** is professor of political science and director of the Marist College Institute for Public Opinion in Poughkeepsie, New York, a post he has held since 1978. He co-authored *The Cuomo Factor: Assessing the Political Appeal of New York's Governor* (Marist Institute for Public Opinion, 1986).

**Jim Norman** is polling editor at *USA Today*, a position he has held since 1987. Before assuming this post, he contributed to the Washington section of the paper and was its original Weather Page editor.

# Vote For The U.S. House Of Representatives, 1994: The Group Story

## Mitofsky International Exit Poll of November 8, 1994

| | Voted Democratic | Voted Republican |
|---|---|---|
| **By Gender** | | |
| Male | 45% | 55% |
| Female | 53 | 47 |
| | | |
| **By Gender/Race** | | |
| White Males | 40 | 60 |
| White Females | 46 | 54 |
| Black Males | 85 | 15 |
| Black Females | 92 | 8 |
| | | |
| **By Gender/Marital Status** | | |
| Married Males | 43 | 57 |
| Married Females | 48 | 52 |
| | | |
| **By Gender/Employment** | | |
| Employed Males | 43 | 57 |
| Employed Females | 56 | 44 |
| | | |
| **By Region** | | |
| Northeast | 54 | 46 |
| Midwest | 45 | 55 |
| South | 46 | 54 |
| West | 55 | 45 |
| | | |
| **By Locality** | | |
| Large Urban | 69 | 31 |
| Small Urban | 52 | 48 |
| Suburban | 46 | 54 |
| Rural | 46 | 54 |
| | | |
| **By Incumbency** | | |
| Democrat Incumbent | 57 | 43 |
| Republican Incumbent | 41 | 59 |
| Democrat Open Seat | 54 | 46 |
| Republican Open Seat | 41 | 59 |
| | | |
| **By Living Standard** | | |
| Getting better | 66 | 34 |
| Getting worse | 35 | 65 |
| Staying about same | 48 | 52 |
| | | |
| **By Vote in the 1992 Presidential Election** | | |
| Bill Clinton | 84 | 16 |
| George Bush | 12 | 88 |
| Ross Perot | 36 | 64 |
| Someone else | 40 | 60 |
| Did not vote for President in 92 | 46 | 54 |

# The Group Story/continued

|  | Voted Democratic | Voted Republican |
|---|---|---|
| **By Age** | | |
| 18-24 | 55 | 45 |
| 25-29 | 46 | 54 |
| 30-39 | 47 | 53 |
| 40-49 | 50 | 50 |
| 50-59 | 48 | 52 |
| 60-69 | 52 | 48 |
| 70 and older | 52 | 48 |
| **By Race/Ethnicity** | | |
| White | 44 | 56 |
| Black | 89 | 11 |
| Hispanic/Latino | 61 | 39 |
| Asian | 53 | 47 |
| **By Party ID** | | |
| Democrat | 88 | 12 |
| Republican | 9 | 91 |
| Other | 45 | 55 |
| **By Ideology** | | |
| Liberal | 83 | 17 |
| Moderate | 58 | 42 |
| Conservative | 21 | 79 |
| **By Clinton Job Approval** | | |
| Approve | 83 | 17 |
| Disapprove | 19 | 81 |
| **By Country Assessment** | | |
| Generally going in the right direction | 73 | 27 |
| Seriously off on the wrong track | 34 | 66 |
| **By Confidence in Government's Ability** | | |
| A Great deal of confidence | 83 | 17 |
| Some confidence | 60 | 40 |
| Little or no confidence | 25 | 75 |
| **By Education** | | |
| Less than HS | 61 | 39 |
| HS Grad | 53 | 47 |
| Some College, but not 4 years | 47 | 53 |
| College Grad | 43 | 57 |
| Post Graduate Study | 53 | 47 |
| **By Denomination** | | |
| Protestant | 43 | 57 |
| Catholic | 51 | 49 |
| Other Christian | 49 | 51 |
| Mormon | 31 | 69 |
| Jewish | 69 | 31 |
| Something Else | 67 | 33 |
| "Nothing in particular" | 58 | 42 |

# The Group Story/continued

|  | Voted Democratic | Voted Republican |
|---|---|---|
| **Whites** | | |
| Protestant | 38 | 62 |
| Catholic | 48 | 52 |
| Other Christian | 34 | 66 |
| Mormon | 25 | 75 |
| Jewish | 71 | 29 |
| Something Else | 59 | 41 |
| Nothing in particular | 58 | 42 |
| | | |
| **By Family Income** | | |
| Under $15,000 | 57 | 43 |
| $15,000-29,999 | 53 | 47 |
| $30,000-49,000 | 51 | 49 |
| $50,000-75,000 | 44 | 56 |
| $75,000-99,000 | 45 | 55 |
| $100,000 and higher | 41 | 59 |
| | | |
| **By Other Characteristics [from list where** | | |
| **respondent checked if applicable]** | | |
| Born again/Evangelical Christian | 39 | 61 |
| Married | 46 | 54 |
| Without health insurance | 53 | 47 |
| Support the NRA | 32 | 68 |
| Someone in household in a Labor Union | 64 | 36 |
| Parent of child under 18 | 46 | 54 |
| Attend religious services once a week | 44 | 56 |
| Gay/lesbian/bisexual | 66 | 34 |
| Employed full time | 48 | 52 |

# Sample Sizes for Basic Demographic Groups

## VNS Exit Poll, November 8, 1994

| | | | | |
|---|---|---|---|---|
| **Sex** | 11,179 | | **Education\*** | 5,317 |
| Male | 5,385 | | Less than H.S. | 288 |
| Female | 5,794 | | H. S. Graduate | 1,190 |
| | | | Some College | 1,511 |
| | | | College Graduate | 1,404 |
| **Age** | 11,219 | | Postgrad | 924 |
| 18 - 29 | 1,614 | | | |
| 30 - 44 | 3,794 | | **Party ID** | 10,575 |
| 45 - 59 | 3,267 | | Democratic | 3,832 |
| 60+ | 2,544 | | Republican | 3,782 |
| | | | Independent | 2,578 |
| **Race** | 11,205 | | | |
| White | 9,678 | | **Ideology\*** | 5,276 |
| Black | 956 | | Liberal | 934 |
| Hispanic | 375 | | Moderate | 2,355 |
| Asian | 108 | | Conservative | 1,987 |
| | | | | |
| **Income** | 10,046 | | **Religion\*** | 5,364 |
| < $15,000 | 989 | | Protestant | 2,152 |
| 15,000-30,000 | 2,144 | | Catholic | 1,590 |
| 30,000-50,000 | 3,009 | | Other Christian | 806 |
| 50,000-75,000 | 2,228 | | Jewish | 191 |
| 75,000-100,000 | 914 | | None | 383 |
| over $100,000 | 762 | | | |

\*Education, ideology and religion were asked of only half the sample.

9840

Printed by Hall & Bill Printing Company, Willimantic, Connecticut